BUT NOT JIM CROW:

Family Memories of African American Loggers in Maxville, Oregon

Pearl Alice Marsh, Ph.D

Copyright © 2019 Pearl Alice Marsh

Publisher
Pearl Alice Marsh

Patterson, CA 95363

Printer
Ingram Spark
www.ingramspark.com

Edited by
Kristen Hall-Geisler
Indigo Editing
917 SW Oak St., #207
Portland, OR 97205
www.indigoediting.com

Book Cover and Book Design by Linda McCrae Bauck, Wallowa, OR

ISBN: 978-0-578-48863-9
Library of Congress Cataloging-In-Publication
Marsh, Pearl Alice
1. But Not Jim Crow: Family Memories of African American Loggers in Maxville, Oregon.
The author developed three main centers to interview and gather stories and information from the decendants: Portland, OR, Sacramento, CA and Swanee, Georgia. Tho loggers were recruited from the Deep South to work for Bowman-Hicks Lumber, Co. in Maxville, located in remote northeast Oregon. Chapters include Migrating with the Company, The Families and Their Roots: The First-Generation African Oregonians, The Memories, memories of fifteen decendants, and one original loggers's interview, with a few contributions by local residents.

Includes index

All photographs read from left to right.

Information in this book should not be used for legal reference.
Facts have been verified when possible but in many cases the stories stand as written from the memories of the many authors. This book is a collection of stories and is accurate as far as the memories of those telling the stories.

Front Cover photograph: Photograph of Maxville workers. See page 1 for a detailed caption

Title Page: A photo of the children of Mattie and Jessie Langford, Mary and Amos Marsh, Sr., and Dorothy and Alvie May. Courtesy Pearl Alice Marsh.

Back Cover: Top Left: Photo of children of families who moved from Maxville to La Grande, OR. The Joseph Hilliard, Sr. children are among the first two rows. Full caption on page 79. Courtesy Joseph Hilliard, Jr. Middle right: A building being moved by Bowman-Hicks, from an old site at Palmer Junction, on the Grande Ronde river, to the newly built town of Maxville. Maxville was a company town built by Bowman-Hicks for their workers to live in.

DEDICATION

This book is dedicated to the intrepid women and men of the log cutters' and sawmill workers' families who migrated from the Jim Crow South to northeast Oregon during the Great Depression to make a better life for themselves and their descendants, whose memories are recorded in these pages.

CONTRIBUTORS

Lucille Mays Bridgewater, Joseph Hilliard, Jr., Rosie Thomas Gray, Seretha Lane Marsh Jefferson, Nadine Patterson Kelly, Kerry King, James Lester Lane, Frank Wayne Marsh, Pearl Alice Marsh, Nathaniel Mays, Robert Minor, Katherine Cook Ramsey, Kay Marsh-Wyrick, Luella Anderson Mazique

Contributors to Amos Marsh, Jr. Remembered
Gail Davidson Fineberg
Dale Johnson
"Coach" Don Wilson

EPIGRAPH

History looks kindly on those who preserve the smallest fragments of memory and pass them on to the next generation.

L-R: Unknown, Adolf "A.D." Williams, David Allen Williams, Unknown, Unkown. Adolph and David are not related.

TABLE OF CONTENTS

ABOUT THE AUTHOR

Pearl Alice in front of the Bowman-Hicks company houses in Wallowa. c. 1949.

Pearl Alice Marsh was born in La Grande, Oregon and lived in the town of Wallowa until the age of twelve. She is the daughter of Amos Marsh, Sr. and Mary (Patterson) Marsh and the granddaughter of Joseph "Pa Pat" Patterson, Sr. and Arie "Ma Pat" (Spears) Patterson, well-known African-American loggers and spouses in the area, and is a former president of the Maxville Heritage Interpretative Center. Her work documenting Oregon's Black logging history has been featured in Oregon Historical Quarterly and on Oregon Public Broadcasting's Think Out Loud. She is the first African American woman to earn a Ph.D. in political science from the University of California at Berkeley, and she served with the U. S. House of Representatives International Relations Committee as a Senior Policy Advisor with expertise in African political, economic, social, and development issues until her retirement in 2013.

ILLUSTRATIONS

PREFACE

The writing and preservation of historical African American rural life in Oregon barely exist, due to Oregon's history of restrictive laws limiting the number of African Americans in the state and the small number choosing to be farmers, agricultural workers, loggers, and small-town residents. This rural population was "ordinary"—working-class people, small shopkeepers, and religious folk, not the kind of people who write their own history or about whom history is written.

Courtesy Lisa Lindsey, Wallowa

Nez Perce Indians in this photo are Jim Williams, Mrs Jim Williams, and one of Chief Joseph's wives called "Traveling Lady," They are standing in front of a traditional teepee in regalia. The Joseph band Nez Perce called Wallowa County their home, even after they were driven out in 1877.

This particular Oregon history is a "history from below," a history of common people.[1] It is community history and family history. It is stored, coded, and recalled in the memories of generations as they descend from the original settlers. It is a fragile history that changes from generation to generation and often is lost. It is not documented in the pages of mainstream newspapers or books, nor is it preserved in archival collections of photographs.

Thus, this book was conceived as a memory project to recover and reconstruct the history of a rural community of African American loggers who came to a railroad logging town, Maxville, Wallowa County, Oregon, between 1923 and the 1940s from memories of their aging descendants. The memory project was based upon "the interpretive authority of ordinary people,"[2] thus giving power to the fragments and short memories of individuals to tell a community's story.

The memory project had five basic aims:

1. To explore the historical events that led to the migration of African Americans to Wallowa County

2. To document Bowman-Hicks Lumber Company's practice of transplanting African American labor from the South to Wallowa County and the development of the company town named Maxville

3. To provide fresh insight into Oregon's diverse African American community

4. To place the African American loggers' oral history within the context of other early Wallowa histories, such as those of the Nez Perce, homesteaders, foresters, and white sawmill laborers

5. To examine the story from the anecdotal perspective of the descendants

The personal stories were contextualized through extensive research using historical newspapers, public records, census records, and the recorded memories of others.

---

1 E. P. Thompson, "History from Below," *Times Literary Supplement*, April 7, 1966, 279–80.

2 Jacquelyn Dowd Hall, *Like a Family: The Making of a Southern Cotton Mill World* (Chapel Hill, NC: University of North Carolina Press, 2000).

ACKNOWLEDGEMENTS

This work would not have been possible without the participation of the authors who descend from the African American loggers who migrated from the Deep South to a railroad logging town named Maxville in Wallowa County, Oregon, in the 1920s through the 1940s. Their patience during a protracted period of research and writing has encouraged me throughout the development of this book.

I am especially indebted to colleagues at the Wallowa History Center, Mary Ann McCrae Burrows, Sally Goebel, David Weaver and Linda McCrae Bauck, who supported my project goals and who worked actively to provide me with research in the center's archives.

I am especially indebted to Linda McCrae Bauck who designed the book and located the volumes of local historic photos and meticulously identified people by using contacts throughout the area, especially Mary Ann Burrows at the Wallowa History Center, local school records and facial recognition technology. Naming "ordinary people" in this project was a high bar but she met it.

I want to thank S. Renee Mitchell, Creative Revolutionist, who helped me tremendously with an early draft of this book and provided me with unequivocal support when it was needed.

I would like to thank Editor Eliza Canty-Jones and the Oregon Historical Society for granting permission to re-publish my father's memoir.

I am grateful to friends in Wallowa and Enterprise whom I interviewed and who gave me additional perspectives on the experiences of our community. They are Wes Conrad, Shirley Carper Doud, Gail Davidson Fineberg, Rafer Guillory, Zane Haney, Dale Johnson, Jack Goebel and John Burns. Jimmy Collins and Thorval Burrows met with me informally for morning coffee at the Blonde Strawberry Restaurant (originally Burrows Café) to confer about local history during this and other related projects. I enjoyed reliving childhood memories with my first-grade classmates Susan Roberts, Kay Landreth-McKinney, and Sandee Collins Jeffers; my second-grade friend Linda McCrae Bauck; and the younger Francine Guillory.

I wish to thank Bill Woodman and Joe Haddock of La Grande, who made themselves available for interviews to help examine the La Grande experience.

I want to thank Priscilla Steele, CSR, for recording and transcribing each interview and her delight in the opportunity to participate.

I am grateful for the professional editing and publication consultations from the staff of Indigo Editing with whom I worked: Ali Shaw, Kristen Hall-Geisler, Laura Garwood, Dehlia McCobb, and Susan DeFreitas.

No one has been more important to me in the pursuit of this project than my sister Kay Frances Marsh-Wyrick. Without her, I would not have been able to produce and display my photo exhibit in Wallowa, travel to Wallowa County and Portland, Oregon, multiple times, or sustain my spirits and commitment.

I want to thank colleagues Prof. Hardy Thomas Frye for early conversations on race and labor and James Lacy for sharing research on African American Loggers in Sloate, CA.

Lastly, I would like to thank my ancestors and elders-my parents, grandparents, aunts, uncles, and friends, whose love, guidance, and experiences came to life in my present world to research and write this book. They are the ultimate heroes of this project.

Pearl Alice explaining "The Memory Project" to a group.at Wallowa City Hall Conference Center.

Chapter I Introduction

This collection of memories captures childhood experiences of first- and second-generation descendants of African American logging families who migrated between 1923 and 1945 from the Deep South to the railroad logging town built and owned by the Bowman-Hicks Lumber Company—Maxville, Wallowa County, Oregon. The memories were collected via a series of interviews conducted in 2016 and 2017. They tell of a unique moment of racial and ethnic adjustment in the long quest for freedom and equality from early to mid-twentieth century rural Oregon. The experiences recalled by these descendants and others span the time between the 1920s and the late 1950s.

The African American families who came to northeastern Oregon were part of the Great Migration of African Americans that took place between 1916 and 1960, when economic opportunity and harsh segregation pulled and pushed millions of African Americans to leave the rural South for cities in the North, Midwest, and West. By 1960, when the migration ended, more than five million people had left their homes, creating one of the largest internal population shifts in US history. [1]

The general history of African Americans in Oregon is fairly well documented, including a concise summary by the Oregon Encyclopedia's article "Blacks in Oregon."[2] While the urban migration, particularly to Portland where most African Americans lived, also is well documented, the rural migration, particularly to logging and sawmill communities, is less so. [3]

Courtesy Smithsonian Magazine, September 2016 electronic version

A family migrating out of the south by automobile.

---

1 Stephanie Christensen, "The Great Migration (1915–1960)," December 6, 2007, BlackPast.org, http://www.blackpast.org/aah/great-migration-1915-1960.

2 Darrell Millner, "Blacks in Oregon," The Oregon Encyclopedia, updated October 1, 2018, https://oregonencyclopedia.org/articles/blacks_in_oregon.

3 Portland Bureau of Planning, The History of Portland's African American Community: 1805 to the Present, February 1993. https://www.oregon.gov/oprd/HCD/OHC/docs/multnomah_portland_AlbinahistoryofafricanAmericancommunity.pdf

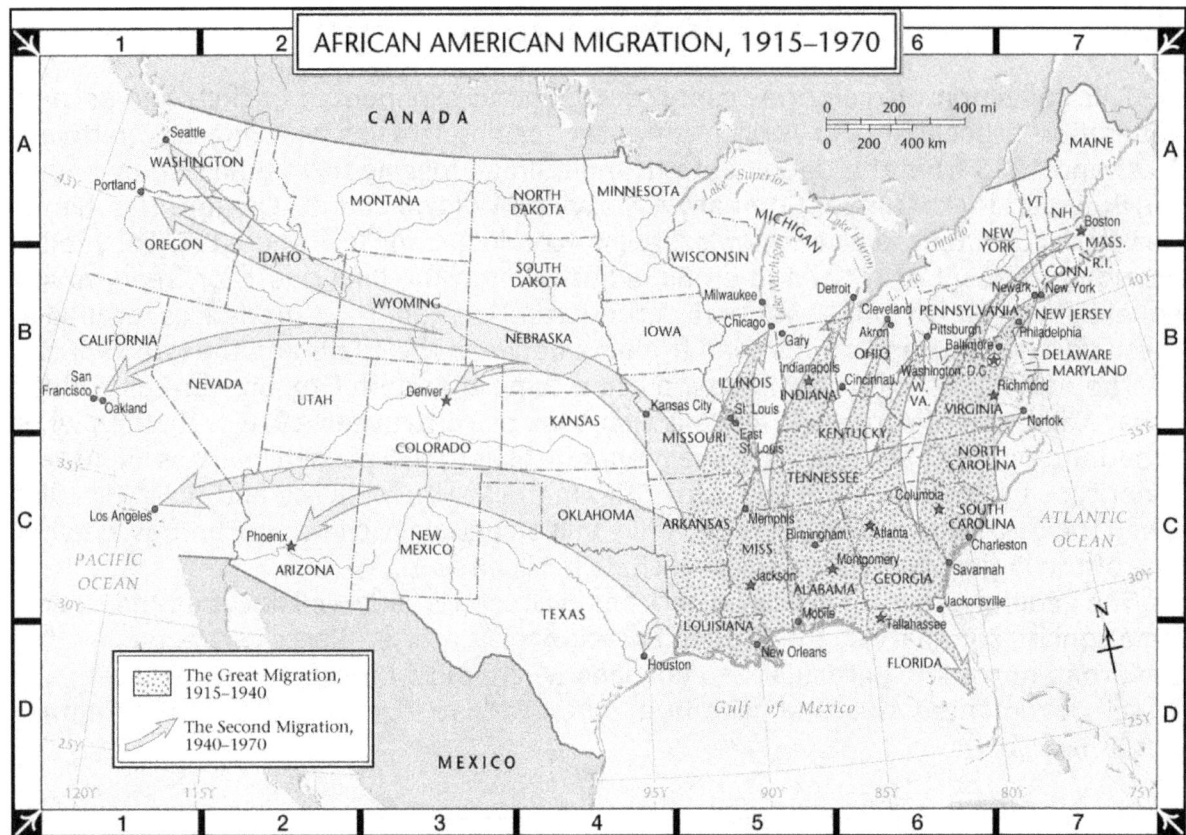

Destination cities for African-Americans during the Great Migration (1915-1970), © 2003, Pearson Education.

Like others in the Great Migration, the African American parents, grandparents, uncles, and aunts who came to Maxville did so to escape harsh economic and social conditions in the South. Generally, northern sawmill and logging jobs offered higher incomes than in the South, where wages were 15 to 25 percent below the national average.[4] Jim Crow segregation laws and practices separated African Americans and white people in order to protect white social and economic supremacy. [5]

White violence was another determining factor for the exodus. On Christmas Day, in Eros, Louisiana, logger Amos Marsh's extended family was struck by violence. Two white men, D. J. Sanderson and Jack Bagell, killed relatives Mary L. Taylor Caldwell and Carrie Caldwell.

A party of white men came to the Taylor house over a dispute they had with them over a dog. Not finding the Taylor men, the party argued with and shot the Taylor women. They killed sisters Mary L. Taylor Caldwell and Carrie Caldwell and wounded their mother and a sister-in-law. There was a near shooting of Mary's baby but one of the men prevented that from being carried out. The baby, named Willie Charles-Caldwell, was found on the porch with his dead mother. The baby's father Willie Caldwell took care of the baby, refusing to give him to anyone else to

---

4 Chris Kromm, "Our Progressive Legacy: The Southern Wobblies," *Facing South: A Voice for a Changing South*, May 6, 2005, https://www.facingsouth.org/2005/05/our-progressive-legacy-the-southern-wobblies.html.

5 "Examples of Jim Crow Laws—Oct. 1960—Civil Rights," Ferris State University, Jim Crow Museum of Racist Memorabilia, accessed February 9, 2019, https://ferris.edu/HTMLS/news/jimcrow/links/misclink/examples.htm.

raise, but Willie Charles died nine months later of some childhood malady. [6]

While moving to majority-white Wallowa County, group migration of African American kin and neighbors afforded these families an opportunity to reconstruct in a safer environment the stability of their southern communities based on their customs and institutions. They were able to "live in the South up North" while becoming Oregonians.[7] Connections with friends and family from larger cities like Pendleton, Portland, Walla Walla, and Tacoma, who visited frequently, also expanded this "southern home" for the new residents.

For the loggers and their families, being transplanted into a white, rural sawmill town presented both challenges and opportunities. At that time, Oregon was far from perfect when it came to race. However, these migrant families found a social space where they could experience a degree of liberty, freedom, and social interaction with white fellow-working-class families that they had not previously known.

In an interview, Ester Wilfong, Jr., whose family migrated from Arkansas, recalled going from La Grande to Maxville in the early 1940s to visit African American logger Joseph Patterson, Jr., and his wife, Helen. Wilfong noted attending a dance in the small neighboring town of Promise:

> *We went up to Promise to some function, and while there, there was a dance going on. We just sat and watched the [white] people dancing—a different kind of dancing than what Joe and Helen had done—but they did get up and do a little number or two, but it all went well.* [8]

Although they had greater freedom, some still did not want to risk making what they perceived to be unnecessary waves with their white neighbors. There were dividing lines that African American men would not cross regardless of cordial interracial moments. Thorval and Mary Anne (McCrae) Burrows recalled in a conversation with Linda (McCrae) Bauck that the black men in town would not let Lee Burrows' wife, Myrtle, wait on them at the service station - they always asked for "Mr. Lee" [Burrows]. Occasionally an outsider, in their eyes, showed up to threaten the social balance.

Earl Fleshman tells the story about a card room owned by Earl Haney, who was originally from West Virginia, and who also had the only pool tables in the county. African American and white men socialized and gambled together there for years.[9]

> *The card room at the back of Haney's pool hall was fully integrated, but on one occasion, about 1949, a "gentleman of color" came to Wallowa from someplace in the southern Midwest and became somewhat of a fixture in the card room.*
>
> *One day, Amos Marsh [an African American] flagged down the Wallowa County Stage Line bus at the railroad crossing and asked [the driver] Charley if he could buy the man a ticket to St. Louis. Charley said that he could only give him a ticket as far as La Grande but assured them that he would see that the ticket for the remainder of the journey was purchased.*

---

6 Account shared with Pearl Alice Marsh by Yevette Richards, as told to her by her cousins Arlena Caldwell and Joe Caldwell, the later-born children of Willie Caldwell in a subsequent marriage, Choudrant, Louisiana, 2017.

7 Isabel Wilkerson, *The Warmth of Other Suns: The Epic Story of America's Great Migration* (New York: Vintage Books, 2011).

8 Ester Wilfong, Jr., interviewed by Gwendolyn Trice at the Maxville Heritage Interpretive Center, http://www.maxvilleheritage.org/learn/transcription/.

9 Zane Haney, interview summary, June 2015

When they arrived in La Grande, Charley asked why Amos had given him the money for the ticket. The gentleman said that it was his money and that the men of the black community had taken it from him and given him the choice of going back East by bus or by freight.

A few days later, Charley had the opportunity to ask Amos what the story was. Amos explained that up to that point, relations between the black and white communities had always been pretty good, but this character was "a no good southern n***er" who was cheating at cards and that his misconduct reflected on the entire black community. So he had been rather firmly requested to go back where he came from. To the best of my knowledge, that is the only time Amos was heard to use the "n-word" in that manner.[10]

Several of these interviews include firsthand encounters with Southern Jim Crow laws. Two families, after the tragic deaths of their mothers during childbirth, moved back to Louisiana permanently and had to be taught by local relatives how to live with strict racial segregation. Other families traveled to the South on vacation and had to learn survival skills for their brief sojourn into the netherworld of possible life-threatening situations. Through their experiences, these descendants were able to draw the contrasts and similarities between living in the North and the segregated South.

The African American loggers' descendants narrate the joys of family and community life in Oregon despite the constraints of some segregation, such as housing, prejudice, and in the earlier years, the menacing specter of the Ku Klux Klan. Given the era, some of the predictable acts of racism they encountered were deliberately malevolent and some were born out of ignorance. But Oregon also provided relative personal freedom and a new beginning that these African American trailblazers did not find under Jim Crow.[11]

Bowman-Hicks Lumber Company, their employer, did not enforce segregation in Maxville as strictly as other company towns. Comparatively, the Oregon-American Lumber Company in Vernonia had a more highly diversified workforce than Maxville, and it had more rigidly enforced racial separation and inequality within the town.[12]

In the South, there was little room to navigate beyond the rigid constraints of the Jim Crow system. But in these isolated communities of Maxville, Wallowa, and, as the families migrated further, La Grande in Union County, they could challenge some boundaries of race and space.

Most efforts to test the waters were successful, such as shopping in local stores, playing interracial baseball, creating interracial friendships, and attending public events along with white residents. During Prohibition, African Americans in Maxville and La Grande even found "freedom" to violate liquor laws, as did their white neighbors, by selling illegal moonshine. Other efforts were not so successful, like getting a haircut in the local barber shop or, in the 1920s, attending the first school with white children or living in residential company quarters together.[13]

These memories are not a definitive narrative on race relations in Oregon, the Pa-

---

10   Caro Fleshman, Facebook Messenger note to Pearl Alice Marsh, October 2, 2017.

11   Elizabeth McLagan, *A Peculiar Paradise: A History of Blacks in Oregon, 1788–1940* (Athens, GA: Georgian Press, 1980).

12   Edward J. Kamholz, Jim Blain, and Gregory Kamholz, The Oregon-American Lumber Company: Ain't No More (Stanford, CA: Stanford General Books, 2003), 85–87.

13   Gwendolyn Trice, "Maxville," The Oregon Encyclopedia, updated March 17, 2018, https://oregonencyclopedia.org/articles/maxville/.

cific Northwest, or the United States. However, they document mostly joyful memories and some instances of interracial social solidarity. They also offer inspiring stories of the larger historical steps on the long march to freedom and equality in the United States. While not generally noted as being of consequence in race relations theory, they recall social bonds and enduring friendships forged with some neighbors in the white community. These interactions were a social map that helped the descendants and their elders navigate the wider world and access a social space for both African Americans and whites to mingle peacefully.

One descendant of a white logger identified the "internal moral code" she learned from generations of her family that helped open the pathway to establishing interracial friendships.[14]

Through these African American descendants' stories, we learn that social and cultural pride, strong family and community bonds within the African American community, and interracial friendships can be guideposts for raising minority children successfully in America and hopefully a vector for changing the racial norms of the community defined by prevailing social strife.

---

14 Conversation with childhood schoolmate, Francine Guillory West, at Tamkaliks Celebration, in Wallowa, Oregon July 2017.

CHAPTER II MIGRATING WITH THE COMPANY

Courtesy Delores Johnson Smith

This photo is of Maxville workers. Don Riggle, wood's boss is 3rd from right. Others have not been identified. The back row of men are standing on a stump and yellow pine that was felled. There are fourteen black sawyers and ten white men, with at leastsix, two-man crosscut saws visible, ten scale sticks, axes, mauls and wedges. The following names have been copied from a time tablet that Mr. R.H. Baxley, foreman, kept on the men. The entries were made by pencil so legibility has faded. Mr. Baxley is not in the photo so possibly he took the photo.These names may or may not be of these men, but it may help someone to help identify them.

1942: H.C. Cummings, Leroy Wilfong, Tommy Wright, Gred Brauer, Will Anderson, Alvie Marsh, Emerson Young, J.M. Johnson, N.H. Skillings, Eddie Burnett, Ivany Sasnett, Jeff Saunders, Edward Lonnie Powell, Jessie Langford.

1947: R.H. Baxley, Fred Samuel, Roosevelt Donley, Amos Marsh, Joe Lowry, Ford Livingstone, Odell Sasnett, Julius Coleman, D. Walker, Jessie Langford, Ester Wilfong, D.E. Roninson, Richard Brunett, Willie Sivia, Hosea Lowry. From Tne North Woods, Vol. 1, p. 287, by Orvalla Carper Hafer.

In 1910, there were 83,000 African American timber workers in the South, with Louisiana boasting the second-largest timber industry in the country.[1]

In the late nineteenth century, as farming proved increasingly unprofitable, African Americans found alternative sources of employment in the forests. Even at the height of segregation, African American entrepreneurs became managers and owners of timber companies. In 1910, there were 195 black owners of timber companies, and 111 were foremen. African Americans comprised about 25 percent of all employees of the forest industry, which now provided year-round employment, though always at lower

---

1   Donna Fricker, "Historic Context: The Louisiana Lumber Boom c. 1880–1925," accessed May 24, 2015, http://www.crt.state.la.us/Assets/OCD/hp/nationalregister/historic_contexts/The_Louisiana_Lumber_Boom_c1880-1925.pdf; Thomas R. Cox, The Lumberman's Frontier: Three Centuries of Land Use, Society, and Changes in America's Forests (Corvallis, OR: Oregon State University Press, 2010), 252.

wages than for whites.[2]

As company logging practices depleted timber, whole communities of African American and white workers packed up and moved to new places where they could find work.

Starting in 1923, African American loggers from the South were recruited to Wallowa County, Oregon, by the Bowman-Hicks Lumber Company. The loggers, prior to coming to Oregon, originated in Arkansas, Louisiana, Texas, Mississippi, Alabama, Georgia, and Florida.[3]

Bowman-Hicks was a Missouri-based firm with large sawmill operations in Loring and Oakdale, Louisiana, and major interests in the Oakdale & Gulf Railway. Bowman-

Courtesy Newt Ashby Collection at the Wallowa County Museum

Store and office in winter, Maxville, Oregon.

Hicks was incorporated with capital of $50,000 in June 1900 by H. Bowman, C. R. Hicks, B. C. Bowman, and others.[4] It was a subsidiary of the large S. H. Bowman Lumber Company of Minneapolis.[5]

After closing its sawmills in Louisiana, Bowman-Hicks found one of its next opportunities in Wallowa County, Oregon.

In 1922 Bowman-Hicks purchased the Palmer Lumber Company operation at Camp 5 in the north woods of the Wallowa Mountains. In May 1923, the company purchased the Nibley-Mimnaugh Lumber Company and other local timber holdings.[6]

Bowman-Hicks became the first of two Oregon timber firms known to intentionally recruit a large number of African Americans into its industrial workforce. The other

2   James G. Lewis and Robert Hendricks, "A Brief History of African Americans and Forests," USDA Forest Service, March 21, 2006, https://www.fs.fed.us/people/aasg/PDFs/African_Americans_and_forests_March21%202006.pdf.

3   Based on US Census data.

4   "New Corporations," *St. Louis Republic*, June 28, 1900.

5   A history of the Bowman-Hicks Lumber Company and its subsidiaries can be found in the biography of Samuel H. Bowman, the patriarch.

6   "Bowman-Hicks Overhauling Wallowa Mill," *La Grande Observer*, August 9, 1923.

company was the Oregon-American Lumber Company located in Vernonia, Oregon,[7] which was later purchased by Long-Bell Lumber Company in the 1950s. In neighboring Northern California, the Long-Bell Lumber Company bought out Abner Weed's mill[8] and recruited workers from its mills in Louisiana and Alabama, paying each worker's $89 train fare to the Northwest. By the mid-1920s, one thousand of the six thousand residents of Weed were black.[9] Long-Bell also was headquartered in Missouri with major sawmills in Louisiana. [10]

Bowman-Hicks hired Henry Newton Ashby to supervise the development of its western expansion. Before coming to Bowman-Hicks, Ashby worked as the manager of sales in the tie and timber department at Long-Bell, and he had hoped to move west to oversee its Northwest expansion. But Long-Bell executives passed him over for a promotion, so Ashby planned to retire. Then the Bowman-Hicks job came along.

After setting up new Bowman-Hicks headquarters in La Grande in 1922, Ashby's first responsibility in Wallowa County was to build a new company town to accommodate both workers and management. He established the town of Maxville high in the north woods near the Nibley-Mimnaugh Lumber Company Camp 5 logging site in a large, expansive area known as Bishop Meadows. The new town was built with all the physical features of company towns of that era, including a post office, medical dispensary, company store, schools, hotels, family housing, horse barn, baseball field, clubhouse, blacksmith, and roundhouse to turn the log train engines.[11]

On a drive to view the new town, the editor of the *Wallowa Sun* newspaper described Maxville:

> *Recently we bumped the bumps on the road to Promise. We slipped through slithers of slippery slime and sought a road in the wilderness. And then all of a sudden we came across a town, newly transplanted in a place where a year ago we saw a buck and his family of does grazing. The north woods is getting all jazzed up. Neat blue grey houses are sitting comfortably on wide streets. A large hotel is being built. A club house and some stores are under construction. An engine puffed up with a string of regular flat cars. Civilization has penetrated the wilderness and Wallowa has a brand-new neighbor.*
>
> *The new town, which they call Maxville and we will continue to call Bishop Meadows, will be interesting to watch. Here we have a southern community set down in an environment of mountains and canyons. It is a hothouse flower transplanted into a snow bank. The camp is typically southern. Their community has a central open court to insure coolness. When the snow comes, it will be filled to the eaves with a variety of coolness which will be a curiosity to many of them. They will find in super abundance the stuff with which they kept their mint juleps cool and shaved ice up to their eyebrows.*[12]

---

7   Kamholz, *The Oregon-American Lumber Company*, 86.

8   "Weed," accessed February 16, 2019, http://nailhunter.com/lbhistory.htm.

9   James Langford, Black Past, Afrian Americans in the Shadow of Mt. Shasta: The Black Community of Weed, March 15, 2010, https://www.blackpast.org/african-american-history/african-americans-shadow-mt-shasta-black-community-weed-california/

10   Helen King, "The Economic History of the Long-Bell Lumber Company," thesis submitted to Louisiana State University, 1936, http://ereserves.mcneese.edu/depts/archive/FTBooks/king.htm

11   Gwendolyn Trice, "Maxville, Oregon (1923–1945)," BlackPast.org, http://www.blackpast.org/aaw/maxville-oregon-1923-1945; Trice, "Maxville,"; Linda Carlson, *Company Towns of the Pacific Northwest* (Seattle: University of Washington Press, 2003); Thad Sitton and James H. Conrad, Texas Sawmill Communities, 1880–1942 (Austin, TX: University of Texas Press, 1998).

12   D. M. Major, "Maxville—Alias Bishop Meadows," *Wallowa Sun*, 1923.

Courtesy Arkansas State Archives

Pine Bluff, Jefferson County, Arkansas early in the twentieth century. The Jefferson County courthouse can be seen to the right.

Maxville soon had a population of about four hundred people and was one of the largest towns in Wallowa County. While building a new company town, Ashby's second responsibility was to increase the workforce to accommodate the expanded operation. He inherited a local all-white workforce, but with a responsibility to maximize lumber output and profits, he needed additional reliable and experienced labor. He decided to recruit good workers based on skills from the region he knew best: the South. Among these were African American logging railroad builders, loggers, and sawmill workers.

As the African American workers were recruited directly by the company to Maxville, workers were paid bonuses to entice other family and friends. Some came from the Cady Lumber Company in McNary, Arizona, which had moved its operations en masse from McNary, Louisiana. In 1924, Cady stopped cutting timber in Louisiana and purchased a mill in Cooley, Arizona, on the White Mountain Apache Reservation. He renamed the town McNary and transplanted an entire sawmill and eight hundred people—skilled loggers, mill labor, and their families—from McNary, Louisiana.[13] Almost all the labor was African American.[14]

Courtesy Denver News - Denver Library Digital Collection

Ku Klux Klan members and a burning cross, Denver, Colorado, 1921.

By recruiting African American workers, Ashby faced a potential threat he knew well from the South: racism. White settlers—pioneers, homesteaders, migrants, and immigrants—had moved into Wallowa County from both northern and southern states as well as Europe decades prior to the arrival of African American loggers. Wallowa

---

13   Jamie Lewis, "McNary, Arizona: A Town on the Move," Peeling Back the Bark (blog), Forest History Society, May 7, 2012, https://fhsarchives.wordpress.com/2012/05/07/mcnary-arizona-a-town-on-the-move/.

14   Lewis, "McNary, Arizona," and Abraham S. Chanin, "McNary: A Transplanted Town," *Arizona Highways 66*, no. 8 (1990).

County residents had plenty of inflammatory images of African Americans in the local newspapers and in the notions they brought with them.[15] Dating back to the late nineteenth and early twentieth centuries, syndicated commentary, travel journals, entertainment features, and news articles about "negroes" helped shape local perceptions. In the town of Joseph's Aurora newspaper, an 1895 article by William C. Elam decried the "flood of negro talk that has discolored our recent literature.[16]

Racist jokes characterizing African Americans as childish, simple, and lazy were common fare.[17] And local theater performances included minstrel acts.[18]

Courtesy Ronee Stone
Henry Newton Ashby, supervisor of Bowman-Hicks Lumber Company, Wallowa operation. Photo taken at Wallowa mill.

In a 1929 newspaper article about a moonshine bust in Maxville, the sheriff noted in racially paternalistic language of the day:

Negroes are just like a bunch of kids and it's hard to do anything with them," said Deputy John Hemelwright when speaking on the raid by county officers and other officials on the Negro settlement at Maxville last Thursday evening about eight o'clock. "About all we did," he continued, "was to give them a good scare, for they certainly are afraid of the law.

[The officers] descended on Maxville and searched through the Negro settlement there, making two arrests. Some beer was found in one of the shacks and one negro was arrested for possession of liquor. A negro woman was also arrested for selling a pint of booze. The two, however, were not brought back to Enterprise by the officers but were told to remain in Maxville until they were sent for. The officers told them they must cut out the bootlegging and gambling.[19]

Occasionally newspaper articles were more enlightened, such as a 1924 report noting the invention of the soda fountain by a New York City–based African American confectioner named Sambo Jackson,[20] which resulted in his accidental invention of ice cream in the early 1800s.

What's more, Wallowa County was not a blank racial slate before the African Ameri-

---

15 "Analysis of 'Jazz' Music: Described as an Outgrowth of the Negro Love of Syncopation, and Belongs to Race," *New York World*, in Wallowa *Sun*, October 7, 1920; "High School Students Present Entertainment" (including Negro Monologue by Mrs. J. F. Morelock), Wallowa *Sun*

16 "False Dialect: Our Negro Stories Are Declared to Be All Wrong," *Enterprise Aurora*, July 26, 1896.

17 "Good Short Stories," Wallowa *News*, August 8, 1902

18 "Minstrel-Vaudeville Given by Local K.P.'s Is a Great Success" (included J. O. Kindle imitation of a negro preacher), Wallowa *Sun*, February 1, 1923.

19 Orvalla Carper Hafer, "Maxville Negroes Raided Thursday," *Joseph Herald*, October 17, 1929, in *North Woods of Wallowa County* , Vol.1, 2015.

20 "Soda Fountain Inventor," Wallowa *Sun*, December 6, 1924; "Ice Cream 100 Years Old," *Refrigeration*, March 1920, 37.

Courtesy Pearl Alice Marsh
Commissary tickets for the company store at Maxville.

cans arrived in 1923. First, the US military defeated the native Nez Perce and moved them from Wallowa County to a reservation in Idaho.[21] Second, a local criminal gang massacred Chinese workers in 1887 at Deep Creek on the Oregon side of the Snake River in Hells Canyon, not far from Joseph in Wallowa County, after the people had been imported to work in the county in the 1880s.[22]

In 1921, the resurgent Ku Klux Klan migrated from Northern California to Oregon and spread rapidly throughout the state. Civic, business, and religious organizations and local labor unions provided the perfect network to spread Klan ideology.[23]

Once the Klan had firmly planted itself in Union and Wallowa Counties, it created a major problem.[24] Crosses were burned regularly throughout the region—La Grande, Island City, Elgin, Imbler, Palmer Junction, Wallowa, Lostine, Enterprise, and Joseph. The Klan's targets included Catholics, immigrants, Jews, Mormons, Chinese, and African Americans.[25] According to its ideology, Catholic was synonymous with immigrant, white immigrants weren't considered American, Jews and Mormons weren't Christian, Chinese immigrants were an opium threat, and African Americans were bootleggers and moral miscreants.

In 1922, the La Grande Klan waged an economic boycott against "Catholic, Jewish, and foreign-owned businesses." A vote recount was demanded, claiming "illegal Catholic primary voting."[26]

By the early 1920s, the area's small African American community in La Grande was also in the KKK's crosshairs. The 1920s US Federal Census recorded only 20 African American residents, which increased to 39 by 1930. The total city population for the same decennial periods was 8,077 and 9,757, respectively.

At a meeting on October 23, 1923, after announcing a planned cross burning, the La Grande KKK did the following:

Motion made and carried that a committee be approved to take up the mat-

---

21   Daniel J. Sharfstein, *Thunder in the Mountains: Chief Joseph, Oliver Otis Howard, and the Nez Perce War* (New York: W. W. Norton & Company, 2017), and Kent Nurbum, Chief Joseph & the Flight of the Nez Perce: The Untold Story of an American Tragedy (New York: Harper-Collins, 2006).

22   Nokes, R. Gregory, *Massacred for Gold: The Chinese in Hells Canyon* (Corvallis, OR: Oregon State University Press, 2009).

23   David A. Horowitz, ed., *Inside the Klavern: The Secret History of a Ku Klux Klan of the 1920s* (Carbondale, IL: Southern Illinois University Press, 1999); Information on the holdings of the "Ku Klux Klan La Grande, Oregon Chapter records, 1922–1923" can be found online at Archives West, http://archiveswest.orbiscascade.org/ark:/80444/xv23071.

24   Horowitz, *Inside the Klavern*, 32.

25   Horowitz, *Inside the Klavern*.

26   Horowitz, *Inside the Klavern*, 18

ter of Negroes on the north side with the city officials.[27]

On November 21, 1923, a "Committee on Negroes" presented a petition to the La Grande City Commission to complain about "Negro drunkenness." And in April 1924 there was a complaint filed with the State of Oregon Labor Commission against Bowman-Hicks for bringing in "dark men" to work when there were "white men needing jobs."[28]

While African Americans were not the only targets, the sight of cross burnings must have posed a major existential threat to the small African American population in La Grande, most of whom had migrated from the Deep South. Reports of Klan activity in Wallowa County are documented in local

Negroes Favored—

C. H. Gram, state labor commissioner, has received a letter from James H. Johnston of La Grande asking if anything can be done to stop the Bowman-Hicks Lumber company from shipping in negroes to take the place of white labor. Johnson claims the company brought in 14 negroes on April 9 and that there are many idle white men at La Grande. Gram says there is nothing that can be done to stop the company from bringing in the dark men. The Bowman-Hicks company is a Kansas City concern.

News clipping from the Oregon Statesman, April 15, 1924.

newspaper articles. Some ascribed the most hardcore racial attitudes in Wallowa County to southerners, including those working in logging.

During the early 1920s, Wallowa County KKK rallies regularly drew several hundred people. At that time, there were around 10,000 residents in the county and roughly 1,700 in the town of Wallowa. According to the 1920 census, there were no African American residents at that point; however, out of 2,486

Courtesy Wallowa History Center

Frick's Bakery. located on the left, site of one of the crosses burned in Wallowa. The Christian Church, locted on the right, was particularily supportive of the KKK at one time. The street in front of the bakery is Main Street and also Highway 82. The elementary school is just visible behind the tree on the left.

households in the county, 319 heads of household were immigrants, who also were primary Klan targets.[29]

The *Wallowa Sun* newspaper reported several cross burnings during that time, signifying the presence of the KKK in the county.[30] One of the crosses was placed near

27 Howoritz, *Inside the Klavern*, 131.

28 "Negroes Favored," Oregon *Statesman*, April 14, 1924.

29 US Federal Census, Wallowa County, Oregon, 1920; Horowitz, *Inside the Klavern*.

30 "KKK Crosses Notify City of Klan Activity," *Wallowa Sun*, January 18, 1923.

the Frick's Bakery, owned by German immigrants Ottmar and Anna Frick, while another was located on the cement bridge near the creamery. That spring, the Reverend W. A. Gresham of the Christian Church of Pendleton arrived to speak on behalf of the Ku Klux Klan and to lecture on the organization's ideals.[31]

Another prized KKK speaker, the Reverend V. K. "Bearkat" Allison from the Christian Church in Lebanon, Oregon, had a reputation as "the most powerful and popular anti-Catholic lecturer in the state."

The Wallowa Christian Church was a key organization for the Klan to spread its hate message. Reverend W. A. Gresham of the Pendleton Christian Church was a popular speaker throughout both Union and Wallowa Counties. He often lectured on "Americanism," a theme that the Klan was pushing.

In January 1924, a group of hooded KKK members showed up at the Wallowa Christian Church, said prayers, and presented the minister with $100.[32] In February 1924, at a large meeting in Enterprise of Klan members from all over eastern Oregon,[33] the

Courtesy Wallowa County Museum

This picture was taken at Maxville, north of Wallowa, in 1926. At that time is was said to be the only Negro school in Oregon. Pleasant Stoudamire is the teacher. The picture was submitted by Curtis Christy, former Wallowa County school teacher, now residing at Fountain, Florida.

The pupils in the picture are: Mattie Jones, Sterling Jones, Louis Jones, Luster Lane, Mattie Lee Lane and Pressie Stoudamire.

---

31 "KKK Speaker Coming," *Wallowa Sun*, March 15, 1923; "KKK Lecturer Tells of Ideals of the Klan," *Wallowa Sun*, March 22, 1923.

32 "Klansmen give $100 to Church in Wallowa, OR," *La Grande Observer*, January 26, 1924.

33 "Wallowa Klan Gets Charter," *La Grande Observer*, February 9, 1924.

Wallowa chapter of the Ku Klux Klan got its charter to be known as the Wallowa County Klan. And on May 2, 1924, Klan men and women paraded up and down Main Street in Wallowa while a fiery cross burned on the hill south of town.[34]

There is one report of a Ku Klux Klan incident in Maxville. In an interview, Alan Dale Victor recalled,

> *Well, it would probably be about the middle '20s. A group of Ku Klux Klan members with their hoods on showed up at Maxville. MacMillan, who was the superintendent, and Jim Crowley, who was the woods boss, they told them to get the hell out of Maxville. They said, "Don't you people ever come back." Jim Crowley says, "Maybe you guys have a mask to fool us," but he said, "I know who you are." He said, "I don't ever want to see your face around here again." So that was the end of the Ku Klux Klan [in Maxville].[35]*

Courtesy Orvalla Carper Hafer

Maxville, 1937. L-R: Helen Wisdom Johnson Prince Collins, daughter of Nellie Coats Wisdom Henderson, Adolph "A.D." Williams, Ona May Hug, Dave Allen Williams, Nova Jean Henderson Heyduck, and Nadine Patterson Kelly, (Adolph and David Allen are not related.)

Among some newspaper editorial opinion leaders, there was pushback to the Klan's race ideology, especially when it came to military recruitment.

Read the roll call of the army that marched under Old Glory to victory on any field, from Concord to the Argonne, and see what it would be if the rule of the "Klan" had been enforced. A negro, Crispus Attucks, was the first to give his life for the republic; a Jew, Hayman Salomon, provided funds for the support of the struggling Continental Army when other means could not be found. French and German leaders fought under Washington. On every page of the nation's history are written names that could not get onto the roster of the Klan.[36]

Later, in 1943, Enterprise Chieftain editor Gwen T. Coffin penned the following indictment of US military recruitment for World War II:

---

34 "Klan Members Parade on Main Street Tuesday Evening," *Wallowa Sun*, May 2, 1924.

35 Alan Dale Victor, interview by Gwendolyn Trice, Maxville Heritage Interpretive Center, http://www.maxville-heritage.org/.

36 "Americanism and the Klan," *Wallowa Sun*, October 29, 1921.

While we are pleading and fighting for the rights for the downtrodden and under-privileged peoples of Europe and Asia, we still tolerate racial discrimination within our own country.

So far as we can learn not a single negro has been called for military service in Wallowa County although there are several who are in the same classes from which previous calls have been filled.[37]

Besides the threat of racial violence from the KKK, Ashby faced the possibilities of white-led labor strikes against the company from the International Workers of the World (IWW), a union organizing in the timber industry throughout the Pacific Northwest. Just before the Bowman-Hicks purchase, Nibley-Mimnaugh was hit by an IWW strike.[38] For Ashby, even labor unrest of short duration posed a threat to his new company.

His mixed-race workforce posed another management challenge. His white workers were unused to working with African Americans and might demand preferential treatment. Meanwhile, the African Americans were a prime target for the IWW organizers. The IWW, also known as "Wobblies," had "stood with the Negro." In its southern publication The Voice of the People, editor Covington Hall regularly urged "white workers in the South to remember how racism had always been used by the ruling class to divide black and white to injury of both."[39] Though limited in influence, in the South the Brotherhood of Timber Workers' constitution welcomed African American membership.[40]

There was one external factor working in favor of the company owners against the IWW. Wallowa County was difficult for the IWW to organize due to its isolation, particularly in winter months, and the strength of the regional Loyal Legion of Loggers and Lumbermen (Four Ls), a company union founded in 1918 during World War I by the US War Department.[41] Maxville was part of "Four Ls District 11," comprised of Umatilla, Union, Wallowa, Grant, and Baker Counties and headquartered

Courtesy Pearl Alice Marsh
Amos Marsh, Sr. at Wallowa, Oregon.

37   "Democracy at Home," editorial, *Enterprise Chieftain*, February 11, 1943.

38   "Strike of Loggers Proves to be a Part of the General May 1st I.W.W.," *Wallowa Sun*, May 3, 1923; Philip S. Foner, Organized Labor and the Black Worker (Chicago: Haymarket Books, 2018).

39   Phillip S. Foner, "The I.W.W. and the Black Worker," *Journal of Negro History 55* (January 1970), 44¬–64.

40   James C. Maroney, "Brotherhood of Timber Workers," Texas State Historical Association, June 12, 2010, https://tshaonline.org/handbook/online/articles/ocbbb.

41   Harold M. Hyman, *Soldiers and Spruce: Origins of the Loyal Legion of Loggers and Lumbermen* (Los Angeles: Institute of Industrial Relations, University of California, 1963).

Brookhaven, Mississippi.

in Baker.

In the face of that dual challenge, Ashby's best bet was to recruit workers outside the unionized northwest and locate the expanded workforce, including African American loggers, in remote Maxville, the company town under his control. So he looked to the South, where both he and Bowman-Hicks had experience and contacts. Ashby started recruiting experienced workers—without regard to race—who were unspoiled by the radical unionization of the IWW.

Ashby was unsure what kind of reception his mixed-race workforce would receive in the new Bowman-Hicks location. But as the principal authority governing Maxville, he had an obligation to maintain social peace among the workers and their families regardless of race.

Upon the arrival of the first African American loggers in April 1923, Ashby armed himself and met the loggers with armed guards at the La Grande train station to assure their safe passage to the logging camp. Ashby had the workers spend the night in La Grande and then escorted them to Maxville the next day. After initial selective recruitment, Ashby paid a bounty to newly hired workers to recruit friends and family members in order to avoid hiring unknown militant union members. Aggressive recruitment attracted an additional forty to sixty African Americans.[42]

The absence of serious racial conflicts in Maxville was characteristic of most southern sawmill towns, as noted in early twentieth-century company towns in Texas:

> *Because of the effectiveness of the lumber companies' control of their towns, few serious race incidents marred the sixty-year history of Texas boom-era lumbering, and no mob of outraged workers ever looted and burned a company's office or commissary store. In truth, visitors often remarked upon the degree of companies' social and economic control over their mill towns.*[43]

Against this backdrop, Ashby had to set the tone for race relations between African American and white workers and their families in Maxville. Consistent with Bowman-Hicks's southern-based policy and company towns in all industries, Ashby segregated the housing and schools in Maxville along class, ethnic, and racial lines. A good example of this kind of segregation is the sawmill town of Weed, California, where Long-Bell Lumber Company recruited workers.[44] This practice also was consistent with the heav-

---

42 Trice, "Maxville, Oregon: 1923–1945."

43 Sitton and Conrad, *Nameless Towns*, 80.

44 Mark Oliver, "From The Quarters to Lincoln Heights: The Untold Story of Far Northern California's African Ameri-

ily segregated racial and anti-immigrant climate at the time. Mining town sections in Virginia, for example, carried names such as Pink Town (American-born white), Colored Hill (African American), and Hunk Town (Eastern European immigrants). [45]

One white resident of Maxville recalls her childhood anticipation of the arrival of African American families, who would live in segregated housing quarters beyond the commissary.

We were all pretty excited when we learned that about 100 black families were moving into camp. I had never seen a black person. The school room was abuzz when I got there. We were told that the black kids would have their own school, that we were absolutely not supposed to go past the commissary. There were now two camps.

My first glimpse of black people came when I was on the steps of the commissary and a young black man came with his little girl. They went in and ordered the same things that Mom usually sent for: potatoes, canned milk, coffee, cabbage and carrots. Maybe they weren't so different![46]

The management decisions and personal style of Ashby and local Bowman-Hicks managers accounted in large measure for the absence of reported racial incidents in Maxville. By all accounts, Ashby was considered a "good man"[47] who respected African American workers and promoted social fraternization, even though he represented a segregated southern company. His management team also reflected his management philosophy. Among them were Superintendent J.D. MacMillan, woods bosses Joe Crowley and Don Riggle.

Don Riggles' daughter, Ronee Stone, remembers,

One day my dad shared that he always carried a gun in a holster when he was out in the woods. He became a woods boss for Mr. Ashby and one time when he was visiting with one of the black loggers, the logger asked him, "Are you still afraid of us?" "What do you mean?" replied Don. "Well, you are still carrying your gun, so we figure you're still afraid of us!" "Oh, no," said Don, "I carry this to protect us!" My dad had tears in his eyes when he told me this story. He thought how sad it was that all that time those men thought it was because he feared them.

In his memoir, Amos Marsh, Sr., an African American log cutter, recalls Ashby sending him out to instruct astonished white workers on demarcating timberlines.

Old man Ashby had given me the authority to show some white guys that come out there, gypos or contractors to haul logs, their lines. He showed me the tract of timber they was to haul. He told me to show it to them and I did. They didn't know all of that. So, when I went to show it to them, they say, "What did Mr. Ashby say?" They wasn't gonna do nothin' on my word.

I says, "That's what Mr. Ashby told me to tell you. I'm just working like the rest of you."

"Well," they said, "you got a pretty big job here, ain't you?"

---

can History and Film Guide Companion," film guide companion, http://markoliver.org/fromthequarters/TheQuarters.pdf.

45   "Company Towns: 1880s to 1935," *The Social Welfare History Project*, Virginia Commonwealth University, updated March 12, 2018, https://socialwelfare.library.vcu.edu/programs/housing/company-towns-1890s-to-1935/.

46   Elizabeth Huffman Mata, "Our Family History Excerpt," *North Woods of Wallowa County Vol. 1*: 27.

47   I heuristically define "good man" as someone trustworthy with a strong internal moral code capable of acting counter to the negative norm.

I said, "No, I'm just like the rest of them, cutting logs."
But I'm able to take them out there on the man's word and show them where their lines was. They thought I was a "big nigger."[48]

Ashby also hired African American Willie Cook, from Brookhaven, Mississippi, to work as an electrician for the mill in Wallowa. He gave African Americans the opportunity to establish independent hauling companies, known as "gypos." One African American logger, William Lee Thomas, owned logging trucks. In addition to driving a truck himself, Thomas hired local drivers before his wife's death required him to move his family to Louisiana.

Logger Walter Patterson recalled:

I worked in the mills, cut logs, drove logging trucks, right there in Wallowa. You know that colored guy had them logging trucks there? What's his name? William Lee? You know William Lee Thomas. His wife died. She was young.[49]

Bonds between African American and white loggers were forged for practical reasons. Integrated labor processes of the timber enterprise in the woods and the danger of the work meant they depended on one another for their safety. Local newspapers routinely chronicled incidents from loss of limb to loss of life related to lumbering. In June 1936, Hoy Carman, a white young man, was badly injured in the woods. Lafayette "Lucky" Trice, an African American logger, carried him a mile to where his father was working, and then the two of them carried him another mile and a half to their Ford truck.

Hoy Carman, 19-year-old son of Mr. and Mrs. P. V. Carman, was badly skinned and bruised Tuesday when a falling tree struck him on the back, rendering him blind and unconscious for a short time while working on a logging road at Camp 5 at Vincent.

At the time of the accident, Hoy and two companions, Mr. Trice a negro, and Melvin Smith were on a caterpillar working the road. Melvin Smith, seeing the tree which was being felled coming in their direction, yelled and Hoy ducked quickly thus escaping it striking him squarely on the head. As it was it hit him on the shoulders and back skinning and bruising him badly and tearing his clothes in shreds.

Mr. Trice, alone, carried the boy a mile to where his father was working and then the two men carried him a mile and a half to their Ford pickup. They placed springs and a mattress in that and laid the lad on it and brought him out over the Smith Mountain road. At the Ashby cabin in the canyon they phoned Dr. Gillstrap of La Grande and he met them in an ambulance on Cricket Flat.

The doctor told Mrs. Carman they had taken several X-rays and had found no broken bones but that Hoy would have to remain in the hospital for 3 or 4 days and it would probably be 2 or 3 weeks before he would be able to work.[50]

At home in Maxville, African American and white women befriended one another around domestic work to fortify their families—spiritually and materially—against the harsh and isolated living conditions. Some of them shared gardening, canning, cooking,

48 Amos Marsh, Sr., interview with Pearl Alice Marsh, Wallowa, Oregon, July 1993; Pearl Alice Marsh, "A Black Logger's Journey: Jackson Parish, Louisiana, to Wallowa County, Oregon," *Oregon Historical Quarterly* 116, no. 4 (Winter 2015): 500–521.

49 Walter Pete Patterson, interview with Pearl Alice Marsh, July 22–24, 1991, Bly and Wallowa, OR.

50 "Lad Seriously Hurt by Falling Tree," *Wallowa Sun*, June 18, 1946.

Courtesy Orvalla Hafer

Housing the company provided for the black loggers that came with the Bowman Hicks Lumber Company from the South; Louisiana, Mississippi and Arkansas. Notice the pigs running loose in the foreground and the clothes on the clothes line between the houses. Those quarters, as well as the black children's school, were located on the north side of Maxville near the railroad and in the area where the water exited the ponds into the canyon. Domestic water flowed from a spring three miles south of Maxville, through a three inch pipe, to the big houses of the company men. The other houses had water piped to outside faucets. 2011 "Where There's a Will, There's a Way," Promise calendar, by Orvalla Hafer.

Note: Hogs figured prominently in all pioneer/frontier households throughout Wallowa County and were an important food source.

quilting, sewing, crocheting, and child care. This interdependence forged interracial bonds that were unlike those in other cities, towns, and industries.

Bowman-Hicks drew racial lines in housing and education out of its own tradition as a southern town and perhaps to appease some southern white workers living in Maxville. Maxville's housing and schools were segregated racially, and company-sponsored baseball teams were organized separately for African Americans and whites, though they played against each other.

Other amenities and activities, such as the commissary and social hall, were not segregated. And company-sponsored social events were celebrated community-wide, regardless of race. A 1927 newspaper article mentioned a few of the Fourth of July party organizers without noting the ethnicity of the loggers; Fred Warrior and R. L. Baggett were African American and the Wises were white.

Maxville, too, is to celebrate the 4th of July with a celebration to last three days and beginning Saturday, July 2nd, according to announcement brought to town Monday by Mr. Fred Warrior, an [African American] logger originally from Arkansas,[51] who was making local arrangements for the fete that will include a big

---

51   An African American logger originally from Pine Bluff, Arkansas.

Courtesy Stan Walker,

This shows the early Maxville Camp before the town was built. The single men lived in the railroad cars. There were double bunks on both walls and a walkway in the center. Single men continued to live in these bunkhouses after the town was established.

barbecue, dances, foot races, greased pole, greased pig, and similar exciting novelty and athletic events.

Fred Warrior is to be the manager of the barbecue and R. L. Baggett is the manager of the dance and refreshments.

Music for the dance will be provided by Mr. and Mrs. Wise[52] of Maxville. Dancing will be in the public hall. A prize will be given to the best dancer. An invitation is extended to everyone to attend.[53]

In the beginning, Maxville had two company-sponsored baseball teams—an African American and a white team—reminders of the way Jim Crow laws heavily circumscribed baseball in the Deep South. An example is the following Georgia law:

Amateur Baseball–It shall be unlawful for any amateur white baseball team to play baseball on any vacant lot or baseball diamond within two blocks of a playground devoted to the Negro race, and it shall be unlawful for any amateur colored baseball team to play baseball in any vacant lot or baseball diamond within two blocks of any playground devoted to the white race.[54]

Courtesy Agnes Lively Fuller

Opal Lively Fuller believes this is the baseball diamond at Maxville. It is typical of all the baseball diamonds of the time.

---

52 Per local historians Sally Goebel and Zora Belle Roley, the Wises were white and lived on Smith Mountain in the 1920s.

53 "Maxville to Celebrate 4th," *Wallowa Sun*, June 16, 1927.

54 "Examples of Jim Crow Laws," Ferris State University.

Courtesy Fred Hill Historical Photos Collection and Eastern Oregon University Digital Collection
La Grande, Oregon, c. 1920-1940.

Unlike in the South, the Maxville African American team played against local white teams in Wallowa and Union counties.

The Maxville Colored Giants, who were to have come to Enterprise to play, will be here next Sunday to meet the Knights of Pythias team, according to present arrangements. Heavy rains made impossible on the previous date. The game is set for 2:30 o'clock on the fairgrounds and admission will be charged to pay the expenses of both teams. Three games have been played by the lodge teams of Enterprise and Wallowa and the interest was sufficient to suggest a continuation of the sport, with an outside club. The Negro boys of Maxville are expected to put up a strong game and it will be worth seeing.[55]

By 1941, the town of Wallowa fielded an interracial team that was managed by an African American named Goldman King.

The Wallowa Wildcats newly organized baseball team under the management of Goldman King and comprising talent both white and colored, will play its first exhibition game on the Wallowa Diamond next Sunday April 6, with another local team their opponents.

The Wildcats won the opener at Promise last Sunday, defeating the Promise Promiselanders, 14 to 6.[56]

Ad from the *Wallowa Sun* about 1926 for an upcoming baseball game between Maxville and Wallowa teams.

In addition to integrated baseball games, African Americans were featured along with whites in

---

55 "Maxville Negro Boys to Play Ball Sunday," *Enterprise Chieftain*, June 27, 1929.

56 "Wallowa to Play First Game Here on Sunday," *Wallowa Sun*, Thursday, April 3, 1941.

the local newspaper, at times for the most mundane activities.

Wallowa Sun February 7, 1929. "Ben Taylor of Enterprise attended the play Friday night."

> Note: Benjamin Taylor was a local African American man born on July 22, 1905, in Oklahoma. In 1920, when he was fifteen years old, he lived with his family in Crane, Oregon. His father, Gus, worked as a section hand for the railroad company. His mother, Anna, was a housewife and mother. He had one brother and five sisters. Benjamin probably moved to Enterprise in the mid-1920s, and he graduated from Enterprise High School. In 1930, Benjamin worked as a janitor in a garage in Enterprise. He stayed in Enterprise until around 1940 when he moved to Fresno, California. He died on February 11, 1966, in Fresno, California, at the age of sixty, and was buried there.

Wallowa Sun, December 30, 1930. "Ben Taylor and Minnie Lee Holland were married at La Grande on Thursday Dec. 23. The groom works at the Frees garage in Enterprise. The bride came from Oakland, California. Friends extend best wishes.

Wallowa Sun, February 11, 1932. "Henry Carper, Lacy Trump, and Bob Baggett [African American] butchered a hog Thursday."

Wallowa Sun, October 8, 1936. "Mrs. Lillie Baggett [African American] returned last Sunday from Brookhaven, Mississippi, where she had gone to visit her mother, Mrs. Beulah Griffin, who has been seriously ill. Mrs. Baggett reported her mother somewhat improved when she left. Before returning to Oregon, she also visited friends in New Orleans.

Courtesy Pearl Alice Marsh
Photo of Moses Blinks.

The arrival of African American relatives from the South also was worth noting in the local newspaper.

Mose Blinks arrived from Louisiana to live with his two daughters, Mrs. Carrie Hudson and Mrs. Mary McDole.[57]

Newspapers reported when African American loggers participated in recreational contests at local fairs alongside whites.[58]

"La Grande Pair Sawing Champs" , *La Grande Observer*, July 6, 1939.

Unofficial log sawing champions of northeastern Oregon today were J. L. Langford and Ester Wilfong of La Grande, sturdy Negro team who sawed two cuts from a 22-inch log at the Baker Mining Jubilee in 1 minute, 8 seconds to best the largest field of sawyers ever to take part in the Jubilee. They won $125 by their prowess.

Second place was taken by a team from Seneca, with a California duet winning third honors.

Other La Grande teams were Lonnie Powell and Robert Mack; Fred Brown and Fred Samuel; and Ed and Joe Mobley.[59]

---

57 "112-YearOld Negro Arrives at Maxville," *Wallowa Sun*, September 4, 1941.

58 The African American log cutters are identified as La Grande residents, which is where Bowman-Hicks Lumber Company was headquartered. Langford and Wilfong and their families were living in La Grande.

59 Langford and Wilfong lived in La Grande; Powell, Mack, Brown, Samuel, and the Mobleys lived in Maxville.

When the gas-fueled chainsaw was introduced to Wallowa County, the local distributor challenged the best local crosscut team, Amos Marsh and Jessie Langford, to a contest. According to Edsel White of La Grande:

> When they first started using power chainsaws to cut logs, they were two-man saws. There was a fella and his son up there at Joseph. They were demonstrating the power chain saw to sell.
>
> They came down to Wallowa and wanted to sell one to Amos Marsh and Jessie Langford. Amos and Jesse told them, "If you can fall a tree with it, buck it and limb it as fast as we can with our [manual] crosscut, we'll buy it."
>
> Amos and Jesse went out in the woods and picked out two trees about the same size. Amos and Jesse beat them. They beat them with the crosscut. And they didn't buy one of them two-man power saws.[60]

Over time, the harsh weather and social and cultural isolation from fellow African Americans pushed most families down the mountain from Maxville to other towns. Some moved to Wallowa and a few to an unincorporated area called Wade Siding, later named Water Canyon after Ashby built his private home and residences for workers. Most African Americans moved about fifty miles west from Maxville to La Grande in neighboring Union County, which had a small but thriving African American community.

While the men continued to work in Wallowa County, wives and children lived, worked, and went to school in La Grande. The men "batched"[61] in Maxville and later Wallowa during the week and then returned to La Grande on weekends.

Some women pursued their career aspirations as well. Atrice Hilliard, for example, had taught school in Mississippi but was not credentialed to teach in Oregon. Hilliard entered Eastern Oregon College and, while working and raising a family, earned her degree. She never taught but was employed as the librarian at the junior high school.

Courtesy Pearl Alice Marsh

Old Bowman-Hicks company house in Wallowa. Houses for the black workers was located acoss the railroad tracks by the Bowman-Hicks lumber mill.

---

60 Edsel White, interview by Pearl Alice Marsh, La Grande, Oregon, May 14, 2015.

61 Lived alone as bachelors.

Marion Hawthorne also pursued an advanced college degree. In 1949, under her previous married name McClain, she joined the La Grande Little Theater. She had enjoyed theater in her hometown of Brunswick, Georgia.[62] Though relegated to the role of maid in plays, she took pride in the part she played in La Grande's civic and cultural life. In 1953, a newspaper headline declared, "Meeting Has Inter-Racial Significance" when Hawthorne was a guest from the Boyd Memorial Baptist Church and gave a very helpful and impressive devotional.[63] In 1958, she was installed as the president of the Greenwood School Parents and Teachers Association.[64]

La Grande was an important railroad hub for the region, which enabled African Americans to venture from the South into Union County. In 1920, there were seven African American families and about twenty boarders who worked for the railroad company as janitors, cooks, teamsters, coal shovelers, machine shop sweepers, or firemen.[65] By 1930, the number of households had doubled to fifteen families.[66] By comparison, in 1930, there were twenty-three African American households in Maxville, but that number dwindled to four by 1940, while the number of La Grande's African American households grew to thirty-six.

Families in La Grande found kinship and social solidarity in churches, social clubs, fraternal organizations, cafés, and juke joints. The population was not large enough to break down into social classes, but there were institutions and activities that loosely demarcated social boundaries. People flowed in and out of churches, but membership in the Masonic Lodge and Order of the Eastern Star fraternal organizations was controlled by a set of strict criteria that many in the community could not meet.

In April 1944, men from Wallowa and Union counties organized the Masonic-affiliated Rocky Mountain Lodge #5 F&AM.[67] Grand Masters Ernest J. Brown and Sgt. L. W. Sims of Spokane assisted in setting up the group. Officers were Jack Gillespie, Worshipful Master; Fred S. Samuel, Senior Warden; Robert L. Baggett, Junior Warden; Roosevelt Coney, Secretary; Robert Mack, Senior Deacon; William Lee Thomas, Treasurer; Amos Marsh, Tyler. Other members were Joe Patterson, Sr., James White, Lester Lane, Fred Samuel, and William M. Torrence.[68] The Masons and Eastern Stars gathered in the hall above Dave's Market to perform their rituals and organize charity events.

Parents who used to live in Maxville sent their children to integrated schools in La Grande and felt reasonably comfortable allowing them freedom to go to town alone, shop in stores, and attend movie theaters without barriers. While the families experienced new personal liberty, there were still social realities of racism in the schools, physically segregated housing, and little tolerance for interracial romantic relationships. For African American children, particularly the males, becoming teenagers increased the chance of white violence in response to any perceived interracial romance.

Interracial marriage between African Americans and whites had been banned since

---

62 "Kiss and Tell Cast Readies Play for Presentation Here on Saturday," La Grande Observer, April 20, 1949.

63 *La Grande Observer*, "Meeting Has Inter-Racial Significance," September 08, 1953, page 3.

64 "Candlelight Ceremony Held for Greenwood PTA Officers," *La Grande Observer*, May 29, 1958.

65 US Federal Census, 1920.

66 US Federal Census, 1930.

67 "Colored Masonic Organized Here; Holds Meeting," *La Grande Observer*, April 25, 1944.

68 Other members of the community were installed as members over the next decade.

1862 in Oregon. The law forbidding whites to marry anyone one-quarter or more black[69] was not repealed until 1951. However, interracial marriage was not illegal in the state of Washington. So Lonnie Powell, who was African American, and Dorothy Juanita William, who was white, both from Maxville, married in Walla Walla on January 25, 1941. The ceremony was officiated by a Salvation Army officer and witnessed by a fellow African American logger and his wife, Adam and Isoria (Blinks) Hart.[70] After the wedding and perhaps a celebratory meal at a local café, the newlyweds promptly returned home to live in Maxville with no reported controversy.

A more challenging interracial incident occurred in the early 1940s between an African American man and a married white woman. Over time the two became too careless with their romantic relationship, given the small size of Wallowa. One afternoon, a group of white men chased the man, who found refuge in the home of Joe Patterson, Sr.

When the white men arrived, Patterson went out to meet them with his .30-30 Winchester lever action rifle. The men explained, "We just want to talk to him, Joe."

Patterson responded, "Well, there ain't going to be none of that down here."

When the white men left, Patterson told the African American that he had to leave because the African American community did not need that kind of trouble.[71]

Years later, in the late 1950s, Wallowa High School Coach Don Wilson recalled that Amos Marsh, Jr., who went to school in Wallowa from first grade through high school graduation, didn't have any romantic girlfriends.

> I think maybe that was just a line you didn't cross. The girl in Enterprise, she and Amos were friends. Don't know how close friends. Don't know anything about it. But I do know that after one basketball game, they had a milkshake bet. And she bet on Enterprise and Amos on Wallowa. And they played the ballgame down here and Wallowa won the ball game. So they went down to Burrows Café, and they were sitting at the counter having a milkshake. And I was cleaning up after the kids left, and I came home, and I got a phone call.
>
> I think I got two or three women calling up and told me I had to talk to Amos because he was down there with a white girl. I said, "She's paying off a milkshake bet with her friend." "Well, you ought to talk to him. He shouldn't be down there with a white girl.[72]

Historical newspapers and other records document some notable progress of individual African American loggers after their Maxville experience. Willie Cook and Lafayette "Lucky" Trice are perhaps the most notable pioneering men for what is recognized as opportunity and success beyond racial barriers in northeastern Oregon. The family of William and Earmine (Barnett) Torrence achieved more notably than many families of either race.

Willie Cook, who as noted earned his electrical credentials, worked as an electrician for the mill in Wallowa and became the first African American to hold an electrical contractor's license[73] in the state of Oregon. Eventually Cook left Maxville for Pendleton, where he started his own business, Cook Car Clinic. After success as a businessman

---

69   Oregon Racial Laws and Events, 1844–1959, accessed February 16, 2019, http://www.ode.state.or.us/opportunities/grants/saelp/orraciallaws.pdf.

70   Marriage license recorded in Walla Walla, Washington.

71   This event was witnessed by a descendant who wishes to remain anonymous.

72   Don Wilson, interview by Pearl Alice Marsh, July 2015.

73   Obituary: Dr. Reverend Willie P. Cooke, Pastor Emeritus Shiloh Baptist Church, , Octobeer 2, 2012, private Family Document (unpublished).

Courtesy Irene Barklow collection, Wallowa County Museus

The Palmer Logging Company donkey loader. Bowman-Hicks purchased this loader from Palmer and would have used it in the same way. Lucky Trice was a log loader for part of the time he worked for Bowman-Hicks.

in Pendleton, he went on to head the historic Shiloh Baptist Church in Sacramento, California.

Lucky Trice migrated to Maxville with his father and brother in the mid-1920s. He worked on a skidder in Arkansas before coming to Oregon. In Maxville, he worked on building the railroad and as a log loader. He left logging and embraced the opportunities afforded in La Grande. After being honorably discharged from the US Army in 1945, Lucky was hired as a special police officer by the city of La Grande.[74] He went on to become a successful entrepreneur, establishing Lucky's Furnace Cleaning Service, and he became an honored member of La Grande's white civic community.

La Grande railroad employee William Torrence and his wife, Earmine, brought their children from Smackover, Arkansas, in the late 1920s to work for the railroad company. Their son Willie, Jr., born in 1915, became an active member of the high school sports teams in La Grande, setting records in the javelin and high jump. In May 1938, Willie received his bachelor of arts degree in social sciences from the University of Oregon, where he majored in psychology and was pledged into a medical honorary society. Their daughter, Ellen Torrence, graduated from the University of Oregon in 1941 with a bachelor of science degree. She became a recreational director for the American Red Cross and was stationed in New Guinea, Australia, and the Philippines. Both Torrence boys, Willie and James, also had distinguished careers in the US Navy.

Later, Amos Marsh, Jr., the oldest son of Wallowa's Amos Marsh, Sr., and his wife Mary (Patterson) Marsh, became a star athlete at Oregon State University and went on to play professional football for the Dallas Cowboys and Detroit Lions. Amos, Jr. and Mary's second son, Frank Wayne, graduated from Oregon State, and their daughter, Pearl Alice, became the first African American woman to earn a doctoral degree in political science from the University of California at Berkeley.

---

74   "Trio Jailed Here on Drunk Charges," *La Grande Observer,* October 22, 1946;
"Police Fill Jail as Roundup of Men as Drunks Made:, *La Grande Observer*, November 20, 1946.

CHAPTER III   THE FAMILIES AND THEIR ROOTS
THE FIRST-GENERATION AFRICAN OREGONIANS

Courtesy Irene Gartzke and her son Jack Shine

In this photo a building is being moved from Palmer Junction, on the Grande Ronde river to Maxville after Bowman-Hicks purchased the holdings from Nibley-Mimnaugh. We don't know if this building would be used for storage, housing or other outbuilding. The back window appears to have a curtain on it. There are eight working men in the photos, some of whom may be black. Notice the skids the building is sitting on, the log harness used to lift the building, the donkey (machine) lifting it and men with ropes and cables guiding the load. Note the steel rails and flatcar with chains dangling from the timbers. A flatcar will be moved under the skids, the building will be anchored and transported to Maxville.[1] (See maps in the Index.)

_____
1   The North Woods, Vol. 1, p.30.

This historical background is intended to contextual-ize this collection of youthful memories of contributors who recount intrepid adventures into the white world as children, as they navigated an integrated environment barely known to their parents. These experiences provided evidence of progress in the social transition for their families from rigid southern segregation to "freedom."

The scraps and patches of memories shared in this collection start in the 1920s with hand-me-down-stories told by first- and second-generation descendants of their elders. They detail the genesis of voluntarily uprooting from the South and participating in the extended family migration. Stories from the late 1930s, the 1940s, and the 1950s are firsthand memories of children who lived in and visited relatives in Maxville, Wallowa, and La Grande. After Maxville closed as an incorporated municipality in 1933,[1] the community continued until the late 1940s, using neighboring Promise as its post office.

Courtesy Edsel White & Wallowa History Center
Promise postoffice on the William Sannar homestead, c. 1937

_____
1   Trice, "Maxville."

In the late 1930s, a lot of the town was dismantled, sold off to local buyers and many buildings moved down the mountain to Wallowa.

I still remember the time when my dad, Charlie Goebel, and Columbus Fisher hauled those houses from Maxville. It was 1937, '38, and '39. I was about five. When my brothers and sisters were in school, I would ride with my dad in his truck.[2]

My dad had a '36 Ford truck with a single axle, an eight rig up, and a logging trailer on it. He hauled logs and lumber the year around. Those homes had been hauled out there on the railroad. But, Dad hauled them out exactly the way we hauled logs. Out of the 58 houses we hauled, we only lost one.

Courtesy Goebel Family Collection

Charley Goebel's logging truck, c1936.
L-R: Unknown, Jack Goebel, and his father Charlie Goebel

The last remaining families migrated down the mountain to Wallowa while the majority moved to La Grande in neighboring Union County. Friends, family, and associates of the African American loggers continued to flow in and out of northeastern Oregon for work until the Portland area shipyards opened for employment during World War II.

This collection of memories provides an impression of early race and community in Wallowa and Union counties through the experiences of the decendents through the 1960s. Some of the experiences may lend themselves to a broader understanding of emerging race relations in Oregon, while others depict experiences peculiar to the facts of their individual situations. These memories collectively do not constitute a theory of race relations in Oregon. There is plenty of research and writing on that topic.[3] Nor is it a complete recollection of racial interactions in Wallowa and Union counties, as the descendants can only tell their side of the story from their experiences as children. Rather, the memories detail how these individual families navigated the interstices of freedom within the context of race, community, and law and created a new life beyond their restrictive origins in the South.

These migration stories are of two communities: one of African Americans in Maxville and Wallowa in Wallowa County and the other of African Americans in La Grande in Union County.

The Maxville-Wallowa story is about living and growing up in a working-class company logging town. As the African American population dwindled, there remained only one African American family with children, the Marshes, who left Wallowa in 1958.

The La Grande story is about growing up in a more conventional small Oregon town

---

2   Interview with Jack Goebel by Pearl Alice Marsh, Recorded with NoNotes.com, Patterson, CA and Wallowa, OR, March 5, 2019.

3   Robert W. O'Brien and Lee M. Brooks, "Race Relations in the Pacific Northwest," Phylon (1940–1956) 7, no. 1 (1946): 21–31; Alana Semuels, "This Racist History of Portland, the Whitest City in America," Atlantic, July 22, 2016; Michael James Hamberg, "Flood of Change: The Vanport Flood and Race Relations in Portland, Oregon," master's thesis, Central Washington University, accepted Spring 2017.

with multiple factors contributing to the African American presence, including the railroad. The last African American family remaining in La Grande was the Trices.

These little-known and short-lived African American experiences would be lost without written recollections. These memories are their stories of freedom, hope, and resilience.

THE FAMILIES

The collection of memories represents the migration pattern of African American extended families and their friendship networks leaving the South for Oregon.

THE LOWRY-MAYS DESCENDANTS: PINE BLUFF, ARKANSAS

Courtesy Robert Minor

Hosea and friend standing in front of the frozen water fountain at Wallowa Lake.

The first three memories are those of the descendants of Hosea and Lucy (Tate) Lowry from Pine Bluff, Jefferson County, Arkansas. They were among the early Bowman-Hicks Company recruits.

Pine Bluff was farming country, and the Lowrys were farmers. After the Civil War ended, African Americans were given access to some confiscated and abandoned farmland to establish and manage their own farms.[4] In December 1895, the family patriarch, Jefferson Lowry, born in 1865 in Oklahoma, homesteaded forty acres of land in Jefferson County, Arkansas.[5] Jefferson and his wife, Phoebe Trice, were Hosea's parents. Cotton was the major crop. As the timber industry grew, the Lowrys and other farmers rotated seasons between farming and work in the sawmills.

The timber industry in Arkansas developed in all directions after the Civil War. The abundant forests of the state made it possible over the years to produce lumber, kraft paper, fine paper, newsprint, chemicals, charcoal, and many other products.[6]

Cotton was seasonal and vulnerable to disease, weather, and price fluctuations. Wages in the timber industry were more stable.

When the opportunity came in 1923 to move west with the Bowman-Hicks Lumber Company, Hosea Lowry, along with some of his cousins, the Trice family, moved west.

Hosea was born September 29, 1887, and Lucy Tate, his wife, was born April 2, 1902, both in Pine Bluff. The couple married April 18, 1918. Hosea died on January 16, 1978, in La Grande, Oregon, at the age of eighty. Lucy died on March 25, 1954, in La Grande

---

4   "Agriculture," The Encyclopedia of Arkansas History and Culture, accessed February 9, 2019, http://www.encyclopediaofarkansas.net/encyclopedia/entry-detail.aspx?entryID=385.

5   General Land Office records, US Bureau of Land Management, US Department of the Interior, accessed February 9, 2019, https://glorecords.blm.gov/details/patent/default.aspx?accession=AR0440__.350&docClass=STA&sid=du4r2uqh.ay0.

6   "Timber Industry," The Encyclopedia of Arkansas History and Culture, accessed February 9, 2019, http://www.encyclopediaofarkansas.net/encyclopedia/entry-detail.aspx?entryID=2143.

Picking cotton in the south.

at the age of fifty-one. Both are buried in the Island City Cemetery. Hosea and Lucy had six children during their marriage: daughters Obie (1919), Johnnie B. (1921), and Georgie (1927), and sons T. J. (1925), Hasker (1926), and Oscar (1926).

Nathaniel Mays, son of Georgie (Lowry) and Will Mays, was in 1946 the first African American baby born in the hospital in Enterprise, Oregon. He recounts the migration story of his grandparents, Hosea and Lucy, from Pine Bluff to Maxville. Lucille Bridgewater, his sister, recalls visits to Maxville as a young girl. Robert Minor, son of Obie (Lowry) and James Monroe "Butch" Minor, was born in 1940 in Pine Bluff, Arkansas. His memories, published here, are a summary of a brief interview in which he discussed growing up in La Grande. Robert passed away in 2016 in Portland, Oregon.

COOK-THOMAS DESCENDANTS: , MISSISSIPPI

The two memories in this section are those of the descendants of Cook family loggers recruited from Brookhaven, Mississippi.

The Cooks were farmers. Ancestor Willie P. Cook, born in 1876 in Indiana, and his wife, Beaulah Dora (Adams), born in 1883 in Mississippi, owned their own farm. The

Courtesy Veronica Cook-Ramsey
Alex Cook, logger at Maxville, 1940.

family farmed and invested in the boys' education as they grew up.

After Robert L. Baggett lost his first wife, Bobbie, in Maxville, the community sent back to Brookhaven for a willing "mail order bride," Lillie Mae Trummell (Cook). After Lillie and Bob married, the Cook family followed their older sister to Maxville: Alexander, known as "Alec," Theola, Willie, and Hattie Louise. Hattie Louise, called "Louise", came from Brookhaven to Maxville through this family's "chain migration." That is how Louise met and married William Lee Thomas.

Rosie (Thomas) Gray, whose memories are the first in this section, is the daughter of Hattie Louise (Cook), born August 21, 1922, in Brookhaven, and William Lee Thomas, born October 15, 1911, in Mansfield, Louisiana. Louise and William Lee were married on November 26, 1940, in Wallowa. He died February 3, 1993, in Marshall, Texas, at the age of eighty-one. She died as a young mother March 9,

1948, in Union, Oregon, at the age of twenty-five.

The next memory from the Cook family is Katherine (Cook) Ramsey's. She is the daughter of Alexander and Ella (Dillon) Cook. The memory is a summary from an interview conducted before Katherine passed away in 2016 in her home in Richmond, California.

HILLIARD DESCENDANT: BROOKHAVEN, MISSISSIPPI

This memory is from Joseph Hilliard, Jr., whose father, Joseph, Sr., was recruited from Brookhaven, Mississippi, by Frank Cook. His mother was Atrice (Smith) Hilliard (See photo page 72). Both parents were born in Brookhaven, Mississippi. Joseph, Sr., was recruited to Maxville by Willie Cook, a family friend. Joe and Atrice left their children, Carolyn and Harold, in Mississippi with grandparents as they moved to Maxville.

Atrice's father, Jessie Smith, attended Philander Smith College, a historically black college in Little Rock, Arkansas, in the 1920s. His brother, Frank, also attended college and went on to become the mayor of Minifee, Arkansas. Atrice followed in her father's footsteps and became a schoolteacher.

KING-LANE FAMILES: PEASON, LOUISIANA AND SHONDLOO, LOUISIANA

Theses memories are from descendants of the King and Lane families from Louisiana. The Lane family also lived in Florida. Like other states, Louisiana boasted both farming and timber industries. The "anchor" family in Maxville for the King-Lane family was Adam and Isoria (Blinks) Hart. Both were born in Arkansas. After Adam and Isoria moved to Maxville, her sister Carrie, who had lived in Louisiana and Florida, migrated to Maxville.

Kerry's parents were Goldman King, born on July 15, 1905, and Mattie Lee (Lane) King, born on December 1, 1915. Both were born in Louisiana. He died on March 12, 1994, in Sacramento, California, at the age of eighty-eight and is buried in Fair Oaks, California. She died on July 20, 2002, in West Sacramento, California, at the age of eighty-six. Goldman and

Courtesy Kerry King
Mattie Lee (Lane) King, wife of Goldman King and mother of Kerry King.

Courtesy Kerry King
Goldman King

31

Mattie Lee had three children: Ida Mae, Kerry, and Samuel. Kerry King is the oldest of the memoirists in this collection.

James Lester Lane is the descendant of Lester Lane, born April 13, 1917, in Shondlee, Louisiana, to his mother, Carrie, and her husband. James' mother, Dorothy (Kent), was born in 1919 in Florida. Dorothy and Lester were married in Washington County, Florida. They had three children during their marriage: Dorothy Lee, Rhoda Jeanette, and James Lester. Lester died on December 28, 2007, in Stockton, California, at the age of ninety.

Dorothy's second husband was Alvie Marsh, whom she married in Walla Walla, Washington. Dorothy and Alvie had three daughters, Oredia, Seretha Mae, and Ollie Marie. Dorothy died in 1953 in La Grande, Oregon, at the age of thirty-four.

PATTERSON-MARSH: EROS AND ALEXANDRIA, LOUISIANA

The families of the next five memories left Rapides and Jackson Parishes in Louisiana to work in the timber industry in McNary, Arizona, before migrating to Maxville. Louisiana boasted one of the largest timber industries in the country in the late nineteenth and early twentieth centuries. Sawmill towns owned by companies moved whole communities after depleting timber in an area. As mentioned previously, McNary shared that fate. After shutting down, the company had moved all of its workers and much of the sawmill to Cooley, Arizona, and renamed it McNary. The Pattersons followed the company.

Joseph Patterson, Sr., was a widowed preacher in Louisiana when he met and married Arie Spears Took, a widow with two daughters. The family moved to Arizona to work and then moved on to Wallowa County, Oregon, with their four boys and two girls.

The unmarried Marsh men left Jackson Parish, Louisiana, and migrated the way

many in that era did—they hoboed out of Louisiana to Arizona. From Arizona, they were recruited by Bowman-Hicks to come to Wallowa County, Oregon. Amos Marsh met and married Mary Patterson in Arizona. The descendant memories from this conjoined family are Nadine Patterson Kelly, Amos Marsh, Jr., Frank Wayne Marsh, Pearl Alice Marsh, and Kay Frances Marsh.

Courtesy Pearl Alice Marsh

L-R: Arie Spears "Ma Pat" Patterson, Aaron Patterson, Helen Vercher Patterson, Joseph "Pa Pat" Valley Patterson. Arie and Joe are husband and wife and Aaron and Helen are husband and wife.

ANDERSON: WAYCROSS, GEORGIA

Little is known about the community origins of Will Anderson in Georgia, but we know he was born September 9, 1895, in Waycross, Georgia. By the mid-1930s, he and his family were working in the timber industry in McNary, where the Pattersons and Marshes worked. He married Frances "Frankie" Spikes, who was born January 13, 1908, in Texas.

Will and Frankie's oldest child, Bessie Mae, was born in 1928 in Arizona. When Bessie was two years old, the family migrated to Maxville, where Will worked as a log cutter for Bowman-Hicks Lumber Company. After moving to Oregon, they had the following children: Helen (1929), Mayola (1932), William (1933), Gladys (1935), Robert (1938), Mildred Lee (1940), Janet Lee (1948), Joyce Marie (1943), and Luella Jean (1945). Luella Anderson Mazique's memories appear in this book.

Will Anderson died August 19, 1957, in Multnomah County, Oregon, at the age of sixty-one. Frankie Anderson died June 6, 2000, in Portland at the age of ninety-two.

CHAPTER IV OUR MEMORIES

These memories begin with the personal narrative of Amos Marsh, Sr., an African American log cutter who, beginning in 1939, worked for Bowman-Hicks Lumber Company in Maxville, Oregon. Marsh's journey began in 1932, moving from his family's farm in Jackson Parish, Louisiana, to McNary, Arizona, then to Kyberz, California, and finally to Maxvillle.

Amos Marsh was born on July 6, 1908, in Eros, Louisiana, the third child of Albert and Ollie (Elmore) Marsh. He had two sons and three daughters with Mary Rutledge Patterson between 1939 and 1948. He died on August 26, 2001, in San Jose, California, at the age of 93.

AMOS MARSH, SR. [1]

I left Louisiana back in 1932. We lived in Jackson Parish. Our family wasn't making a living farming and times were getting worse every year. We had a good farm, over 80 acres, but the man wouldn't buy from black farmers until the price dropped to nothin'. The Ku Klux Klan was ridin' too and my oldest brother Ed and some cousins had started to have run-ins with them. Mama and Papa decided it was best for us to leave. If the South had worked for us farming and the Klan hadn't been ridin', I never would have left Louisiana. That's how whole families moved. If my Uncle don't be in Arizona, I wouldn't have went there. And, if I hadn't gone to Arizona, I wouldn't have met Mary and got married.

Every Tom, Dick, and Harry was hoboing' and going somewhere. I had two bits in my pocket my cousin Tommy give me. I said, "I'm going some-

Courtesy Pearl Alice Marsh
Amos Marsh, Sr. as a young man, with Idella Williams and an unknown friend.

where, Tommy. I don't know where, but I'm leaving. You can't make a living down here."

Every time you looked up there was a freight train loaded with folks hoboing to somewhere. Looked like blackbirds and robins and crows up on top of the boxcars. Everybody was maneuvering to hop the train, so I got in a bunch up at Cartwright, [Louisiana], between Calhoun and Ruston and just kept going. I almost

Courtesy "Riding the Rails"
Photo of men running to jump on a train during the Great Depression. They "hoboed" from place to place looking for work and a meal.

---

1   Used by permission of the *Oregon Historical* quarterly,

Courtesy Pearl Alice Marsh

Many lumber companies moved employees and their families to new mill towns that included separate hous-ing for black and white workers. This undated photograph is of the "quarters" in McNary, Arizona, where African American workers, including Amos Marsh, Sr., lived.[1]

---

1   Forest History Society. *Marsh, A Black Logger's Journey.*

got killed a few times. I went to get off a train to look for something to eat and mis-judged the speed and boy, it threw me out there and then back up on the train. If I didn't hit standing up and hit that boxcar, I would have went up under that train and there wouldn't have been no more of me.

The authorities couldn't arrest you just for hoboing because there was too many folks doing it. They wouldn't have nowhere to put everybody. They would arrest you though if you doing wrong. Give you a couple of days on the chain gang. I never did get arrested, but saw guys who did. The guys were too tough when we get in the city — stealing and things. They put them on that chain gang. Have to work three or four days. That was about all they give 'em. When they turn them loose, they was glad to get back on a train and get out of there.

I crossed Louisiana, Texas, and New Mexico. I didn't get off the train for good until I got to Williams, Arizona. I know I had an uncle up there, my daddy's brother Frank. He had lived in McNary, Arizona, for a while but his ol' wife, Aunt Clara, didn't like "them niggas," she called black folks, that lived up there.

She was from Arkansas and was bright skinned with good hair and thought she was somebody. She tried to talk cute you know, say, "You can't take 'them niggas' nowhere." Pretty quick, Uncle Frank moved back up there to McNary. And then pretty quick Aunt Clara fell out with "them niggas" again. They had to move.

When I got to Williams, I met a guy that was one of Uncle Frank's good friends, and I asked him did he know Frank Marsh. And he said, "Yeah." "Well," I asked him, "Do you know where he stay? That's my uncle." Word got out that I was hunting him and he started hunting me. We was going around in circles.

When I found him, Uncle Frank was selling hot tamales. He had one of them big containers about yay tall. He set it down, took the lid off, got a long fork, and got me out about four or five. When I finished, he said, "You had enough?"

I said, "Naw, I ain't had enough." He knowed I hadn't eat on the train. I eat up about four or five more before I got full.

In a couple of days, Uncle Frank said, "Ain't no work here." Says, "If this mill was go-ing to run, there would be a job. But they just shut down for the winter." He said, "But you can go up to McNary and look for work." So, I come to McNary.

The first person I met, they called him Pa Pat. He and Ma Pat was living down where the Blacks was, way down in the quarters. The white quarters was up on the hill where I got off the train. The Blacks was down under the hill. They didn't live in the same quarters just like in Mississippi, Louisiana, and the rest of the South. So, I got off the train and went to the Black quarters.

Pa was just like he always been, fat, friendly, jolly, and loud. He asked, "Who are your folks? You got any here?" I told him Uncle Frank sent me from Williams. "Yeah? Come on," he says. Says, "come on home with me."

Then, when we got to his house, he says, "Come on in. Have some supper." I said, "Yeah." I didn't tell him I ain't eat nothing in three or four days.

Got there and his daughter Mary was getting ready to go somewhere. He says, "Ma'y." He called Mary Ma'y, but not Mary like I do. "Ma'y, I brought you a husband."

Courtesy Pearl Alice Marsh
Joe Valley Patterson, "Pa Pat"

Mary looked at me, rolled her eyes and said, "shit." I looked at her, rolled my eyes and said the same thing. Mary went on out of there and went about her business and I ate me some supper.

I got a job in McNary at the sawmill. During wintertime, when things got tight, I would go around there to Ma and Pa's house and eat. I kept fooling around there and started courting Mary. We courted for two years and then got married in [1934] on the twenty-first of June. Ma went with us down to the courthouse. Me and Mary and Ma and Mary's sister Pee Wee went. My brother Louie was there too.

Afterwards, we went to Uncle Frank and Aunt Clara's house in Williams for, I guess you could say, a honeymoon. We got up that next morning and Aunt Clara had breakfast ready. But, you know she was one of them funny kind. When we got up, she told Mary, "Look here what you was sleepin' on." She raised up the mattress and she had about five or six fifty-dollar bills up under there.

Mary said, "Well, it didn't make no difference to me. I didn't want it." Mary was just happy to be married. She wasn't worried about no fifty dollar bills. She would have a lot of them right there at home if I could keep a good job. Aunt Clara didn't figure we knowed nothing, but I bet she had the police outside all night.

Me and Mary got along good in McNary. After we bought our first car, Mary started to drive. She was the first woman around there to drive.

That McLamore fella, he wasn't bad looking. His wife was real good looking too. The McLamores had a car. He didn't allow his wife to drive until Mary got her car.

Somebody asked me, "You going to let your wife drive by herself?" Says, "She might take that car and don't come back." I said, "If she don't want to come back, she could

Courtesy Pearl Alice Marsh
Mary Patterson, age 19.

take it while I go to work and don't come back." I said, "That is no excuse for not letting your wife drive. If your wife don't want to stay, you can't keep her." Everybody finds that out, but some men just wants to be tough. "I ain't gonna give you no rope," they say to their wife.

Mary liked having her own money. She could save too. She used to charge people a few bits to drive 'em up to Pine Top to shop. She had a regular little route and a bunch of no-drivin' people to take up there. She would make a run a few times a week and have a car full. Mary loved to drive and she loved making a little money on her own.

In the election, Mary used to haul people to the polls to vote. She didn't charge them for that. That's the first time I ever voted. I voted for Roosevelt.

People would be getting off from work. Mary would go down, pick up a load, take them to the polls, go back, put them off. They come out of the gate and she carry them up there and right back.

Long as I knowed anything, Blacks liked the Republicans 'cause Lincoln freed the slaves. Things was still real bad after but you didn't gripe cause that's all you was used to. But, after while, people got a little schooling. Mary was the first one to read up a lot of that stuff. She said, "The Republicans ain't freed nobody. They just ended slavery under Lincoln's administration. But, it ain't changed nothin' for Blacks." So Mary got everybody voting for Democrats and I been one ever since.

Work was good in Arizona. We got respectable wages, especially after the union come in. When they first tried to set up the union, everybody was scared the company was going to run them off. One Black guy and some white guys come there and the Black guy got around there among the Blacks and told us, "If you get this union signed up, once you get it, they can't do nothing to you." Some of them kind of believed it but they didn't want to take no chance. I didn't want to take a chance either cause I ain't had nowhere to go if I lost my job. But I signed up anyhow and kind of took the lead in get-

Courtesy Wallowa County Museum
Drinking fountain at Water Canyon. Mr. Ashby's home was about a mile east along on the other side of the river. The fountain was important in the time of no air conditioning in automobiles. Almost everyone traveling through this part planned on stopping for a drink of cold water. This photo was taken before Highway 82 was paved. The fountain was moved and is set up on a lot in Elgin. It was moved when a young girl was hit by a car.

ting others to sign.

When they got enough signatures, fifty-one percent of the workforce, you automatically got a union. The company can't refuse you. So, they got the certain amount of signatures and it automatically become a union. And, it helped a lot. I been union ever since.

My wife's folks, Ma and Pa Patterson, left Arizona and went up to Oregon in [1937]. They moved to Water Canyon. That was up in Wallowa County. Pa and Ma had lived in McNary, Flagstaff, and Phoenix. He had to take Ma down there to Phoenix 'cause she couldn't stay up there in the high mountains. But, that was where the work was. Me and Mary stayed in McNary.

Another logger named Jim Williams — they called him "Fourspot" and his wife "Weedie" — used to go up to Wallowa in the summer to cut logs and then go back home to Arizona in the winter. Pa tried that a time or two — cut in the summer in Oregon where he could make more money. Then the winter come, he go back to Arizona.

The last time Pa went back, the man said, "You going back to Oregon this summer?" Pa said, "I don't know." The man say, "Well if you plan to go back, you had better go now." He didn't give Pa no more job so Pa had to leave Arizona. He just come on back up to Water Canyon and stayed. It probably would have been ten more years with him coming in the summer and going back to Arizona in the winter if the man had let him.

I left Arizona in October of [1938] after a run-in with the law. I fooled around and got accused of selling whiskey to some Indians. The government didn't let Indians buy whiskey, so

Courtesy Vearl Lewis
Jim "Fourspot" Williams and his wife Louise "Weedie" Williams.

some fellas I met was going down to Pine Top buying whiskey and bringing it back to McNary to sell.* Yeah. See, wasn't no liquor in McNary. That was on the Apache Reservation and selling whiskey on the reservation was a federal crime. They sent you to the penitentiary if you got caught. But, go down to the reservation gate and on down to Pine Top, you could buy liquor and sneak it back. Some of the guys sold pints, but I sold half pints. You didn't have to charge as much and Indians could afford them better. I didn't think the man knowed nothin' about us selling whiskey. But, he come arrest me and Johnny Miller and Jerry Mack and two or three more. Put us in jail. They was up there crying, "What they got me for? What they got me for?" I said, "They gonna have to charge us with something."

There was a bunch more down there, too. They set bail at $200 so none of us could get out. We just had to sit. Two Indians, Mary Stone and her old man Wallace, lied and told Mary I was going to the pen. They called theyselves White Mountain Apache. I told Mary not to believe what they was telling her. I didn't want to have no trouble with them when I got out of jail. And, I didn't want Mary to suffer, so I told her she could sell the car if she needed to.

In a day or two, we got a hearing. I saw some Indians sitting over there. One of 'em said, pointing at me, "He sell me whiskey." They had some whiskey bottles sitting there. The ol' prosecutor pointed at the bottles and asked me, "Did you sell this whiskey to these men?" I said, "No, I didn't sell nothin'." I had been selling whisky, but it hadn't happened the way they told it, so I wasn't guilty of that exact charge. I plead not guilty and so did the rest of 'em.

It was the trial day in court. The prosecutor started, "On such and such a day..." When they got to me, the Indian say "He sell me this whiskey." I didn't know that brand. And, it was a whole pint and I hadn't never sold a pint of whiskey in my life. I sold half pints. And he said, "On the twenty third day of August, 1938 . . ." And, on the twenty third day of August, I wasn't even in McNary, and I was able to prove it.

See, I was managing a little baseball team. And, the judge was at that ball game. He said, "Where was you on the twenty third day of August?" I said, "I was in Globe." That's where I was in jail at. "What was you doing here in Globe?" I said, "I had a ball game. I was managing a ball game."

So the judge said he was at that ball game and if I was managing it, I was

there, too.

The judge told me, "I want you to go home and work and take care of your wife and stay out of bad company." He said, "Bad company is the reason you got in trouble." I still got that letter, I believe, in the trunk. And when I got out of there, boy I want to tell you something, I was sho glad. And, the old sheriff, if he could have got me, he would have had them all. He had to turn me loose and had to turn all the rest of them loose.

Courtesy Pearl Alice Marsh
Uncle Louie and Frank Marsh

Some folks said the sheriff arrested us because he was runnin' a liquor operation hisself. Now, I don't say he paid them Indians to set us up, but he was the little sheriff and he could hold stuff over their heads too. I believe he was making money out of the deal somehow.

After I got home, Mary said, "Well, I'm sho glad. I was praying for you and you got out of there." I said, "That didn't get me out. I was innocent of the way they charged me and I proved it. That's what got me out."

Mary had got religion after we got married. Before, she would dance and drink a little beer. After we got married, she got sanctified and all of that stuff. She didn't want nothing after that, no whiskey, no beer, and no wine.

About two or three days after I got out, the sheriff started harrassin' me. He told me I had to get out of town. He was mad I made a liar out of him in court. Well, he made a liar out of hisself.

He said, "Don't you be here in the morning."

I said, "I ain't got to leave."

He says, "Yeah, you gonna leave here."

I told Mary, I said, "I'm leaving here. Don't want to see these 'niggas' no more. I don't want to be around them."

Mary was pregnant with Junior when I left McNary. She stayed in Arizona with her sister Idella — we called her Pee Wee — until I could find work and get us a place to stay.

Uncle Frank had left Arizona and come to Loyalton, California, to work in the sawmill. Louie was in Oroville [California] and my oldest brother Ed was in Quincy,[California]. I had wrote to Louis and told him I was coming. Louie

Courtesy Pearl Alice Marsh
Amos Marsh, Sr. and Amos Jr. at Maxville, Oregon.

Courtesy Pearl Alice Marsh
Frank and Amos Marsh, lived in Maxville, Oregon before the family moved to Wallowa because the school in Maxville had closed.

said the mill gonna start up in February or March so I left Arizona.

I got out there a few months ahead of time. Louie worked at this sawmill in Kyberz, [California].

I stayed there in Oroville until the mill was getting ready to start up in a few weeks. We went up Kyberz and saw the man and he told me, "If all of the old hands don't come back, your chance good as anybody's." A guy name John Shelton and all of them old hands was stacked around there so tight, I knowed I wasn't gonna get on. I could hear them talk, "You going back?" "Yeah, man, I'm going back." I said to myself, "Oh me, I ought to break one of them legs." So, the old hands beat me. I left, and headed on to Water Canyon.

It was January or February when I got to La Grande, [Oregon], first. That was one county over from Water Canyon and Maxville. A bunch of black folks lived there already, mostly railroad workers. They was [segregated] on one side of the tracks just like everywhere else. Soon as I got a break in the weather, I headed to Water Canyon to find a job. Pa was working for Bowman-Hicks Lumber Company and said they might be looking to hire. So, I went with Pa up to see ol' man Ashby. He was in charge and said he would see after they started back to work and saw who showed up. The woods opened up in April and they needed more labor, so I went on up to Maxville to cut logs with Pa.

That summer, after Junior was born, Mary drove from McNary to Maxville. She brought Pee Wee and her boy David Allen and Charlie Smith, Ma's cousin. She put the pistol I had bought her in the glove compartment. She said she sho' was glad she didn't have to use it.

Me and Mary had two boys, Amos Jr., and Frank Wayne, in Maxville, a town in the mountains about 14 miles from Water Canyon, up past Smith Mountain and up to Bishop Meadow. As the boys got closer to school age and Maxville shut down, Mary said we needed to move to Wallowa so they could go to school.

There wasn't a school in Maxville by then.

Other folks were moving to La Grande, Pendleton, and Portland. But, Mary didn't want to move to any of those places. The black quarters were too rough in La Grande, and Pendleton was too far. She wanted to keep her family together and the boys in a small town away from trouble. So, we moved to Wallowa. We rented a house until the Company put in some company houses. I bought three lots in La Grande just in case Mary change her mind. But, she didn't. So, we left and moved to Wallowa.

Bowman-Hicks had brought Black labor to Wallowa County in [1923] when he built a logging camp for his operation and named it Maxville.

Some of the old [earlier arrivals] loggers come out included Bob Baggett, Will An-

Courtesy Newt Ashby Collection at Wallowa County Museum

This appears to be a skid trail landing to load logs on the train as the tracks are visible in the lower right corner. Notice the four horse teams and eight wheel wagons. It appears the road goes over the tracks down in the left corner by the ticket house. Bowman-Hicks switched to logging trucks sometime after purchasing the Nibley-Mimnaugh Lumber Company.

Courtesy Newt Ashby Collection at Wallowa County Museum

A photo of an eight wheeled wagon of the type used by Bowman-Hicks for several years after establishing Maxville.

Courtesy Irene Barklow Collection at Wallowa County Museum

An early logging truck being loaded. This photo was from a logging operation used in Wallowa County and typical of all the logging trucks at the different sites.

Courtesy Pearl Alice Marsh
Hosea Lowry and Oscar "Tell Boy" Lowry.

derson, Adam Hart, Goldman King, Joe Lowry, and Lucky Trice. The first ones to come helped build the labor camp and the railroad. Then they started bringing the log cutters. That's when Pa come.

The woods was booming in Oregon and there wasn't enough cutters to keep the mill running. The Company sent and got Hosea Lowry, Joe Lowry's brother, from Arkansas and he brung a crew. Bob Baggett told them to send and get his family, the Cooks, from Mississippi. Lightnin' [Ivany Sasnett] and his younger brother Odell come from Florida. Some of them others come from Texas, Louisiana, and Alabama. I don't know nothing about how Smokey [Edward Lonnie Powell] got to Wallowa. He say he was born in Pennsylvania in 1898 and then went to Arizona. Everybody went to Arizona at some point. When they got to leaving there, they come to Oregon. The rest of them started coming when more family sent and told them to come. They was making good money then, better than they was making back South.

A lot of these new workers was mostly farmers and sawmill workers and couldn't cut logs but he needed labor. Some they brought could cut logs, though.

They finally got enough log cutters to keep the mill going. By the time they was through, they had Blacks working in the mill and doing some white jobs in the woods. That was around [1942] to [1945].

All of the loggers got along pretty good most of the time. Everybody knew somebody, either family or friends from somewhere else. Pa was real goodnatured. You could hear him laughing a mile away. Smokey liked to do carpentry when he wasn't working. He set up a little shop beside him and Carrie's house and stayed out there every chance he could. He made my gun cabinet that I still got.

Courtesy Pearl Alice Marsh
Ivany "Lightnin' " Sasnett

43

Courtesy *History of Union County*, Bernal Hug at Elgin Public Library
Train load of logs going to the mill on hastily built temporary tracks. This load was being pulled by a Shay engine that was subsequently purchased by Nibley-Mimnaugh and then Bowman-Hicks. The engineer, Ed Gettings, devised a way to haul out an entire days production (21 cars) in one run, although derailment occured from time to time, resulting in injury and death to some workers.

Hosea was alright, but he like to complain too much. He always had something contrary to say, I don't care what was goin' on.

Bob Baggett was the oldest. He was born in Mississippi but he told everybody he

Courtesy Pearl Alice Marsh
Odell Sasnett, Amos Marsh, Sr's best friend. Born 1914 in Georgia.

was from Africa. We believed him too. He used to read them Black newspapers from Chicago. He was sensible, so when we had problems, we could go talk to him and work it out.

Lightnin' was slow as molasses. You couldn't make him move fast if you lit a fire under him. Odell, Lightnin's brother, turned out to be my best friend. After we met, was friends long as I can remember.

Alec Cook was kin to ol' man Baggett through his Lillie. He didn't stick around Maxville long. Didn't like a "company town." And, Goldman King was married to Smokey's wife's daughter.

The Company gave the black workers the hardest most dangerous job, log cuttin', but we was good at it and liked it 'cause it was making a living for our families. It was dangerous work, too. There were a few whites doing black jobs, but no Blacks doing white jobs. The white guys was choker setters, hookers, and log skidders.

Crosscut saw being used at what appears to be a cutting contest. This was the type of saw being used by Amos and his cutting partner.

They drove the Caterpillars and ran all of the heavy equipment.[2]

And they ran the train when we was taking the logs out by railroad and drove the logging trucks when we switched.

I kind of became the head logger in the woods. Old man Ashby give me seniority. I drove the labor truck everybody called the candy wagon. I got the men back and forth to work and decided when we would go and come.

Some white guys come out there and saw me. They was little gyppo contractors who had their own trucks to haul logs. Ashby had showed me the tract of timber they was to haul. He told me to show it to them and I did. They didn't know all of that. So, when I went to show it to them, they say, "What did Mr. Ashby say?" They wasn't gonna do nothin' on my word.

I says, "That's what Mr. Ashby told me to tell you. I'm just working like the rest of you. "

"Well," they said, "You got a pretty big job here, ain't you?" I said, "No, I'm just like the rest of them, cutting logs." But, I'm able to take them out there on the man's word and show them where their lines was. They thought I was a "big nigger."

When we first started cutting logs, we was running a two-man crosscut saw. That crosscuttin' was something. You could get mad, man. You see, that was where you and a partner had to match. Some people never had run a crosscut and never did get real good at it.

I saw a lot of cutters, they both good men, but they couldn't saw together. I saw two guys go out there and when one do this, the other one do that. Yeah, then they both go to trying to saw their own way. But, it just as simple as the nose on your face if both of you know how to pull it. You can make that saw hum. But if you didn't have a good partner, you really didn't make a living.

I started crosscutting with Smokey. I'd go round and round and take my ax and size up the tree. Whichever way she lean, that's the way she'll fall pretty quick. But, you try to go against the lean, you'd have trouble all day.

Smokey wouldn't look for the lean. He went out there one time and marked one for us against the lean. We had a dozen wedges and still didn't have the tree down by quittin' time. He went down to the old shop the next day and got him a croker sack[3] full of

---

2   At the very top of the labor hierarchy were the [hourly wage] loader operators, but not something most wanted because of the long hours. Choker setters were the bottom of the heap - the job was really dangerous and [hourly] pay was not as good. The log cutters were highly self-comnfidentt because of the skill needed and because they were paid by the board feet they cut and the timber was good. They had the ability to set their own hours and make more than the hourly workers on the landings. But it is a really dangerous job.

3   * "Croker sack" is a chiefly southern term for a sack made of coarse material, such as burlap. See Merriam Webster,

wedges and put them down side of that tree. He said, "By God, I'll get her now."

I said, "Yeah? What you gonna do? I tell you what you gonna do. You gonna get somebody else to work with. I ain't gonna put up with that kind of stuff. Go get you somebody else."

So, I sent to Louisiana and got my brother Alvie. Smokey had to find him a partner. He thought he could beat us. Shoot. We eat Smokey up. Cause he tried to buck and bully the trees. He believed he can make it go the way he want it to go rather than the way it ought to go.

When Alvie got there and learned how to work, me and him took over the woods cutting logs. Then Alvie got homesick. Said, "I'm going home." I said, "Well, jeez, why don't you wait until..." "I ain't waiting. I'm going home." He took off and when I heard from him, he was in Salt Lake City. Then didn't go home.

Courtesy of son, James Lester Lane
Lester Lane

Got down there with five or six hundred dollars worth of war bonds, turned around and come back. Said, "I decided I wouldn't go." I said, "Aw, I think you going crazy now." Yeah. So, he come back. He never made na'r 'nother bluster. He worked pretty steady after that. When he did go the last time, he stayed. His wife Dorothy died over there in La Grande in [1955] and he packed up those five kids and moved back home to Louisiana.

Odell and Lightnin' was partners. Lightnin' couldn't do much cuttin' cause he was so slow. Odell could cut but he had never made much money 'cause he had to cut with Lightnin'. Lightnin' raised him and Lightnin' got him a job, so he sawed like him. Odell called me Home Boy all of the time. He say, "Home Boy, I be glad when I can get me somebody else to cut with." Soon as he could, he got rid of Lightnin' and went to cutting with another guy and he went to making more money. Ol' Lightnin' was gonna near 'bout starve to death.

"Odell," I said, "Ain't you gonna go back and help him out?" "No, I ain't gonna go back and pick him up. Let him starve, I ain't gonna saw with him." I say, "Lightnin' ain't got no partner." Odell say, "Well, I ain't gonna saw with him."

Lester Lane come out to cut with his uncle Adam Hart. Somebody told Lester that old man Adam was slow and twist the saw handle when you pulling crosscut with him. And the saw wouldn't slide back. Well, me and

Early gas powered, two-man chain saw.

Courtesy Newt Ashby Collection, Wallowa County Museum

Superintendent's house at Maxville during winter. The two men on the porch are probably mill bosses based on their more formal attire.

Lester sawed together for a little while. And he was tough as a boot. We was making a lot of money.

This photograph shows two tree fallers (or fellers) using a two-man crosscut saw in 1921. It appeared in Timberman Magazine with a caption that reads: "After the undercut is notched, timber fallers go to the opposite side of the tree and saw towardthe notch. The saw kerf is wedged so that the tree will not pinch on the saw."

Old Lady Hart, her name was Izora, said, "Lester, you ought not to do Mr. Hart that way." Say, "You ought to saw with him. Let Mr. Amos get somebody else."

Lester said, "You want Uncle Adam to make some money?"

Izora said, "Yeah."

Lester says,"Well, you go and saw with him."

She hushed then. Boy, that was something.

Me and Alvie was working a two-man crosscut when the two-man power saw first come out. Lightnin' was the first one who bought one. He kept his money tight, you know. So, he had the cash and looked it up in the catalogue and found out where he could get one. He got a money order at the post office and ordered a two-man Maul from Chicago. After he got it, he complained, "It takes all of my time just to get it to run. I can't cut no logs, but I can run it." I laughed and said, "Well, how you gonna make a livin'?" There wasn't no dealership in Wallowa, Enterprise, Elgin, or La Grande to help him out either.

Nobody here knowed how to run one. Him and Smokey got out in the woods and tried to get it to start. Smokey stand out on the stinger and look while Lightnin' crank the motor.* It go dead every time he pull the starter rope. Smokey got tired of standing around while everybody else was throwing a tree. Finally, this other guy we called Squeaky went around and cranked it. Smokey pushed him away and got hold of that stinger. That sucker kicked him back a mile. Oh, that was the ticklingest thing I ever saw.

Courtesy Irene Barklow Collection, Wallowa County Museum

Bate's Mill, c1950s or 60s.

You know, he was nervous anyhow, Smokey was. Well, when he finally crank it, we had to laugh because he didn't know how to run it. After a little while, Smokey told Lightnin', "I don't want no more at that chain saw. I'm gettin' me a partner and gettin' me a crosscut."

After we went to using power saws, I didn't want no more at the old crosscut.

Me and Alvie bought a two-man saw. I thought, well we got it made now. Guy Snyder, who owned the saw shop in Enterprise, come out and set it up. Got it all cranked. At first, we thought we figured out how to run it, but it was running us, just getting the best of us.

About a log or two, the chain was swaggin'. Then, every time you put it on the tree, something catch it and she roll over. Well, we tightened the chain up, got it going again. I had the motor. Alvie, he slick, he didn't ever get on the motor. He stay on the stinger. We get to sawing around there and the tree getting ready to fall. Sometime it still don't fall, and then you try to back the saw out and the top chain catch. That thing will kick you clear out through the woods, too. That motor, that old saw kick back there like that — whoooooooom! Two or three weeks, we needed a new chain.

The first one-man saw come out around [1950]. At first, it was harder than a two-man because you had to control it by yourself. Smokey, he give plumb out trying to run one. They kicked, you know, they would kick him so hard he get sick. He would take that saw and put it up on his shoulder and come down on a log and beat the saw up. Boy, sometimes you be going along there and when the saw drop down on

Courtesy Pearl Alice Marsh
Early gas powered, one-man chain saw.

the log, you think it's going on through the bottom. But it pinch the top chain and kick you, just a jolt right on that kneecap. Holy Christ. Sometimes, I wouldn't look up. I would just shut my eyes and don't let nobody know it done kicked me. I stand around there for twenty minutes trying to get some breath. Boy, that hurt.

One time, that tree spun around right up on the bar and went right where I sat that saw. Fell right across the top. I say, "Uh huh." That's the worst thing I ever done. I said, "It could have fell on me too."

I got pretty good with a one-man saw pretty fast, though. I heard some of the scalers brag about some of the fellows doing such a pretty job throwing trees. They give me credit for doing a lot of that. I didn't always do it pretty, but I get the trees down. Old Man Bob says I limbed better than all of them.

Pa was rough on his saws. When he got it tangled up, he would make a bad mess worse. Then, he would come home and tell Ma, "Take my saw off to the shop," and she and Mary would take it up there and the guy would fix it. Pa would say, "What was wrong with it? What did he say was wrong with it?" Ma say, "He said wasn't nothing wrong with it." Pa said, "Had to be something wrong with it."

Next time, Pa took it up there hisself. Said he just got it and something was wrong with it. Pa would flood it, you know. Them old ones would flood quick. He didn't know how to take the plug out and clean it and clear the cylinder. Guy would start it for him.

Courtesy Pearl Alice Marsh

Amos Marsh, Sr. with a couple Wallowa Friends Wes Conrad and Kenneth Brooks.

Guy and Pa got into it one day. And, boy, I thought the cop was going to have to come. Pa says, "I bought that saw! That's my saw!" Guy said, "But Joe, you don't sup-pose to..." Pa said, "I do what I want to. It's my saw." He said, "I pays you when I come up here and you fix it." The next time he sent it by Ma.

Pa said, "What did he say?" Ma said, "He said you stop trying to work on it." Guy said when something go wrong you bring it up here and he will fix it." Guy said, "But when you tear it up first, then I can't fix it." Pa didn't like that, but he couldn't fix it.

All the log cutters got along pretty good for the most part. But I gets mad some-times, too. I was driving the labor truck we called the candy wagon. Sometime one of the cutters wouldn't get going 'til about four or four-thirty when it is near time to go home. You got to wait until he cut him a few logs.

Once, Old Man Bob Baggett was scaling. I said, "I done cut out for the day." He said, "How do you like waiting around for these other fellas?" And I said, "I don't like it." He

Promise road emerging from the timber on its way to the valley floor and on in to Wallowa. Wallowa is just under the little timbered hill in the middle on the extreme left. This is the road Amos, Sr. used when driving the candy wagon to and from work.

said, "Well go ahead and go home."

Hosea was one of them. Hosea never was a good log cutter, cross cutter, and nothing else. His stuff would break down, but he wasn't gonna quit. He gonna hold everybody up. He run to town with his saw and come back when we was getting ready to go home. After he got it fixed, he gonna cut him some logs anyhow.

I took the candy wagon and took the crew home. Hosea's wife Lucy come by. "I, uh…" You know she talked soft. She say, "I ain't seen Hosea. Was he out there with y'all?" I said, "I don't know where he is. Might have been out there. But he didn't come in with us."

I wasn't ornery. I felt sorry for Hosea after I left him. But, the old scaler said go on home. Says, "We done fooled with him long enough." He said, "I will back you up. Go ahead."

Hosea didn't stay out there all night. No. Somebody went and got him. Boy, you could hear him blowing when he got home that night. I was in the bed and I just went under the cover. I wouldn't have liked that either if they had left me. But, I wouldn't put up with that kind of … But if I knowed it was getting late and I couldn't work no more, I would have come out of the woods with the men. If I knowed they was gonna leave, I ain't gonna stay out there. That's what made me mad. I told him to come on. Hosea say, "Yeah, but I ain't made nothing. I got to make a living just like all the rest of them. Y'all fast and got it made and I gotta make my living too." "Well," they say, "Go in your own car."

Boy, he come out there the next morning and then do you know what? He got right after me. He weighed about two hundred and forty pounds. He was big and heavy, but he couldn't fight. He didn't know how to hit. When he lunged, I took my fist, and hit that sucker as hard as I could and you know, I didn't knock him down. I bounced back. He tried to kick me then and he threw his leg around and I caught it and flipped him on his be-

Town of Wallowa. The schools are just across the fence on the left. The small business district is further down the street. It has remained much the same over the years.

hind. If he had a hit me, I would have been knocked out cold. Everybody was standing around looking.

Well, we come on home. Nobody at the camp knowed what had happened.

But, by daylight next day, everybody knowed: "Them Negroes fighting." But nobody reported it to the boss. The company never did say nothing. Hosea never did like me no more. And he never did try to. I told him when the time come we go home. You can quit the job if you don't like it. Me and Hosea never did get along good after that.

Then, the company finally took the truck away. Everybody went in his own car and you ought to have seen the mess then. Sometimes five or six o'clock in the evening, you hear a saw running. Me and Alvie was always pretty fast with them crosscuts and when we was running chain saws, it didn't run, we was going to go home and get it fixed. When it run, we gonna get some log cutting pretty quick.

When I got to Oregon, there wasn't no union. I got Pa to join but he didn't want to at first. Didn't nobody talk bad about him because he was just like all of them, didn't want to join. But when they see it was going to be a union, they got in. Me and Pa was the oldest two laborers it was there among the working people. Pa was the oldest and I was next in the line of seniority. And we had a pretty big voice. So, when we joined, the rest of them did.

They said Bowman-Hicks wrote old man Ashby or called him from Kansas City, that was where their headquarters was, and told him to spend a million dollars to keep that union out. They wasn't about to recognize a union.

Some of those guys say, "I ain't gonna join. I'm in the company house." The union man told them, "If you sign up for the union, when we get it, the company can't put you out.

Some people like me don't figure he can sweat that long. But, the company give up pretty quick once they got it going. When they knowed anything they was under contract.

The union covered the woods and the sawmill, all of it. It was the IWA [International Woodworkers of America]. They first got the union in the sawmill, but they didn't want just that. We wanted a union for the log cutters too. So, then they had to get one for the woodcutters. It wasn't no two different unions.

Loggers and the mill workers was in separate groups, but it was all unionized. There was problems with one union that covered the whole company. Sometime the woods took a notion they didn't get the contract they want, they could pull a strike. If the mill got the one they wanted, they couldn't run cause the woods crew wouldn't go to work.

The union in Wallowa was good and lasted a long time until some of the workers went crazy. That was way after Bowman-Hicks sold out to J. Herbert Bate's Lumber Company. I had moved to California, because Mike Holloran had stopped his operation up there. I really can't explain just how it went, because I done gone. I was there when the union got there but I wasn't there when this last rhubarb come up. I disremember exactly what it was, but it got real bad.

See, at one time, Bowman-Hicks had a lot of log trucks, hisself. He ran the whole operation. So, when the workers went on strike, they could picket the whole company. But, after Bowman-Hicks sold to Bate's, he started using a bunch of gypo operations to haul logs. The union couldn't picket the gypos 'cause they weren't covered by the contract. So some of the gypos started hauling regardless of the strike. Some workers out there turned their log trucks over, even set some on fire.

Some of the guys in union got mad. When they got a little power, they went crazy. Throwing peoples' stuff around. Some of them got mad because they didn't go through the process of union, bargaining, and setting a strike deadline.

Some of them guys got mad and just went out and pulled the whistle. Called a big wildcat strike. Bates said he would shut the mill down before he conceded to the union. That was a long strike, that last one. Bate's broke the union that time. And he shut it down. Wallowa ain't never been the same.

I stayed in Wallowa with my family until Ed Holloran and Son, the company I worked for, went down. Too many small operations cropped up and he couldn't compete. That was about 1959. Mike moved his operation to California. Smokey, Lightnin' and me, Mary and the kids moved down there with him. We cut logs out of Cisco Grove, not too far from Truckee. Mary and the kids lived in Grass Valley. The boys, Amos, Jr., and Frank Wayne, went off to Oregon State College and Pearl Alice and Kay Frances graduated from Nevada Union High School.

Our daughter, Penny Merle, passed in Grass Valley. I left logging after Mike went out of business in California. I started working in construction. I was about fifty-five years old when John Paye, the man from the employment office, spotted me. He was a nice fella. He said I didn't need to be working that hard any more. I thought this was the worst thing a man could ever do, work out here in this hot sun in construction. But, it ain't no hotter here than it is in the woods when you get out here. And the work wasn't as hard as cutting logs. So, he helped me get into construction. I joined the union and stayed long enough to get my pension. When I turned sixty-five, I told Mary I was going to retire and burn my work clothes and I did.

NATHANIEL MAYS

My name is Nathaniel Mays. I was born in Enterprise, Oregon, on April 16, 1946. I have a cousin who was born later in Enterprise. But our family lived in Maxville. We were part of the African Americans working in the sawmill in Wallowa County. My sisters were Willola—my father's sister Aunt Bennie raised her. Then it would be Lucille, and then it was Velma, Alice, Nazarene. I hope I didn't leave any out.

[In 1946,] African American women couldn't go to the hospital in Enterprise to have their babies. They had to have midwives or drive to the hospital in La Grande. But for reasons not known to me, when it came time for me to be born, they took my mother to the hospital in Enterprise to see if she could deliver me there. I guess the administrator said okay. And so I was the first African American baby to be born there in the hospital in Enterprise.

Now, about how my grandfather Hosea Lowry, an African American logger, wound up in Maxville. He was one of the early African American loggers in the county. They had him working in the sawmill down there in Arkansas. He didn't just go up to Maxville and start working with no experience in the timber industry. But when he went to Maxville, he didn't work in the sawmill; he started to cut logs.

The story that was told to me was that he [Hosea] did regular work as a farmer and sawmill worker down in Jefferson County, Arkansas. But on the side, he was a bootlegger. He and my dad, Willie Mays, made whiskey together. That's how my father met my mother, was through my grandfather.

Anyway, the revenuers came around regularly. That's what they called the government agents who came around to shut down bootleggers. To keep their operations running, the guys making the bootleg would have to pay the revenuers to keep up their sales. The revenuers kept raising the price on what [the bootleggers] had to pay them. Came to a time where Grandpa said he wasn't going to pay any more. While the bootlegging was illegal, so were the revenuers' activities. So they got into a shootout at one of the stills. My grandfather had to leave Arkansas in a hurry. That's how he wound up in eastern Oregon.

He picked Oregon because some of our family was already up there. Grandpa had been up there in 1929. That was the first time he [Hosea] went there. His brother, Joe Lowry—they called him "Lou"—was already up there working in Maxville. Also, his cousins Lafayette "Lucky" and George Trice were working in Maxville.

I don't remember if Grandpa took my grandma with him when he first left Arkansas. I would assume he didn't take her with him when he was running. But she came later.

I can't remember those early years in Maxville too well because I was a small child. We moved from Maxville to La Grande anyway. Most of my memory is around La

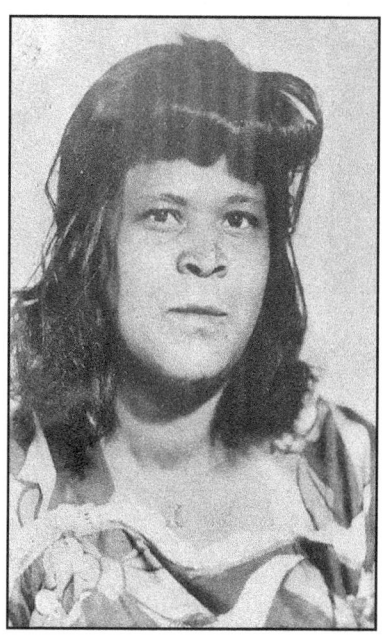

Courtesy Lucille Mays Bridgewater
Lucy Tate Lowry, wife of Hosea Lowrey. Came to Maxville in 1927.

Grande, since that's where I really grew up as a kid. I'd have to think hard and long on Maxville.

But of course my grandparents lived in Maxville. Then they moved to Wallowa instead of La Grande. I can tell you about Wallowa. After we moved to La Grande, we used to visit Wallowa when I was a little kid. It was nothing to go to Wallowa. We were up there all the time. But La Grande was where we lived. My father would go to Wallowa during the week to work, and we would stay in La Grande to go to school.

Religion was a big thing in La Grande. At one time there was more than three churches, [but] each had only about three people in them. My family went to church; I think at one time or another we probably wound up in all of them. The Baptist church was next door to the Hilliards. It was run by R. R. and D. D. Banks, who would come from Hermiston. Reverend Lowe's church was on the corner. And there was one down by the

Courtesy Wallowa History Center

Bowman-Hicks sawmill in Wallowa. Center left, behind the stacks of lumber, are some of the company houses the mill owners had the black loggers live in.

grocery store where the guys would bring in the deer for the rented freezer. They would dress them out in the alley. I think it was the Church of God. But I don't remember any other churches. There wasn't enough black people to fill one church, or half-fill one church.

Everybody had a church. One time we were to go—I forget her name, whose house we were at. They had a wake. I forget who died. The houses weren't big, you know. And they had a wake, and we were sitting there.

But anyway, the coffin was open, and the man just shot up. Yeah. I saw it. I didn't think nothing of it. I was a kid, right? It was the adults that went crazy. Yeah, he was dead. What I was told is that they sometimes do that. Sometimes they have to tie them down to keep them from going back to the position that they always were dead.

As a kid I did kid things, you know. I remember when we went to visit Grandpa and Grandma in Wallowa. The sawmill sat behind the house. And then, we had regular everyday chores when we was up there. Grandma had us doing them. There was a little pump out front where we had to get water. And they didn't have a refrigerator. They had an icebox. You get the big block of ice to put into the icebox to keep everything cold.

We just did kid things up there. Played, you know. Didn't have toys. Whatever toys we had were homemade. There were some things that was done that I didn't do, like pranking. Some of the kids would trick little kids to put their lips on the pump in the wintertime. Their tongue would get stuck, and they would holler. Some of the stuff like that wasn't innocent kid stuff. I remember another time, Grandma gave my brother George a good whoopin'. They were trying to get these two dogs to have sex, and she caught them. She was little, but she was a powerhouse and could give you a good whoopin'.

When we came up to Wallowa, sometimes we would stay a day or two, and sometimes we would go straight back down to La Grande. The time varied. We would go up there on weekends or when school was out.

I remember Grandma would buy milk and put it in the churn. Kids had to sit there and pull that thing up and down, up and down to separate the butter from the milk. Yeah. I hated it.

My grandpa was tall and light skinned. Not pass-for-white light, but a light-skinned man. I remember he would hunt up in the woods in Wallowa County. And his boys, you know, Hasker and Oscar, they were identical twins. They would hunt with him. But the other son, T. J., he didn't really hunt. He'd fish.

So when my grandpa would bring the deer, he'd bring them into La Grande. There was an alley that ran on the side of the store, and they'd have them bring the deer in and hang them up on the hook. And then they would take the skin off and take out the guts, all that stuff.

Life in La Grande as a kid was mostly fun. That's where most of the blacks went to school. In La Grande, everyone went to the same schools. Black kids and white kids played together in school and were friends. But here's one thing about it. I don't care if you were in the first grade all the way up to the eighth grade. If one black kid got in trouble, they would call all of the black kids in and give us a lecture. They would tell us to "learn a lesson from this." They didn't punish all of us, just talked to us.

One time, ol' Johnnie Faye Lawson, one of the white teachers grabbed her. She was about seventh or eighth grade. I remember it was a mean ol' teacher. Probably racist; I don't know for sure. But Johnnie Faye balled a fist up and cold-clocked her. We all had to go to the office.

And we were friends after school. You know as a kid, the racism—I don't think it ever crossed my mind. Because we were doing the same thing they was doing, and they was doing the same things we was doing and everything, you know what I mean? I never felt what you would truly call racism.

I almost drowned in the pool. As a matter of fact, I was there playing in the swimming pool, in the shallow end where you can swim and stuff, and I'm watching them jumping off the diving board. I go over there. Said, "I'm going to jump off the diving board." And I go over there and jump off. Now, I can't swim.

If it hadn't been for Mayola, one of the Anderson girls, I would have drowned. She saved me. She was older than me. Because Mayola was nine years old in 1940, so she was years older than me.

There were a lot of kids. You go to the swimming pool, you pay your little money, and you get your key and all that. So you put your clothes in the locker, and there was no special room or side for black people, for black kids. It was all there together.

Now, my favorite things that I was doing as a young kid in La Grande was probably out there in that swamp. We made rafts out of tree limbs and had fake naval battles and tried to knock people off their raft. That probably would be my favorite time when I was a kid growing up down there. I couldn't swim, but the water was no more than two or three feet deep. It was a swamp.

La Grande wasn't segregated, though, except for where we lived. There was no place we couldn't go. We went to the swimming pool and the movie theater. There wasn't enough blacks there to be for that. There were very few blacks in La Grande. There still are less now, if any.

There was no special place for you to sit in the theater, all that type of stuff. And after school we would go down there at the swimming hole. You know, blacks and whites, just kids.

We didn't fight much with white kids. Didn't throw rocks at them. But one time I do remember this: We were coming from the theater. I forget the name of the theater I'm talking about. One closest to the tracks. And you know how the cars was parked diagonally on the street.

And we were crossing the street in between these cars, and the street sign was out there. And this little white boy was in the back seat of the car, and he call us "nigger." Said, "Look, Mom. Look at them niggers." And my brother Anglee turned around and said, "What did you say?" I guess he opened his mouth up to say "nigger" again, and then Anglee spit in his mouth. But anyway.

We found lots to do around the tracks. Sometimes we would put pennies on the tracks so the train could smash them. And we'd have cable and stuff to make things with. We liked to play with the empty cable wheels too. They'd have a whole pile of them in the train yard. We would get inside, and someone else

A young boy walking on a pair of home made stilts. Notice the rope wrapped around his legs, holding his feet to the stilts.

would push it down the hill, and you'd roll around in it. And we would follow the train tracks up to the drive-in theater and sneak in.

Something else about the drive-in. We used to go around to the cars, usually when people were making out and stuff, the car windows get steamy, and we'd look in, you know. Sometimes we got caught. One time this white boy said, "What if we caught you making out with your girlfriend? What would you do?" Anglee said, "Oh, I'd whoop your ass."

We used to make our own stilts to play on. Here's how we made stilts. Take a long board—two-by-four—and you nail a block on it so you put your feet on them, and it depends on how high it was. You stand next to something to balance yourself. And then you just walk. Yeah. You don't see that anymore.

We were told never to cross the railroad tracks on the stilts. And what happened? I didn't cross them on the stilts; somebody else did. But I got a whoopin' for it too. It was all right to have the stilts as high as you wanted them. The adults didn't complain about them. But don't walk across the railroad tracks with them, though.

We had fun at local festivals too. At the time my brother Anglee was the biggest delinquent in the city. You know [at the traveling carnival], where they have all the games. Once a year they'd have it. Anyway, it's like a carnival circus, but they had all these rides and things you do. And Anglee, he had these guns, these rifles with the cork in the rifle end. And so you pump it up, and it would shoot that cork out. He'd go pick one up and start shooting at the man [running the booth]. Anglee was a bad seed. He never grew out of it.

When we left La Grande and moved to Portland, we were still dressed for the country. We had these combat-looking boots. They had two straps at the top; you laced it up. And overalls. We were still wearing plaid work shirts. And the kids made fun of us. Sho' did.

I got a story. All those people coming out of Arkansas, they had pictures with them on the trains hanging out the windows. It was Kaiser that brought them to Portland. Kaiser had the shipyards up there, building ships. Yeah, and all this timber was going to Portland. The majority of the blacks in Oregon, they trace their family roots in Oregon before '47. Majority of them came from Arkansas.

Some of the people who came out of the South went directly to the shipyards in Portland. But Uncle Lou and Mr. Hosea didn't go to Portland first. Uncle Lou in his later years, he went to Portland. My grandpa never did go to Portland. His last home was always La Grande. He and my grandma are buried in Island City just outside of La Grande.

Courtesy Wallowa History Center

Another photo of housing at Maxville. Notice all the buckets and tubs around the door. It looks like the occupants have built sheds on each ent of the basic structure. Icicles are long because insulation was lacking in the ceilings and walls. In fact, insulation of the time was extra newspapers tacked to the walls or sawdust in the walls.

Courtesy Irene Barklow collection, Wallowa County Museum

Inside of a bunkhouse where loggers lived when "batching" while working for Bowman-Hicks logging company.

Courtesy Paula Helton, Curator Eastern Oregon University Digital Archives

Maxville laundry, c1923. This was just one year before the Lowrys arrived in Maxville. Notice the big tin tub on blaocks above a fire with a stirring stick. The man is using a scrub board in one of the other four tin tubs. More than one tub may have been used for scrubbing, with the rest having rinse water. There is a pile of wood in the background for the fire and a little outhouse conveniently located behind a tree.

Courtesy Wallowa History Center

Photos of housing at Maxville for the loggers. Top photo is bachelor quarters for the Greek loggers. In the quarters below notice smoke coming out of more than one chimney, with a man out back cutting stove wood. A photo of the black loggers housing is located in an earlier chapter.

LUCILLE MAYS BRIDGEWATER

Lucille (Mays) Bridgewater was one of eleven children born to George Louise (Lowry) and Will Mays. The children are Lucille, George, Hosea, Nathaniel, Ivery, John, Velma, Stanley, Alice, Albert, and Nazarene.

Lucille's grandfather was one of the first loggers to arrive in Maxville in 1924. Her grandmother Lucy (Tate) was one of the pioneering women who followed their husbands. His cousin, Arthur Trice, arrived in the early 1920s to help build the logging railroad in Maxville for Bowman-Hicks. Lucille's father, Will, also cut logs for Bowman-Hicks. He moved the family to Portland, but he returned to his home in Pine Bluff, Arkansas, where he remained until his death.

Lucille did not live in Wallowa County as a child. Her family lived in La Grande before settling in Portland. However, she recalls visiting Maxville as a little girl. Though her childhood memories are few, they are quite vivid as she recalls the sights, sounds, and people of Maxville. In her memoir, Lucille recalls fondly her early childhood visits to Maxville and Wallowa to see her grandparents, family, and friends.

Lucille went to school at Greenwood Elementary School in La Grande through the fifth grade. She started the sixth grade in Portland and grew up there for the most part. She attended Washington High School and graduated from Lincoln High School. After graduating from high school, she continued her education by taking classes at Portland Community College.

Lucille worked while in high school and then worked for Crown Zellerbach, now Graphic Packaging International, starting in 1966. She has been there for fifty-two years.

Courtesy Lucille Mays Bridgewater

L-R:Lucille, Alice, Nazarene, Velma.and Georgie Mays, mother.

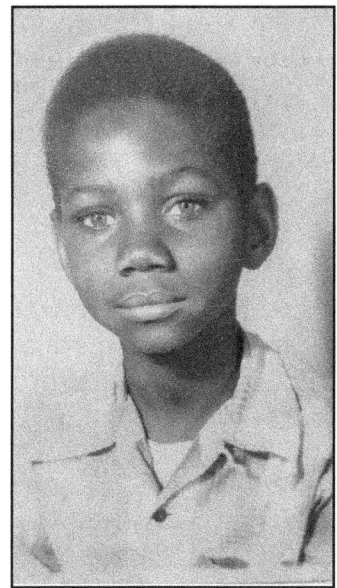

*George Willie Mays, broth-
er of Lucille Mays Bridgewater*

She married Leroy Hudson and they had one child, Leroy Hudson, Jr. In 1973, she married Willie Bridgewater, and they have no children. Lucille has two grandsons, Leroy Hudson III and the late Eugene Lee Hudson. She has one granddaughter, London Skye Hudson.

Lucille grew up a Christian and attended the Church of God in Christ in La Grande. She is now a member of Mount Olivet Baptist Church in Portland. She was baptized in Israel in a sacred place.

For years, Lucille's main hobby was being a seamstress. She took tailoring classes to perfect her work. She is also an avid gardener and has a passion for canning fruits and vegetables, which she shares with friends and family. She walks every day with her dog Lily around Portland, and she enjoys volunteering with senior citizens.

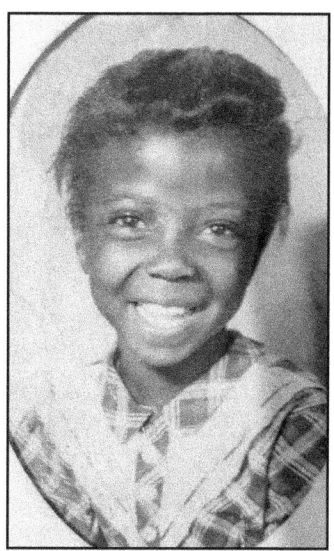

*Lucille Mays Bridgewater,
granddaughter of logger, Hosea Lowry.*

My name is Lucille Mays Bridgewater, and I was born in Pine Bluff, Arkansas, on September 22, 1943. I remember bits and pieces about people from Maxville and Wallowa. Some moved to La Grande, and that is where most of my memories begin.

My father was Will Mays. He worked at the sawmill in Wallowa for Bowman-Hicks Lumber Company. My mother was Georgie (Lowry) Mays. Her name was Georgie and not Georgia. Georgie Louise Mays. My mother met my dad in Pine Bluff, where they got married. She was either fifteen or sixteen years old.

When my parents came out from Pine Bluff to Oregon, my grandparents were already in Maxville. I was eighteen months old. My brother George and I were born in Pine Bluff. And then my brother next to me—his name was Hosea after my grandfather—was born in Portland in either 1944 or 1945. My brother Nathaniel was born in 1946 in Enterprise, Oregon. He was the first black baby born in the hospital in Enterprise. My mother said white people came to the hospital to see the "nigger" baby.

Bate's sawmill, Wallowa, Oregon.

But like my mother, he was light skinned, which they did not expect. Apparently, my mother and father were living temporarily in Wallowa. I'm sure they didn't want to go to Enterprise to have a baby. But Mama went into labor, and that's where they took her. My other brothers and sisters were born in either La Grande or Portland. John, Stanley, and Velma were born in La Grande. Hosea, Nazarene, Albert, and Alice were born in Portland.

My grandfather was Hosea Lowry. He and my father both cut logs or worked in the sawmill for Bowman-Hicks. My grandfather was one of the early African American loggers in Wallowa County. He came from Pine Bluff. He and his wife, Lucy, lived first in Maxville, then Wallowa, and finally in La Grande. They are buried in the Island City Cemetery near La Grande.

My grandmother was Lucy (Tate) Lowry. Everyone called her Mis' Lucy. I wasn't named after her. I was named after somebody on my father's side. But my cousin, Precious, her name was Precious Lucy. She was named after Grandma.

When my grandfather first came to Oregon, my mother wasn't born. She was born in 1927 in Pine Bluff. My grandmother didn't come out here when he first came. And so he had to go back to Arkansas to get her and the family.

My family went back and forth between Oregon and Arkansas back then between seasons. I can't tell you what year they last come back out here to Oregon, but it had to have been after '43 since that's when I was born.

Some of our relatives were the first ones to come out to Maxville to start working for Bowman-Hicks. They came in the early 1920s. My grandfather's cousin, Arthur Trice, and his family came out in 1925. He brought his whole family, wife Ella, and their five children to Maxville.

My grandfather's brother, Uncle Joe Lowry, came to Oregon after my grandfather. We called him "Uncle Lou." That's how families came out, through relatives. My family, the Lowrys, all are related to the Trices.

Let me tell you about Cousin George Trice. I've never known anybody to say Cousin George was married. He lived in La Grande and was the kindest

Courtesy Ronee Riggle Stone

Johnnie Riggle loading a load of logs. c.1930's. His brother, Don, was a woods boss for Bowman-Hicks.

person that you ever wanted to meet. He was always good to all the kids because he didn't have children. But you didn't get away with anything with him. That's just the way that generation was. I think about him all the time, because if I had to really listened to things he told me, I would have gone on to school. He was very encouraging and wanted you to do all kind of things in life.

Newt Ashby Collection, Wallowa County Museum

This is probably a photo of some of the Bowman-Hicks bosses out inspecting timber in the winter.

I remember Grandpa and Grandma lived in Maxville when we came back out from Arkansas and I was a child. We went back to Arkansas after Nathaniel was born in 1946 and came back out here, but only my mom came with the children. My dad never came back to Oregon. He stayed in Arkansas. But we came back out to Portland.

The last time we came out here, we moved to La Grande. I wasn't in school. I started first grade in La Grande. I went from first grade through fifth grade at Greenwood Elementary School. When we first moved from Arkansas to La Grande, we lived with Aunt Obie. And then we lived on Madison Street, and then we moved to Monroe Street. I remember where Reverend Lowe's church was, and I remember where Hub City was. That's the street [where] Jack Gillespie and his wife Ms. Mary lived. We were half a block from downtown, just across the railroad track. Then we moved back on Madison Street next door to the Lawson family.

As I said, my grandparents first lived in Maxville. My aunt Johnnie B. lived up there—Aunt B., we called her. She was my mother's sister. She was married to Ivany Sasnett. He came out with his brother Odell from Florida to cut logs for Bowman-Hicks. We called him Uncle Son. Some people called him Lightnin'.

I never physically lived in Wallowa County, but since my grandpa and grandma lived there, we were always up there visiting them. On the weekends, Grandma and Grandpa would come over to La Grande on Fridays. Any-

Courtesy Pearl Alice Marsh

Ivany Sasnett, husband of Johnnie B., Lucy May Bridgewater's aunt

63

one who wanted to go back up to Maxville or Wallowa would go back with them and stay until on Sunday.

I can remember the houses in Maxville where other black and white people lived. There weren't that many. We'd have to walk equal to about a block between each house to get over to Grandma's house. It was a two-story house. It had a kitchen, a living room, a dining room, and a couple of bedrooms. I know they had at least two bedrooms, maybe three. Of course they had the woodstoves, one for heating and one for cooking. In Wallowa, they had a well where you would get water out of the ground with a pump. They had outside plumbing—the toilet was behind the house.

I remember the main road in Maxville. Of course it wasn't paved. Everything was dusty. Where my grandparents lived was about a quarter mile or so from the main road. The mailman would put the mail down there on the main road, and you would walk down and get the mail. We'd pick it all up out of the box, see if there was any mail for my folks, and then walk back. There wouldn't be any people on the road, and at that time as a kid, I wasn't afraid. Now, after watching a lot of those different ID shows on TV, it just gives you chills thinking about that dry, lonely road because anything could have happened.

Let me describe my grandfather. Grandpa Hosea was a big guy. I would say he may have been at least six feet. And he was real stocky. Not overly big, but stocky. And he was no nonsense. With the kids he was strict, like the parents were in those days. When they said something, that's what you did. But while he was real firm, he was a nice, kind person.

Everyone always enjoyed being around him because he and Grandma were around all the time. They took time with us to do a lot of things. I always said, and I still maintain to this day, any kid that doesn't get a chance to spend time with their grandparents is missing a lot.

My Grandma Lucy was a real kind and sweet person. Mama and the rest of her kids looked like her. Grandma was tall for her generation. She was about five seven. She wasn't thin, but she wasn't big either. She was medium size.

When we'd come from La Grande on our way to Maxville, we'd always stop in Wallowa at that general store, Shell Mercantile. I think that building is still there. They sold dry goods and food. My grandparents would let each of us choose a treat. I always chose bananas. As a child, I always liked bananas. Then we would go up the mountain to Maxville, and I would

Courtesy Pearl Alice Marsh
Greenwood Elementary school in La Grande, Oregon where Lucy went to school 1st through 5th grade.

Courtesy Kasey Adkins

The type of old had pump the households would have used before indoor plumbing. This old pump would need to be primed by pouring water into it to form a seal before it would pump water. This pump came from an old homestead house near Wallowa and today kids fill the tub for play.

be eating bananas.

I remember going fishing up in Maxville. There was a little pond, and occasionally Grandma would take us fishing after dinner. We would walk down to the pond. Well, there wasn't nothing to do up there except go fishing. I don't remember anything but catfish. After we caught the fish, Grandma cooked them the next day.

When we were visiting Maxville, most of the kids had gone. The kids we knew, their parents and grandparents left Maxville and moved to Wallowa.

I heard a lot of stories as a kid when we visited Maxville. There wasn't much for grown-ups to do in the evenings, so they just worked, came over to one another's houses and visited, and went back to work. We always used to sit around on the porch or in the yard and laugh and talk. One story I remember very well, and I never have forgotten it.

One time we were in Maxville, and it was in the evening, you know, dark. And they had baked sweet potatoes and asked us if we wanted some.

And I said, "Yes."

And at that time you had to eat it if you asked for it. So I said, "Yeah, I want one." I didn't know I didn't like baked sweet potato that much, but I had to eat it. From that point on, I've never eaten baked sweet potatoes. I eat sweet potato pie and a few candied yams once a year, but not baked sweet potatoes. They made me eat that sweet potato, and that was it.

My grandparents never spanked me. Never. All they had to do was look at you, and that was it. As far as my father goes, he wasn't there while I was growing up, so I never got a spanking from him.

I only got in trouble one time. I remember once my mother got on me because she had gone to the store. I was fixing dinner plates. My brother Nathaniel was there and said something that made me angry. I threw a case knife at him and broke the window. When my mother came home, she spanked me.

I didn't have chores except washing dishes and washing the venetian blinds when it was my turn. Each of us old enough had to do dishes for one week and the blinds every couple of months. Our mother came back to check, and if it wasn't done properly, we had to do them over. I didn't have to go out and mow the grass, but we all had chores. My mother did laundry, but we had to iron and fold our clothes. All of my brothers know how to cook and take care of the house.

Georgie Lowry May, daughter of Lucy Tate Lowry. The Lowrys and Trices are cousins.

So with me being the only girl and five boys, I was treated special. I was always the good kid. I can remember some things my mother got on me about that I did. But I never got any spankings or anything like that.

Everyone from La Grande used to go up to Wallowa to visit the country people. Uncle Son moved from Maxville and lived in Wallowa. While he lived in Wallowa, they bought a house, and Aunt B. lived in Portland. I don't recall them living in Maxville, and I don't remember B. living in Wallowa with Uncle Son. They got a house up in Portland, and Uncle Son lived in Wallowa.

Uncle Butch worked in the sawmill in Wallowa. His name was James Monroe Minor, but everyone called him Butch. He was my Aunt Obie's husband. When he worked up there, he came back to La Grande on the weekends. Aunt Obie and Uncle Butch never lived in Maxville, but they lived in Wallowa briefly. Uncle Butch would come and work up at the sawmill in Wallowa and go home to La Grande on the weekends.

I remember visiting Wallowa. All of the African American people lived in a single row of houses on the highway and across the railroad from the sawmill. Ma and Pa Pat's house was next door to Grandma's house. There was Grandma's house, Ma and Pa Pat's house, and then the Marsh house. They were virtually identical company houses. At the end was Uncle Smokey and Ms. Carrie's house.

I remember the Langfords—Jesse and Mattie. Their children were Betty Lou and then Donald, and they had several others. I just remember the nicknames. It was "Rabbit" and "Man" and then "Peaches." That was Betty Lou. And then Shorty. Rabbit was Jesse Lee, Jr.

There was nowhere to go in Wallowa except those houses. We'd usually be at the Marsh house or Ma Pat's house. We visited Kay Francis, Pearl Alice, Penny Merle, and their two brothers, Amos, Jr., and Frank Wayne. We just ran back and forth between the houses. Back and forth. That was all we did. Ten steps between houses.

After we moved to Portland, we'd go down there two or three times a year, first to La Grande and then Wallowa. Pa Pat would be working in his garden. That's when Macy, his niece, was there. The Marsh family had moved to California.

We always went by to see Pa Pat because he was the only one there. Then when Macy came, that was him and her, and we'd always go down to see them. I have pictures of her too. With him and his collard greens, you know. I remember when my grandmother and Ma Pat would cook greens. They would say "save me some pot liquor." They would soak corn bread in it and eat it.

❖　❖　❖

We went to the Church of God in Christ in La Grande. Brother Isaac Lowe had a church. Brother Lowe and his wife, Sister Beatrice Lowe, were some very nice people. They had a son named Paul. He lives somewhere up in Seattle. Elder Lowe's church had food. He didn't have a café, but he sold some food on the weekends: fish sandwiches, potato salad, and homemade ice cream.

I remember the fish sandwiches and mustard. I love fish and mustard today. They would cook whiting fish, slap some mustard on it between two slices of light bread, and that would be so good. And then homemade ice cream. When I eat fish to this day, I want light bread. I don't want whole wheat bread. That's what we called it, light bread.

We went to Brother Isaac Lowe's church. Then we went to Brother and Sister Jenkins' church. The only time we would go to Boyd Memorial Baptist Church was for some special program or Bible study during the summer.

The Banks brothers, D. D. and R. R., ran the Baptist church. They didn't live in La Grande. They lived in Walla Walla, Washington, and Pocatello, Idaho, and came over to La Grande to hold church celebrations periodically. They used to say, "Pass the offering plate," then leave.

Brother and Sister Jenkins had a church. Everyone had a church. Two people over here, one over there, three over here, you know what I'm saying. Everyone had a church.

Courtesy Lucille Mays Bridgewater

Lucille's brothers L-R: Nathaniel, George, John, Ivory, Albert, Stanley

I remember the Alvie Marsh family. They had a daughter named Dorothy Lee. They lived over Dave's store. That's where they were living when their mom passed away. She was in the hospital. I was over spending the night with them when they called and said she had passed away. She was so young. That was really sad. I can still remember them crying.

There was the large Anderson family in La Grande. The parents were Will and Frankie. There were twelve kids in the Anderson family. Only two of them are alive now.

La Grande was a small community, so any personal discord struck the community. After Fred and Lucille Samuel divorced, he married Cousin Velma Butler from Baker. Lucille married Mr. Julius Coleman from right there in La Grande. I remember Billy, Lucille's grandson, and his mother. Her name was Mattie Ruth.

Ruby and Odell Sasnett adopted their son named Bobby, and last time I saw him was at their funerals. Ruby died first. We went to the service, and that was the first time I had seen Bobby since we were adults.

When we left La Grande, I think we were still living on Madison. We only lived those three places. And then we moved to Portland. So that's what I remember about Maxville and Wallowa. Even though my memories are small, since I was a child, they are fond memories and will stay with me always.

ROBERT LEE MINOR

Courtesy Robert Minor
Robert Minor in his army uniform.

Robert Lee Minor was born on October 4, 1940, in Pine Bluff, Arkansas. His father was James Monroe Minor, and his mother was Obie Lowry. They had five children: Precious, Lillie Jane, David, Robert, and Anglee. James died on December 24, 1994, at the age of eighty-nine, and Obie died on December 2, 1994, at the age of seventy-five, both in Portland, Oregon. Robert died on July 10, 2016, also in Portland, at the age of 75, and was buried there.

Robert went to elementary and high school in La Grande and graduated from Washington High School in Portland. He later served in the army.

Robert and Bessie Johnson had two children, Alterina Wilson and Robert Wilson, Jr. Robert, Sr., and Lorene Stephens married in 1968 in Vancouver, Washington. They have two daughters, Jacqueline and Regina. Robert, Sr., then married Velma Rhomas, and the couple adopted a daughter, LaSha.

Courtesy Robert Minor
Robert Minor placed fifth running the 100 yard dash in this Oregon State track meet.

Robert worked at Pacific Northwest Bell until he retired. He attended St. Paul Church of God in Christ and then Power House Church of God in Christ. He enjoyed going to church. He also liked to fish and sit on his porch.

Note: The memories in this contribution by Robert Minor were not based on a recording. They were taken from notes during an informal discussion about his memories.

Robert Minor was born in 1940 in Jefferson County, Arkansas. His parents were James Monroe Minor and Obie Lucy (Lowry) Minor. His grandparents were Hosea Lower and Lucy (Tate) Lowry.

Robert moved with his parents to

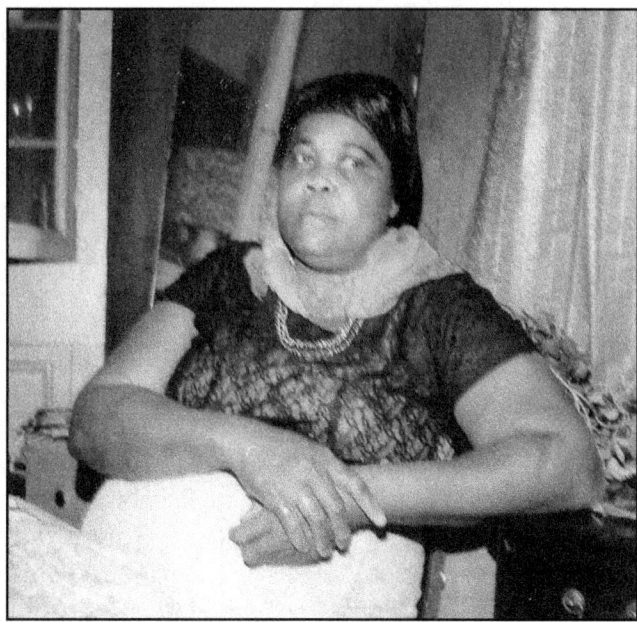

Courtesy Robert Minor

Obie Lowry Minor, Robert Minor's mother.

Wallowa County, Oregon, and lived in Maxville for a short while before moving to Wallowa. Robert attended the first and second grades in Wallowa. His family then moved to La Grande, where he attended the third grade in 1953. Robert's favorite Christmas present as a child was a little white car he could ride.

After the Minor family left Maxville, Robert remembers going back to visit his grandparents and friends and finding Maxville very nice. Robert used to go deer hunting with his grandfather, Hosea Lowry, but Robert never killed a deer himself.

His grandmother Lucy was kind, caring, and gentle. Robert loved his grandmother's cakes, especially her chocolate cakes and vanilla cakes, which were Robert's favorite. Robert loved going fishing in the summer with both his grandparents.

To earn money, Robert washed store windows in La Grande when he was about thirteen or fourteen years old. He earned fifty cents per window, which was very good money for a kid at that time. He used his own brush, squeegee, and bucket. He washed windows at J.C. Penney's, Red Cross, and the drugstore.

Robert never ran into much racism growing up. Everybody got along.

In high school, he played football as a left end and basketball as a right guard and ran three distances in track: 100 yards, 220 yards, and 440 yards. He was fast. He ran against his friend from Wallowa, Amos Marsh, Jr., and beat him. The Minor family moved to

Courtesy Nancy Baker

Lillie Jane Minor, daughter of James and Obie Minor and sister of Robert.

Courtesy Wallowa History Center

Wallowa Elementary, First grade. Teacher Hattie Fisher.
Front Row, L-R: Patty Milligan, Bonnie Lindsay, Unknown, Shirley Henry, Darnell Abrahamson, Mary Ann Murphy, Sandra Baird, Unknown, Billie Blaisdell, Duane Berry, Betty Lou Langford?, Coral Manns, Unknown.
Middle Row: Janice Dougherty, Dorcas Johnson, Darrell Thomas, Lowell Armon?, Shirley Sater, Unknown, Sharon Dailey, Unknown, Unknown, Vera Lampkins, Milton Wade, Harry Cummings.
Top Row: Lawrence Prince, Mary Ann Moores, Ernest Boyd, Darrell Skillings, Greg Johnson, Robert Minor.

Portland when Robert was a senior in high school, and he graduated from Washington High School. He then served in the army in Georgia and South Korea.

Robert married Velma Taylor on March 1, 1986, in Portland. He worked for and retired from the telephone company. His job was to install phones in residential homes.

ROSIE THOMAS GRAY

Rosie Lee Thomas was born in La Grande, Oregon, the daughter of Hattie (Cook) Thomas and William Lee Thomas. Her parents met in Maxville and married in Wallowa, Oregon. The family had six children: Robert, Rosie, Sylvester, Ernestine, Norman and Loletha, all born in La Grande. Her mother died in childbirth in 1948, and her father died in 1993 in Houston, Texas.

Her father was a log cutter for Bowman-Hicks before he started his own trucking business as a log hauler. Her mother was a young homemaker.

Rosie attended elementary school briefly in Wallowa. After her mother died, her family moved to Louisiana, where she attended DeSoto Parish Elementary School. She then moved to Houston and attended Kashmere High School, but she graduated from McClatchy High School in 1961 in Sacramento, California.

Courtesy Rosie Gray

Thomas children. Back row, L-R: William Sylvester, Rosie, Loletha, and Robert Louis.
Front row, L-R: Norman and Ernestine

Rosie married Handy Gray in January 1965. They have two children, Verna Williamson and Freddie "Butch" Douglas. Rosie worked as an administrative assistant at UC Davis Medical Center before she retired. She now works part-time for a nonprofit agency, Center for Fathers and Families in Sacramento, where she's the office manager.

Rosie loves golfing and fishing, though she doesn't do it as much as she did when she was younger. She attends Shiloh Baptist Church, where she has been a parishioner for fifty-nine years. Her uncle, Rev. Willie Cook, pastored Shiloh for many years.

My name is Rosie Gray, and my father, William Lee Thomas, was a Maxville logger, and my mother was Hattie Louise Thomas. Her maiden name was Cook. My dad was from Mansfield, Louisiana. He met my mom in Maxville. She lived with my Aunt Lillie and Uncle Bob.

We lived in Wallowa, but I barely remember much. I was born in La Grande in 1941 and left in 1948. Basically, that's about all. I don't remember much because my mom died when I was six and a half years old and my baby sister was two days old.

Courtesy Rosie Gray
William Lee Thomas

I remember us living in a little white house on the corner somewhere in Wallowa, with a coal bin in the back. And I remember living at the Weaver Bridge. We used to go fishing with Dad at Weaver Bridge. My dad used to love to fish. So it's only a couple times because we weren't there that long. And then we moved to Louisiana after my mom died.

We used to have the stream on the side, and my mom would catch trout. There was a thicket on this side, and the deer used to come up to the fence.

I remember starting first grade in Wallowa, and Mrs. [Hattie] Fisher was my teacher. I only went a half a semester. I would have to take the school bus to come into Wallowa to school. And this white girl sat there with her nose up the whole way. I remember that.

Courtesy Pearl Alice Marsh
Hattie Louise Cook Thomas, wife of William Lee Thomas, mother of Rosie.

My dad drove a logging truck. He used to come by the house with this big truck and all those big logs on it. My dad made snow ice cream when we had snow.

I remember Ma Pat and Pa Pat, and I specifically remember going over to their house. They always had food. I don't remember too much more than that. I knew he

Courtesy Wallowa County Museum
A General Motors logging truck, c.1930s, as the license plate is dated 1939. This logging truck is of the general time that William Gray had his logging business in the 1940s.

73

Weaver pond, down by Weaver's bridge where Rosie went fishing with her family.

was a big man, but I don't recall his voice.

The Langford family lived in the big house on the end of the row. We called one of the Langford boys "Rabbit". He and my brother Sylvester were playing with a butcher knife, and he stuck the knife through his hand.

After my mother died, my grandmother came from Louisiana, picked all six of us up, and took us back to Louisiana. So I really didn't have that much personal contact with my dad after that. That was in 1948.

Dad would always call and write and would always send money to Louisiana. And then I remember him moving to Klamath Falls. And then not long after that, my dad moved to Houston, Texas. I guess at that time he started working with Southern Pacific. I'm trying to find a happy childhood. Well, I remember when my grandmother came to pick us up after my mother died in '48. My uncle who was from Mississippi came, and that was a beautiful week. He took us from Mansfield to Mississippi for a week. My uncle was Willy Cook.

I was so young when we moved to Louisiana. But I enjoyed it when my uncle took us from Mansfield to Brookhaven. Mansfield was the country, but my uncle had a car. We didn't have one with my grandmother. But it was kind of neat living with my grandmother.

We raised hogs, and we would kill them in the fall. And we had a smokehouse. We would smoke our own bacon and hams and make our own sausage. We'd use the small intestines and smoke it. At that time, it wasn't much fun, but now I'm glad that I had that experience. I learned a lot. Hard work made me who I am today. So, I would say my time in Mansfield with my grandmother was pretty nice.

Then my grandmother died, and we all moved to Houston with Dad. He retired from Southern Pacific and died at the ripe old age of ninety-three on December 17, 2004.

Courtesy Wallowa History Center
The donkey jammer was used on the railrod tracks to move and load logs. Later jammers were used from truck beds at log landings. See photo under Lucille Bridgewater's story.

KATHERINE COOK RAMSEY

Katherine Cook Ramsey was part of the Baggett-Cook family from Brookhaven, Mississippi. She attended Wallowa Elementary School from 1940 to 1944. Ms. Blanche Billings was her teacher.

After leaving Wallowa, Katherine's family moved to Portland, where she attended school and graduated from Jefferson High School. After high school, she attended Methodist Central State College in Wilberforce, Ohio, a historically black college, and majored in English and sociology. She earned a bachelor of science in education (BSEd) in 1953 and graduated cum laude. She was a member of the Alpha Kappa Alpha sorority.

After she graduated, she moved to Berkeley, California, and lived with her uncle Frank and aunt Magnolia Cook. She worked on the Treasure Island Naval Base in a typing pool. Then in 1960 in San Francisco, she worked as a keypunch and verifier operator. Professionally, she became a social worker in the county of Alameda, where she rose to a supervisory position.

Courtesy Veronica Ramsey-Swift
Valarie & Katherine Cook, Maxville, 1939.

Katherine met her husband, Leroy Allen Ramsey, Sr., at a dance at the California Hotel in Oakland, which was a stylish social venue in the city. He served as a fighter pilot in the Korean War and earned the rank of lieutenant before retiring. After retirement, he worked for the State of California.

Katherine and Leroy had twin daughters, Veronica and Valerie, born in 1956, and two sons, Leroy Allen, Jr., in 1957 and Robert in 1958.

Katherine grew up in the Methodist Church and attended Downes Memorial Methodist Church in Oakland. She became a Jehovah's Witness in 1970.

Katherine was a fabulous seamstress and made clothes for her daughters. She also knew how to crochet, but her passion was sewing. She was very compassionate and embraced those who did not have much. She currently resides in Richmond, California.

Note: The interview with Katherine Cook Ramsey was not recorded. It is summarized from handwritten notes taken during a brief interview on December 6, 2014.

Courtesy Veronica Ramsey-Swift
Ella Mae Dillon Cook

75

Courtesy Ronee Riggle Stone
L-R: Jack Riggle, son of Don Riggle, woods boss for Bowman-Hicks, Catherine and Valerie Cook, daughters of Alec and Ella May, and Verna Coleman.

Katherine Cook Ramsey is the daughter of Alexander Ozias "Alec" Cook and Ella Mae (Dillon) Cook. Katherine was born on March 2, 1931, in Brookhaven, Mississippi. Her parents had two daughters, Katherine and Valerie. The family moved from Brookhaven to Maxville in 1939 and after one year moved to Water Canyon.

Several members of the Cook family came to Maxville to work around 1940. The first of the family to move was Lillie Cook, who came around 1934 as a "mail-order bride" to marry Bob Baggett, one of the older men in Maxville. He was born in 1875 in Mississippi and had been married previously to Bobbie Baggett, who presumably died in the early 1930s. Mr. Bob and Mrs. Lillie were living in Maxville in 1935. Several years later, she sent for her sister Theola Cook Coleman and her daughter Verna Eloise Coleman, who still lived in Brookhaven. After Theola and Verna arrived in Maxville, other members of the Cook family came, including her sisters Hattie Louise "Louise" and Logia Agnes "Logie" and her brother Alexander.

Katherine's father came to cut logs but did not like the work or living in a company town. He came to Oregon because you could make more money. In Mississippi, he sometimes made one dollar a day. In addition to disliking the work and the town, Alec and Ella Mae did not like that the school was closed. Their daughters went one full year without going to school. So they left Water Canyon and moved to Pendleton. There, he became a bricklayer. They later moved to Portland.

A second brother, Willie Phillip Cook, left Mississippi but went to Sacramento, California, instead of Maxville. He married Mary Alice Bryant, and in 1946, they moved to Pendleton, where Katherine's family lived. Willie did not log; he was a businessman. He was the first African American licensed electrical contractor in Oregon. He also established an auto body shop in Pendleton called the Cook Car Clinic.

Courtesy Veronica Ramsey
Logia Agnes Cook Babin. She is Alex Cook's sister.

Katherine's uncle Bob Baggett was one of the original African American loggers recruited to work for Bowman-Hicks Lumber Company in Maxville. Mr. Baggett was a section foreman for the company and presumably in charge of the African American workers. In 1940 he was working as the caretaker for the Bowman-Hicks properties in Maxville after the operations shut down. When Katherine and her family would visit Uncle Bob, he would walk the sisters

Katherine Cook report card, 1940-41.

Courtesy Veronica Ramsey-Swift

through the woods and introduce them to the birds, animals, and plants they had not seen as children in Mississippi. After Bob Baggett died in 1936, Lillie remarried Robert Terry and had four children.

Katherine's mother, Ella Mae, worked for Jeannie Gail Ashby, the wife of Henry Newton Ashby, who was the manager of the Bowman-Hicks Lumber Company operation in Wallowa County. In 1940, the Ashbys built a new family home on top of the hill at Water Canyon and moved there from La Grande. A few African American loggers and their families lived down the hill alongside the Wallowa River.

Katherine Cook Ramsey remembers Water Canyon as a beautiful place.

Courtesy Linda Bauck

The Ashby's place in the Wallowa River canyon at Water Canyon. The houses ore the original houses, only the sign is new.

JOSEPH HILLIARD, JR.

Joseph Hilliard, Jr., was born in 1946 in La Grande, Oregon, to Joseph, Sr., and Atrice (Smith) Hilliard. Joseph and Atrice migrated from Mississippi to Maxville but then moved to La Grande because Atrice was unhappy with the small town.

Joseph and Atrice had six children: Carolyn Jean, Jimmy Carol, Harold "Buddy," Joseph, Jr., Ted Stevenson, and Jerry Duane.

Joseph, Jr., attended Greenwood Elementary School in La Grande. After graduating from La Grande High School, Joseph went to Eastern Oregon University, where he earned a degree in business administration. After working for eight years, he then went to the University of Washington, earning a master's degree in public administration. Next, he attended the Industrial College of the Armed Forces, where he earned a master's degree in national resource strategy.

Courtesy Pearl Alice Marsh
Atrice Smith Hilliard

Joseph married Celia Rankins in 1972. They have two daughters: Malaika, who was born in Nairobi, Kenya; and Tendayi, who was born in Rahway, New Jersey. Celia and Joseph are the proud grandparents of three very active boys.

Courtesy newspapers.com
Joe Hilliard, Jr. photo from the La Grande Observer, March 9, 1963

Joseph pursued a professional career in government, first with the Peace Corps, where he served in Kenya as associate director of administration, then Malawi and The Gambia as country director. Later he joined the US State Department as a member of the diplomatic corps. His career took him to Venezuela, Bangladesh, Malaysia, Italy, Cuba, and Panama.

Outside of his active life, Joseph has a keen interest in golf and precolonial African history. But much of his time is spent with his grandchildren

❖   ❖   ❖

My name is Joseph Hilliard, Jr., and I was born in La Grande, Oregon on January 22, 1946. My father was Joseph Hilliard, Sr., and my mother was Atrice Marie (Smith) Hilliard. Both of my parents were born in Brookhaven, Mississippi. My siblings, Carolyn Jean and Jimmy Carol, both

La Grande Observer, March 2, 1944. Hospital Notes, St. Joseph's hospital: "Dismissed:.... Mrs. Joe Hilliard and infant son of Wallowa ...."

La Grande, Observer, Sept. 5, 1962. (Article listed turnout for La Grande Football) "The rest of the squad ncludes seniors ... Joe Hilliard .... Sophomores .... Ted Hilliard ...."

were born in Brookhaven and stayed there until my parents could send for them after they moved to Oregon. Harold Eugene—we call him "Buddy"—was born in La Grande in February of 1944. Ted Stevenson was born a year after me, and Jerry Duane came along a year later.

My parents saw their job as ensuring that their kids were good and respectful and were grateful to them for the choice they made to relocate to Maxville in 1943. Our family was programmed to succeed. We had done well in the South in spite of Jim Crow constraints. So moving west provided my parents a greater opportunity to open doors for their children.

They were clear-eyed about the racial situation in Oregon, but despite the obvious, figured that life was so much better in Oregon that we had no good reason to complain. In fact, my dad told us plainly and often that, even in Oregon, certain jobs were reserved for whites and that we shouldn't expect to get one of those no matter how hard we tried. Well, thank goodness for my mother. As far as she was concerned, I was going to make it to the top, and she was the one I listened to. But even she applauded accomplishment more than effort, and there is a distinct difference. "Oh, he's probably somewhere with his head in a book" was the usual answer when someone was looking for me—and that was not meant as a compliment.

So how did we manage to find ourselves in Maxville, Wallowa County, Oregon? Well, Willie H. Cook, a family friend, moved out there from Brookhaven in 1943 and convinced my father to follow him with talk of big money and better living conditions. So Joe and Atrice scraped enough cash together for train fare for the two of them, with plans to send for Jimmy and Carolyn as soon as they could. I don't think they thought life in the Northwest would be much different from the South—if they gave their new home much thought at all. Being part of a segregated black community was all they knew, so why would it be any different in Oregon? They were in for a rude awakening.

"Nothing up here but white people and sheep" wrote my father in his first letter back home. In fact, they disliked Maxville so much that they planned to move back home as soon as their finances would allow—a plan that never materialized because in the next five years, their brood grew from two to six. After the initial shock, they quickly realized that Oregon presented more and better opportunities than Mississippi.

Though we grew up in Oregon, us kids didn't much like the Northwest either, largely because of the size of the black community. When we complained, Mama would say, "You're lucky you aren't in Promise"—a town in Wallowa County that she made sound even smaller than Maxville. Matter of fact, we couldn't complain about anything without hearing one tall tale after another about how much worse it

Courtesy Joseph Hilliard
Mary Gellispie, grandmother of Joseph Hilliard, Jr.

79

Courtesy Fred Hill Historical Photos, Eastern Oregon University Digital Archives
The old La Grande High School building scheduled for demolition in 1990.

was for them growing up down South. Thus it was that we learned to count our blessings.

My mother didn't talk very much about life in the logging camp because, truth be told, she started looking for a way out almost as soon as they unpacked. She was the driving force behind moving out of a lively Brookhaven area, so it was not surprising that she found Maxville a bit tedious. So she issued an ultimatum to Dad Joe, which went something like this: "I can't take it. I'm moving. You stay here. I'm going." And go she did, finding a house in La Grande. In order to make ends meet, she worked hard, taking every odd job she could find from cleaning hotel rooms to washing store windows.

My brother Ted, and I believe Dad Joe, traded in his power saw shortly after he realized felling trees in the woods was not his forte. The only story we remember him telling about Maxville was about his narrowly escaping serious injury while loading a big logging truck. After that incident, he found a job in the machine shop, which was more in line with the work he did in Mississippi. Nonetheless, he still wasn't happy because of his separation from Mama, so eventually he found a job in La Grande with the Union Pacific Railroad.

Initially we didn't have relatives in Oregon, but my paternal grandmother and stepgrandfather, Mary and Jack Gillespie, decided to stay when they brought Jimmy and Carolyn out West to join Mama and Daddy. My grandmother Little Mama's brothers—James, Jesse, and David—joined them later.

We drove to Mississippi in '53, with the eight of us squeezed into an old '49 Buick, suffering three of the most arduous days any of us had experienced. Once there, we stayed exclusively on my grandfather's farm because Daddy and Mama didn't trust us around southern white folks. It was fine with us, because life on the farm was so different from the "city" life we knew. It seemed like we were living with the animals. Big Papa plowed his fields strapped to a mule named Bill. He raised pigs, chickens, and cows as well. We learned the sounds Big Papa made to make the mule go and stop, got our water from a well, and saw watermelons growing in the fields for the first time. We were so excited we would go out and pick them up, breaking the stems, ensuring they

Courtesy Irene Barklow collection, Wallowa History Center

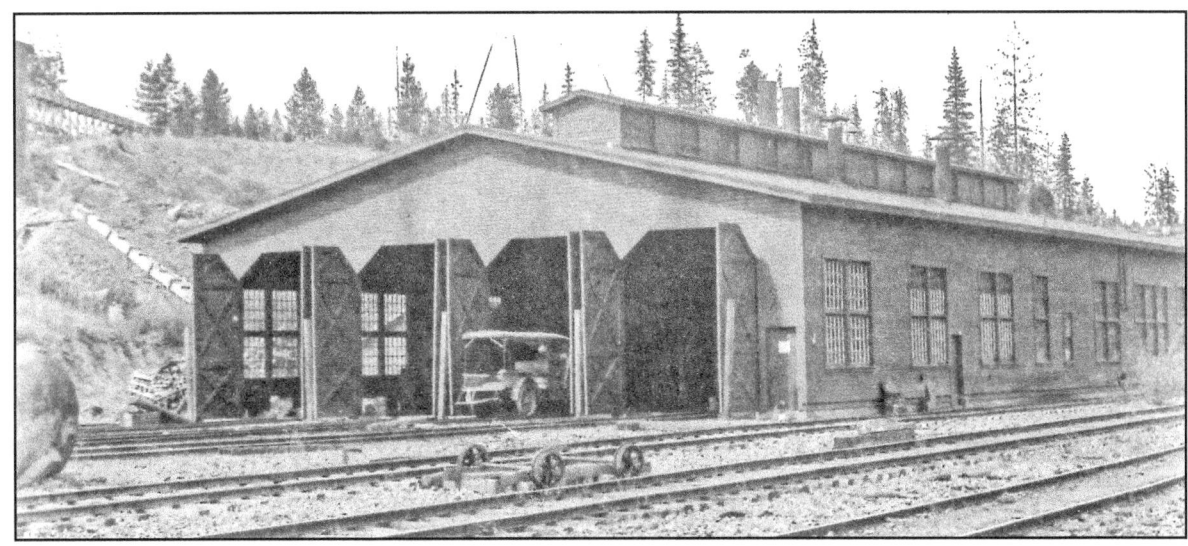

Bowman-Hicks engine house, Camp 5.

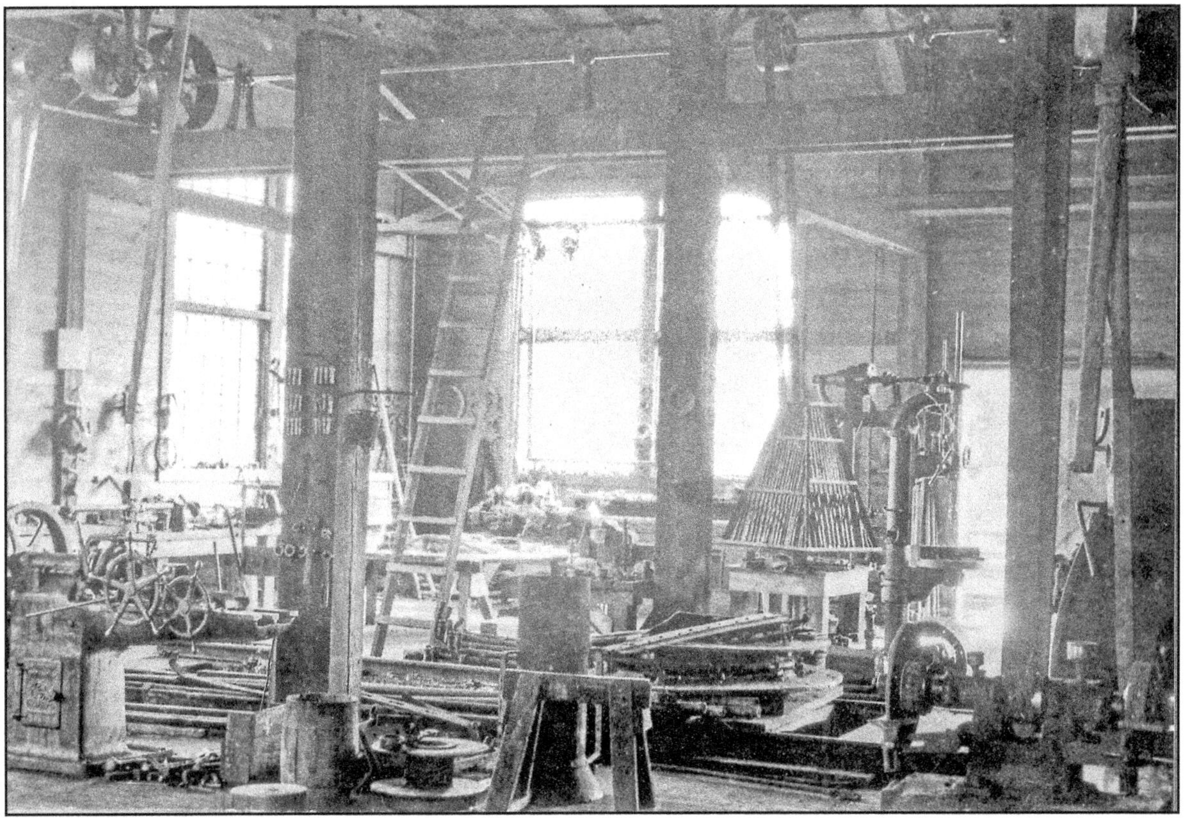

Courtesy Irene Barklow collection, Wallowa History Center

Bowman-Hicks machine shop, next to the engine house.

would rot in the field rather than ripen on the vine. When my mother yelled that we were wasting good melons, our grandfather just said, "Leave them alone, Atrice. They don't know." How great was that? Our grandparents down there wouldn't let our parents touch us no matter what we did.

From that one visit to Brookhaven, I realized my parents had brought their culture north with them. They raised us according to the world they knew in an effort to keep us safe. Raised us to be good and respectful kids, and if that led to success, fine. But challenging authority was out. We knew that in case of a disagreement, our parents would generally side with the adult—especially if the adult was a teacher. So we accepted whatever elders or teachers told us. I look back at it and think we should have pushed back when the time was right, but that was never expected of us, and we never did.

Odell Sasnett, Johnny Lawson, Alvie Marsh, Will Anderson, and others lived in La Grande and worked in the woods in Wallowa County. Their power saws sometimes awakened us on Saturday mornings as they felled excess trees in the neighborhood and then cut them up for firewood to heat their homes and fuel wood cooking stoves. We knew they cut logs for a living, but I don't remember hearing them talk shop. They may have, but trouble awaited kids who showed too much interest in "grown folks' conversation."

I remember visiting Wallowa a couple times. Pa Pat with the laughing eyes, big belly, and jolly conversation was unforgettable. I remember the smell of the woods, the green trees, and the bluest sky. We were deep in woods, or so it seemed, and totally isolated. We would sit around talking for a while, and before hitting the road for home,

Courtesy Fred Hill Historical Photos, Eastern Oregon University Digital Archives

La Grande Railroad yards, c. 1940-1960

Courtesy Fred Hill Historical Photos, Eastern Oregon University Digital Archives
Aerial view of La Grande, OR, c.1945-1965.

they always fed us well, with chicken and dumplings always on the menu. My parents persuaded me to stay up there for an extended period when I was about three to keep Little Mama company. Papa Jack worked all day, and she must have been pretty lonely. My memory is not too keen, but I must have missed my brothers dearly. So the first time they took me back home for a visit, I said, "I'm ain't going back." Incorrect English to be sure, but I got my point across. No way were they going to pry me away from my family again.

Papa Jack was a self-taught bricklayer. I don't know if he actually did that type of work in Wallowa, though he may well have. He and Little Mama also decided opportunities were better in La Grande, so they moved into the house next door to ours. My dad loved that because Little Mama cooked him breakfast every morning. I never heard my mother complain, but this must have bothered her. Having six of us to feed must have made it easier to tolerate.

About my impressions of La Grande, and with apologies to Charles Dickens, it can best be described as a tale of two cities: ours hard by the railroad tracks with dirt roads and run-down houses, and theirs with tree-lined streets and well-manicured lawns. How I envied them. I remember hoping that one day I would live in one of "their" houses.

Our house was the meeting place in our neighborhood because folks would always find a reason to stop by. I remember Sam Montgomery would come from Baker to hang out, and Junior Fletcher (my best buddy) came by often to watch TV. (We were one of the first families to get one.) Fletch was afraid to come up on our porch because our dog Skip didn't like him. So we would hear him yelling, "Jimmy Atrice" from a safe distance. Funny how they gave my oldest brother my mother's first name as his middle.

83

I remember Johnny Fae, Mildred Anderson, and my sister Carolyn hanging out together, and the three of them dancing in our living room. We'd have the latest records we could find, like James Brown and the Famous Flames, Garnet Mimms and the Enchanters, Little Richard, Mickey and Sylvia, Sam Cooke, and so many others. I used to love watching them, but I never got a chance to strut my stuff—assuming I had some stuff to strut. Besides, I was much too young to even think about asking one of Carolyn's friends to dance with me.

I recall my father used to buy Ebony and Jet magazines as soon as they came in at the train station. We'd absorb these things as our lifeline to a black community we did not know, but we couldn't wait to introduce ourselves.

I remember the Jet that covered the murder of Emmett Till. The photo of his mutilated corpse haunted me then as it does even to this day. But we never discussed it with our parents or even among ourselves. Because he was murdered in Mississippi, I am sure it reinforced my parents' decision to move up to the Northwest. Further, we were beginning to see the Civil Rights movement take shape with Martin Luther King, Jr., leading the Montgomery bus boycott. We watched the nightly news shows with Walter Cronkite, David Brinkley, and all, but it was foreign to us. That's what it was like for me growing up in that environment. I felt like two different people; I was torn between who I was and where I was, trying desperately to figure out how to make sense of it all.

Christmas was a magical time because it was the one time of year we could be sure of getting, within reason, whatever we wanted. The countdown would start just after Thanksgiving, and our excitement would grow as the days passed. I remember my mother baking her sweet potato and apple pies and cherry pies and peach cobblers. My mouth is drooling now because no one makes them like she did.

On Christmas Eve, we'd all get dressed up for the children's program at the church. Everyone would be there—saints and sinners. We would always do a play and/or recite speeches and prayers from Ms. Torrence's playbook. After church, we would go home and try to get some sleep—which did not come easily. Waking up at 3:00 or 4:00 a.m. was not unusual, but our parents would chase us back to bed. But at six we were up and into the presents. Those were the best of times.

We had three churches in La Grande with each pastor doing his best to provide material assistance to his parishioners where possible. Ours was Boyd Memorial Baptist. Never knew who Boyd was, but we memorialized him every Sunday. We claimed an enrollment of fifty-nine, but the actual number would have been closer to twenty. Our pastor, Reverend D. D. Banks, had churches in Walla Walla, Pendleton, and Hermiston as well as La Grande. We looked forward to the times when one of his churches would host a joint service, because unlike La Grande, the other towns had unattached black girls. So we would pair off after church to arrange dates for the coming weeks and months.

We would have a potluck lunch after Sunday school and before the preaching and singing service. All the ladies cooked their best dishes. Little Mama's fried chicken was to die for, and Ethel Wilfong cooked a mean banana pudding. My mother always cooked mac and cheese and a delicious shrimp salad. And these were just the ladies from La Grande. We would stuff ourselves and then go back for seconds—and thirds while the late

Courtesy Pearl Alice Marsh

Front Row L-R: Unknown, Ted Hilliard, Buddy Hilliard, Joe Hilliard. Row 2: Jimmy Hilliard, Unkown.
Row 3: Carolyn Hilliard, Unknown.
Above Row 3: All Unkown.

service was still going on. The choirs competed too, and ours was never the best. Marion Hawthorn had the most melodious voice, but my mama definitely sang the loudest. We had a young folks' choir too, and Marion's daughter Vinie and her sisters were a cut above the rest of us if you throw Carolyn out of the equation. I was not a good singer, but

Courtesy Fred Hill Historical Photos, Eastern Oregon University Digital Archives
J.P. Barnes Circus parade, upper 4th Street, La Grande, Oregon, c. 1910-1940.

they let me lead one song, and I remember throwing my head back, singing, "It's me, it's me, it's me, O Lord, standing in the need of prayer." I'd be so proud, and everyone would nod approvingly, happy that my song had ended.

Reverend Lowe had the next largest congregation. He couldn't survive on the meager income the church provided, so he doubled as the town gravedigger. And then there was Zedell Jackson, whose church was physically the largest, but I do not know that he had any permanent members. He could really play the guitar, though, so we would hang around outside and listen to him do his thing. His fire-and-brimstone sermons were so entertaining that we would go home and practice his style and delivery.

My mother was a churchgoing woman. She went to gatherings on almost every day of the week, for example, choir rehearsal, Bible study, mission, and prayer meeting. She loved going to church with her friends, and I suppose one could consider her circle of friends a sorority. In contrast, every now and then Dad Joe went on special occasions. Some evenings he would come home with a twinkle in his eye and a touch of whiskey on his breath and persuade Mama to dance to some of his old Count Basie records. What a shock when we first saw how the church lady could shake with the best of them. I'm guessing she atoned by praying a little harder the next time she found herself in the sanctuary.

Everyone—even the sinners who drank wine, played poker, shot dice, and sometimes fought in the alley behind our house—respected the church ladies. They called my mother Miss Atrice, and I never heard them utter a swear word in her presence.

Were there some "rough" folks in our neighborhood? Of course, but they loved us as much as anyone else in the neighborhood and would do anything to protect us. And none of the kids were allowed to hang out at the adult meeting places like George Trice's gambling house in the back alley. My dad liked going over there to drink wine, play dice, and talk smack. They might have been rough, but as far as we were concerned, not at all. They were just friends and neighbors. Matter of fact, my dad had a little juke joint for a while called Little Joe's Café. He and Willie Cook built it just next door to our house. The joint sold fish sandwiches, hamburgers, and sodas. They didn't need a liquor license because everyone brought their own. Mama cooked, and I don't know what all Dad Joe did, though he probably circulated and kept order. Carolyn was responsible for babysitting her little brothers at home, and I can remember going to sleep listening to Big Joe Turner on the loud jukebox singing, "Come on and shake-a your booty cause your booty's all right with me." And I can just imagine how they were "getting down" inside. The business did well for a while, but they closed it because folks started fighting every weekend and my dad didn't want that stuff happening so close to the house.

I remember one time this guy named Cane tried to molest one of the girls. When word got around to Dad Joe, he simply told her mother, "Okay. I'll take care of it." So he went and got a couple of his buddies, probably George Trice, George Fletcher, and Odell Sasnett. They pummeled Mr. Cane severely, so that was the end of that.

I remember a guy named Jim White used to beat his significant other, Maggie Hayman, whenever he had been drinking. She put a stop to it by throwing a lye-based concoction into his eyes, and that was the end of the beatings—and his eyesight. Same thing happened to a guy named Mack Johnson. He was abusing a woman named Bessie Mae Anderson. Rumor has it that after a long and intense conversation with Maggie, Bessie Mae summoned the courage to extract her revenge on Mack. And he had a seeing eye dog the rest of his life. As one might imagine, this had a chilling effect on men in the neighborhood who would mistreat their women.

I remember the Lawson family in La Grande very well. Doll, Jimmy, Maurice, Dean, Johnny Fay, and Andy. They went to Reverend Lowe's church, and I believe they rented a house from him too. It was a big two-story place very near the railroad tracks. I knew Jimmy as an excellent basketball player and, as I understand it, somewhat of a ladies' man.

What stands out about the Lawsons, though, is their job at the D & V Donuts shop. The owners gave leftover baked goods to employees, and often the Lawsons would get so many they would call us over to pick up what they didn't want. Those were beautiful days when we'd get the call. "You guys want some doughnuts?" We would be at the front door with the biggest grocery bag we could find practically before they hung up. My favorite was the cream-filled logs, and Buddy liked the twists. I think the little boys liked the maple bars. The regular glazed were the last to go—but believe me, they went too.

I have to mention Lucky Trice, who was so much an outlier that we really didn't think of him as one of us. I often wonder what he could have accomplished if not for that melanin thing. He was a businessman when most of our parents were cleaners and loggers. I wonder how he financed his business ventures, because banks were not known for betting on unconventional blacks at that time. My guess is he did it all on his own, and with a large family to feed, it must have been a challenge.

When I was in high school, I worked as a busboy at the Tropidara, the fanciest restaurant in town. Obie Minor, Robert's mother, washed dishes there, so we had plenty of time to chat. She told me lots of stories, good and bad, about the grown folks in the neighborhood, but it was clear she really liked and respected my mother.

Obie's house was separated from ours by an alley and an enclosure filled with used tires. There was always something going on over there. They had the best music: B. B. and Albert King, Bobby "Blue" Bland, and others. I loved Obie because she was honest with me in a way that most adults were not, never sugarcoating a thing.

Lillie Jane, her youngest daughter, and I were in the sixth grade together, and I remember us walking home together. She was two years older than me, but those were like dog years. I remember her wearing a waistcoat one time and claiming, "Oh, this coat makes me look like I'm pregnant." And I'm eleven years old going, "What?"

We didn't have air conditioning (no one did), so on some hot summer nights, we would pull our mattresses outside to sleep under the stars. Anglee, Obie's second son, would try to scare us by sneaking up with a sheet over his head. I think that was his way of announcing he wanted to find a place among us to spend the night.

I remember Portland kids coming east to visit their La Grande relatives during summer vacations. We had so much fun they wouldn't want to go back home. We were, to use a current term, free-range kids, wild as lion cubs on the East African savannah. We came and went as we pleased—left the house after breakfast and didn't come in until it was time for the next meal. I have a grandson now who's almost ten years old, and I don't think he's ever been alone. He's always with somebody. In contrast, at five years old, I was already walking to school by myself. That's just what we did. That's the way we grew up.

So out there in that environment, we had time to dream and time to think about making our dreams a reality. We made our own toys and our own fun. In the winter we had snowball fights and made snowmen and skied on ice patches. And I'll never forget walking to school in the mornings after the first snow when everything is white and quiet except for the sound of tire chains on the odd car crunching along on almost-deserted streets. In the spring and summer, we played ball outside and in the fall raided our neighbors' apple, pear, plum, and peach trees. Had to be careful eating those apples because every now and then you'd run up on a live worm.

We were born in La Grande, so interacting with white kids was normal; it was all we knew. There was no real effort to keep us apart when we were in elementary school, though I don't remember ever being invited to a house party.

Vinie McClain was my closest black classmate. Her family lived next door, and we were like brother and sister. They tell me I used to crawl up into her crib and finish off her milk bottles.

From the beginning, Vinie was whip smart, and I showed so little promise that my mother feared Vinie would show me up in class. So she changed my birth certificate (yes, this is true) and started me a year early. One day I was out in the yard making mud pies, and the next I was in Dr. Gregory's office for my physical, and the next in the first grade. Jimmy took me to class the first day, and I remember thinking this school thing was strange because they started calling me Joey when my name was Junior. Then the second day everyone mistakenly thought I knew my way to class. I went to the playground instead. I was having fun out there until someone spied me and came out to say, "Boy, you better get yourself back in that school." Thus, sadly, my life of leisure came to an end—at least for the next nine months.

So grade school was unremarkable, though I was always conscious of being the only black kid in most of my classes. And I remember being ashamed when that chapter on slavery came up in American history. I was embarrassed when there was no good reason to be. Aren't the slave owners and their descendants the ones who should bear that shame rather than the victims? Also, I was always assigned to the slower groups when the classes were segmented. I always took the challenge because I knew at the end of the year I'd prove to be one of the better students. This happened year after year. It was unfortunate that some of the kids who didn't have parents who believed in them would stay in the slow class all year though they were as smart as anyone else.

One day a group of four or five white kids and myself were having a casual conversation with a fully uniformed police officer. We were looking at his service revolver wondering if he had ever killed anyone and asking inane questions when he looked at me and asked my name. I told him, and he responded, "Oh, one of those Hilliard boys, eh?" Then, "You know, we've been told that if one of you guys ever get into trouble, just call your father. What he'll do to you is much worse than anything we would do." My parents liked that story. Reputation was everything to them, and we had a good one because we followed the rules, both written and unwritten.

La Grande was a great place until we entered the teen years, when our dormant hormones began to awaken. And by then, all of the black girls were gone. The Hawthorns, Andersons, Langfords, the Lawsons, and the others—they all left at precisely the wrong time.

There is one threatening incident that occurred over in Elgin. Buddy started playing the piano by ear when he was about three. He played in church and won most of the talent competitions. My parents tried to give him lessons, but he already had his way of doing things and wouldn't change.

He had a band called The Roadrunners, who played for high school dances in La Grande and lots of little surrounding towns. I used to travel with them quite a bit, and one night in Elgin, a small town not more than thirty miles from La Grande, I decided to ask one of my friends from La Grande to dance. About halfway through, I felt as though someone had tripped over my legs but didn't give it a thought. Afterwards a guy named Pat Hammond told me he didn't like what he was seeing and that if I danced with another white girl, he was going to take me down to the river and teach me a lesson. Buddy couldn't hear, but sensing what was going on, [he] stopped playing midsong and came down off the bandstand to tell the guy if it was a fight he wanted, we were all in. At that point, shocked that this young uppity black showed absolutely no fear, Hammond left to round up his boys for some action after the dance.

During intermission Buddy and I managed to get to a pay phone and called my dad. Suddenly his worst nightmare had come true. Taking no chances, he loaded his car with every firearm he could find and headed for Elgin to rescue his boys. Fortunately somebody called the state police, who separated us from the local toughs after the dance and escorted us all the way home. What surprised Buddy and me was that our friends from La Grande never left our side. When we expressed some surprise, one said, "You didn't expect us to abandon you, did you?"

Pat Hammond alone decided he was going to impose his will on us because he didn't think blacks had any rights he was bound to respect. But this night our white friends stood with us. Now, fifty years later, I wonder why we didn't just slip into a car shortly before the dance was over and drive away. But the idea never occurred to either of us. Stealing away was not part of our DNA.

We traveled to Pendleton and Walla Walla when we wanted a date—and that was almost every weekend when we didn't have a ball game. Now you might ask if, in an unguarded moment of youthful exuberance, one or more of us might have dared to date across the color line. Well, yes, it was happening and only a problem if you were found out. To wit, George Fletcher, Jr., not realizing fat meat is greasy, started dating a local white girl and not doing a good enough job of covering his tracks. When her mother found out she was dating this black kid named Junior, she did some sleuthing and determined incorrectly that I was the culprit. So she called Dad Joe and told him he would find me hanging in a tree if I didn't stop dating her daughter. Dad Joe, who was totally in the dark, told her if she bothered his son, she might find her own self up in a tree. I guess he was convincing enough, because we never heard from her again. He was relieved to find that I wasn't the "Junior" in question.

We didn't have trouble with bullies or anything like that during our school years. You see, there were five of us, and though we fought each other from time to time, no one messed with us, fearing retribution from one of my older brothers. Having said that, if we lost a fight with someone our own age, that was a personal problem you were encouraged to revisit. But if someone older bothered me, Jimmy or Buddy got involved, and no one wanted any part of that.

Jimmy was the best athlete in the family, and we all wanted to be him. He was so good his coaches made sure he passed tough classes by providing him answers before he sat for the test. Also, he would "find" the fanciest football shoes in his locker at the beginning of the season and always got the highest-paying jobs during the summer. The faculty really took care of him until his last term as a senior, when his English teacher stopped going along and failed him. The coaches did set him up with a tutor to help him fulfill his requirement and enable him to enroll in college the next fall. But in what was the biggest mistake of his life, he quit going after a couple of weeks. So he didn't graduate, and he's bitter even to this day.

Over in Wallowa, Amos Marsh, Jr., was a few years older than Jimmy, so they didn't get a chance to compete against each other in sports. Jimmy was good, but Amos was so big and so fast that I don't think Jimmy could have stopped him—at least for long. But Jimmy would have never quit or admitted defeat. Amos was, in my opinion, the best athlete to ever come out of eastern Oregon, period.

Speaking of Amos, there was always a lot of excitement in the neighborhood when he came to town for a track meet. The most highly anticipated event was the 100-yard dash where Amos and Robert Minor would face off. The two of them would come flying down the track, but Jim Puckett, this little red-headed kid from Cove, beat them both every time. I think Jim went on to Oregon while Amos went to Oregon State. Once they got to college, Amos beat Jim regularly.

In a December 10 *La Grande Observer* sports column writeup, writer Don Concklin reported that Buddy Hilliard scored 18 points and went on to say, "On defense, the Tigers lived up to their name but whenever the first five combination of Hilliard, Gary Voruz, Cater, Smith and Nice was broken up, the La Grande floor game seemed to get a little ragged. Buddy, Joe and Ted all played sports during high school.

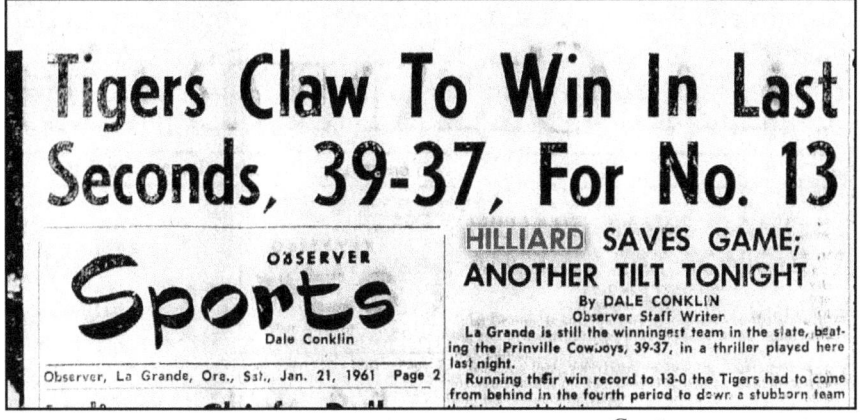

Courtesy newspapers.com

Headline saying Buddy Hilliard has a winning play to win the basketball game for La Grande High School.

My mother taught elementary school in the segregated Brookhaven school system and dreamed of teaching in Oregon too, but her high school diploma was insufficient to provide a pathway to her goal. After cleaning houses and the like for a number of years and hating every minute of it, she decided she had all she could take and enrolled at Eastern Oregon College with elementary education as her major. I was only in junior high when she started, but I recall helping her with her homework when I could. Though she finished four years, she never taught again because of her health. She was, however, the only black woman in the neighborhood to escape the menial labor trap by landing a professional job in the junior high school library. I recall Ted and I dropping by on occasion to take her to lunch. She loved that.

I often wondered what drove her, what made her think she could take care of a large family, work, and carry a full load of classes at the same time. My questions were answered when I learned that her father and his brother, sons of slaves, went to Philander Smith College in Arkansas back in the early 1900s. Big Papa did not finish because my great-grandfather needed him on the farm. Uncle Frank did graduate and served a couple of terms as mayor of Menifee, Arkansas. He was involved in the Civil Rights movement right up through the integration of Central High in Little Rock in 1957. And if you drive through the area, you will find a stretch of highway named for him.

Incidentally, of Big Mama and Big Papa's eight children, four completed college and three taught in the Brookhaven school system even after the schools were integrated. Two have advanced degrees, one in education and the other in chemistry. And one of my first cousins has a PhD in physics from Emory and works in Bethesda, Maryland, for the National Institutes of Health. My mother talked about her family a lot, but I didn't find out about most of this family history until I was an adult.

I've talked a lot about my mother's family but little about the other side. Well, here goes: Little Mama and my biological grandfather never married—in fact, they never even lived together because she was only fourteen when my father was born. So young that Dad Joe thought Little Mama was his sister. When he learned the truth, he called her Mother from then on.

Lamar Hilliard, his biological father, married [then] moved to Weed, California, and later to Seattle, Washington. Like my parents, they had five boys who are about our age, so we had young uncles, all of whom graduated from the University of Washington. While we always were on good terms with them, we felt like outsiders simply because we didn't know them well. In fact, they didn't know we were living in a town so close to Seattle for a long time. When they found out, our Seattle uncles found Dad Joe a job and tried to persuade him to move us north. He says he didn't go because he didn't want to leave Little Mama in La Grande, and it would have been awkward moving her up to Seattle. I have my doubts about that, but I'll leave it there. Suffice to say, us kids were raring to go.

Ted, Carolyn, and I started off at Eastern Oregon College in La Grande. Carolyn majored in secretarial science and regretted the decision because she could easily have handled business administration. She worked as an admin assistant at UC Berkley for a while and, after completing a course in business studies, quit the university to start her own business. Ted graduated from California State University, Hayward, and worked as a computer programmer for the telephone company. After retiring, he started his own consulting business. He says he was much in demand because he knew COBOL when a lot of folks were migrating to PC programming languages.

My first job after I was discharged from the army was as a business consultant in San Francisco with a firm that specialized in providing management and technical assistance to minority businesses in the five Bay Area counties. I loved that job so much that I hated when Friday rolled around. I was the youngest person on staff, and they all treated me like a little brother. The women especially were very protective, thinking my background didn't make me hard enough to cope with the social and work environment in Oakland and San Francisco at that time. I not only survived but thrived, becoming the director of our program within three years. And after a while, I found how enjoyable the weekends could be.

My parents moved to California in 1967. I was studying Spanish in Mexico that summer when I learned that the Selective Service had caught up with me. I was living with a Mexican family who almost freaked out when I told them the news. It was like someone in the family had just been given a death sentence. They tried convincing me to marry a local girl and stay down there because that would be so much better then dying in Vietnam. I'll have to admit that argument made sense, because I was not at all sure I would survive combat in Vietnam. But at the end of the day, I decided to take my chances. I joined up in August of 1967 and finished in March of '69, ending up as a specialist E-5. As luck would have it, I served my one tour of duty as a personnel specialist in Seoul, Korea.

I left San Francisco to join Peace Corps staff as associate director of administration in Nairobi, Kenya, in1973. Now, if I thought my first job was ideal, this gig was close to nirvana. Not only was my work challenging and interesting but I was in the motherland. One of my proudest moments was during a conversation (in KiSwahili) with the wife of one of my local employees; she turned to her husband, asking what was my tribe. I responded I was from the lost tribe.

After I had been in Nairobi for a few months, I had to go home on emergency leave because my brother Duane died. While I was home, I married my sweetheart, Celia Rankins, who came over a couple of months later. I like to say we had a two-year honeymoon. My oldest daughter was born in the Kenyatta National Hospital in 1974. We named her Malaika, which is Swahili for "angel." My next assignment was in Malawi as country director and then on to The Gambia, where my youngest daughter, Marcia Tendayi, should have been born. The medical facilities, however, were such that our doctors insisted we medically evacuate Celia to New Jersey (her parents' home) for the delivery.

After completing the maximum five-year term with PC, I returned to the States, enrolling at the University of Washington in a master's program in public administration. Between my first and second years, I took an internship with the governor's office of financial management and ended up working in Olympia for four years. Seattle was good for us, but I couldn't get living and working overseas out of my system, and I detested the 120-mile daily commute. So I joined the Department of State in January of 1982. In my over-twenty-year career, I served in Caracas, Dhaka, Kuala Lumpur, Milan, Singapore, Cuba, and Panama. In between those assignments, I completed a year at the Industrial College of the Armed Forces at Fort McNair, earning a master's degree in national resource strategy. I retired in 2005, having been promoted to the Senior Foreign Service.

Since I joined this memory project, I have thought a great deal about those of us whose parents migrated to northeast Oregon from the South. We inhabited two diametrically opposed worlds with parents striving to provide better opportunities for their children but not fully understanding what we were facing—and mine never asked. As long as we were respectful of our elders and stayed out of trouble, they felt they had done their jobs. In retrospect, I suppose we didn't share a lot with our parents or raise problems because we figured the status quo was normal; we had no ready point of reference. So each of us developed his own coping mechanisms.

KERRY L. KING

Kerry King was born on October 6, 1932, in Peason, Louisiana, a small sawmill town near Shreveport in Caddo Parish. Her parents were Goldman and Mattie Lee (Lane) King. She had two siblings, Samuel "Sammy," born in 1930 in St. Hill, Louisiana, and Ida Mae, born in 1934 in Florida. Her father was born in Morgan City, Louisiana, and her mother in Shongaloo, Louisiana. The family moved to Maxville when Kerry was a baby.

Kerry graduated from high school in Sacramento, California, and went on to attend the University of the Pacific in Stockton, California, where she studied public relations. Kerry then moved back to Sacramento and worked at Sacramento County Hospital in housekeeping. The hospital later became the University of California at Davis Medical Center. After Kerry retired from the hospital, she worked at the Sacramento International Airport in the security department. She also worked part-time as a census taker for the United States Census Bureau.

Kerry married Carroll Chandler, and the couple had six children: Janice, Kenneth, Rachel, Karen, Carroll, Jr., and Kyle.

Kerry is a devout Christian and attends the Church of Christ in Sacramento. She is an avid outdoors person and loves to fish, hike, camp, and garden—anything that has to do with nature and the outside.

My name is Kerry King. My nickname is "King." I was born October 6, 1932, in Peason, Louisiana. My dad was Goldman King, and he was a logger for Bowman-Hicks Lumber Company in Maxville, Oregon, in the late 1920s. He and my mother married and returned to Louisiana, where my brother was born in 1930.

I remember one story that my dad told us about leaving Louisiana. He had taken my mom to live with his mother so he could go find work. And if I remember correctly, he said she was pregnant with me. My dad caught a freight train, and he had gotten off this freight train and was walking down this dirt road. And this Model T Ford stopped him. Three white men in it. They accused him of stealing a chicken. And he told them, no, he didn't steal a chicken; he had just gotten off the freight train to look for work. They tied a rope around his neck, tied his hands behind his back, and took off. (They had tied the other end to the back end of the whole car.) He had to run to keep up with it. And they were laughing the whole time. Finally they cut him loose. I don't think I'll ever forget that.

My father hated white people. I always wondered why. And then after he told us about that, you know, and I think about it, that was why he hated white people. But all white people aren't like that.

In any case, we had other relatives who came to Maxville in the early 1920s to work as log cutters and housewives. My great-uncle Adam Hart and his wife, Aunt Isoria, came first with my

State of Louisiana

grandmother, Carrie, my mother, and Uncle Lester.

My grandmother married Mr. Freddie Brown in 1926 in Wallowa County. I remember my mother's brothers talking about Uncle Adam. He was a schoolteacher in Arkansas but wasn't making hardly any money from teaching, so he started logging.

My family moved from Louisiana to Maxville around 1932 when I was a baby. In 1935, we lived in Florida, where my sister was born and Grandmother Carrie, Uncle Adam, and Aunt Isoria lived. Grandma had divorced and remarried Mr. Major Hudson in 1934 in Florida, who died in 1940. After 1940, we returned to Maxville, where my widowed grandmother married Lonnie Powell. He was a log cutter.

My father liked to dress well. He always wore a hat. Had to have it on his head. He wasn't that tall, maybe about five feet nine. Short man. Kind of low-key, but he could get angry. He never spanked us or scolded us. It was always, "I'm going to tell your mama when she come home." I can remember my mama had this belt on this rusty nail hanging in the kitchen. And when she come home, he would tell on us.

My dad loved sports. Before he died, he could sit and watch TV—baseball, basketball, whatever the game was on TV, he would sit and watch it.

My father had a brother named Richard who came to live with us in Maxville. There were other brothers who came out as well. He had two sisters, Ida and Beatrice, but they did not move to Maxville. My father didn't talk much about his family.

When my grandmother Carrie married Lonnie Powell, he became my step-grandfather. Before marrying my grandmother, he had a white wife named Juanita. We used to go to her house, and she'd make cookies and let us help. She taught us how to embroider tea towels.

I can remember Ms. Juanita had red hair. And she was cross-eyed. We used to wonder as kids when she be looking at us and one eye be looking somewhere else, "Can she see us and something else too?" So we used to have to be careful because she might. If she can see us while seeing something else, she might go tell on us. I don't know what happened to her.

I remember Maxville being very, very cold. Sometimes my dad and my uncles couldn't get to work because the snow was too high and they weren't hauling any timber. But we kids could play in the snow. Wasn't nothing stopping us from having fun. The other black children that was there was Ms. Mary's [Marsh] kids, Aunt Dorothy's [Lane] kids, and my mom's. That's about it.

Sometimes we couldn't get out, you know, to get meat. So they would go and hunt and kill a deer. And then we all shared it. Everybody in the camp shared it. I remember that. All the kids would gather around because we had to carry the wood and keep the fire going. And they would throw the hot water to clean him. They take the hide off of him. I remember they would hang the deer up by his hind legs. I'd feel so sorry for him, but I ate him.

| Brown, Freddie | 11 May 1926 | Carrie Blinks | H 1708 |

Courtesy Wallowa History Center
Marriage date of Freddie Brown and Carrie Blinks on May, 11, 1926 as found in the Index of Wallowa County Marriages 1887-1983. The certificate is found in Book E, page 1708.

I remember for fun in the summertime in Maxville we would raid Ol' Man Bob Baggett's garden. Mr. Baggett, he was a mean ol' man. I was a child, you know. And he was always fussing and threatening us for going in his yard. I thought he was a mean ol' man. None of us really liked him. Maybe he thought we were bad children.

We would go in his yard, pull up his carrots, and eat them. Radishes and eat them. Pick his tomatoes off and eat them. Another man had an apple orchard. And he caught us up in his tree eating his apples. He ran us off, but that didn't stop us. We'd still do it.

I think about this quite often now. I don't remember his name, but there was this Caucasian man. He was a sheep herder. My brother and sister, they played with the sheep. Played with the sheep just like I did. We'd play with the babies if the mothers would let us get close enough to them. And whenever he would come into the Maxville area, we would find him. He used to tell us stories about France and Germany and, you know, different countries. I remember him telling us about the Eiffel Tower.

Courtesy Kerry King
Bill Baxley and Lonnie Powell standing on the porch of Bowman-Hicks company housing, Wallowa, Oregon. Lonnie was also called "Smokey."

He had a card with the Eiffel Tower on it. I don't know if he was from France or what. He didn't have a family. He was always by himself. And he would make goulash, and we'd all sit and eat. He'd make this fire, and he would take his black cast-iron frying pan and make what he called a "hoecake" made out of flour like a biscuit. And he would sit there and eat with us.

I remember that tick I got from the sheep. I told my mom that I had a bump on me and that it hurt. She looked at it and says, "Oh, Lord, girl. You got a tick." I didn't know what a tick was. But I remember she rubbed some kerosene on it. Put a match to it or put some kind of heat on it, I don't remember. But I remember it came out. It scared me to death. It was still alive. I must have been about seven or eight.

There was no school in Maxville, but there was a white family that had I forget how many children. I remember two of them being around my age. I think there was one boy and one girl our age. Their mother taught them, so she taught my sister, brother, and me right along with her kids. We went to her house. She taught me how to ski. We went bobsledding. Wherever she took her kids, she took us.

There was no black and white. We were just all people up there together. As far as I can remember back then, children just played together, and the white adults mixed with the black adults. At Maxville camp, they did. That other white lady who was my mom's friend. We had to mind her just like we did our parents. Her kids had to mind my mom just like they did their mother. There was no difference. I think the first time I was called the n-word was, I was twelve years old, and I was called that by a black child in Sacramento.

From what I can remember, the white people that were up there in Maxville, they'd hunt and share whatever they had. Their kids came to our house. We went to their house. And maybe those who were living in the city, maybe it wasn't happening that way. But way out in the boonies, who cares.

There was a cookhouse in Maxville, if I remember correctly, for the men that didn't have wives. But mostly everyone that lived up there was a family.

I remember the baseball team at Maxville. In 1941, my father took over managing the first black and white baseball team in the area after his brother, Woodman, who originally organized the team, was killed in a car wreck. The team was named Wallowa Wildcats, though my father and other players lived in Maxville. My dad, Mr. Amos [Marsh], my uncles, Mr. Frank [McClean], and quite a few others played too, like Mr. Joe [Patterson, Jr.] and Mr. Walter [Patterson].

The team traveled. They'd go to other towns and play. Every once in a while, the kids got a chance to go if there was enough room in the car. A lot of times Mr. Amos would drive, and people who didn't have a car, he would take them. We'd go to different towns and play the white teams. There were enough black men for a team.

We used to go from Maxville to Wallowa just to be around more black people. There were a few families living down there. That's where I met Ma and Pa Pat [Arie and Joseph Patterson, Sr.]. Ma Pat was always taller than Pa Pat. A little bit taller than him. There was always food cooking in her house. That's where I met their son, Walter. He played on the ball team too. And their other son, Joe. He played, too.

My mom would get her hair done, but I forget who did her hair. But I know that's why she would go to Wallowa. They would go shopping, but we kids didn't go shopping with them. They went shopping by themselves. We stayed home. We would get a chance to play with [my friend Dave Allen] and his cousins and other kids that were in Wallowa.

After leaving Maxville for good, my mom, brother, sister, and I lived in La Grande with a family for a while. My dad stayed in Maxville. I can't remember these people's names, but they had beaucoup kids, and they all peed the bed. We lived with them for maybe about a year. And then from there, we moved to a town called Beatty, Oregon, on the Klamath Indian reservation and then to Bly, Oregon, which was about thirteen miles away.

Wallowa Sun, April 24, 1941. "Wildcats To Play Enterprise." The Wallowa Wildcats, colored/white baseball team, will play Enterprise at Joseph next Sunday at 2 o'clock. The Wildcats defeated Promise last Sunday 26 to 8 and marks their fourth victory in five starts, their one defeat haveing been at the hands of the Walowa All Stars. Playing for the Wildcats are Sarrett 3b, Roy Cobb ss, Art Lubbes 2b, Goldman King lb, W.L. Thorn as p, Amos Marsh c, R.C. Coney cf, Lester Lane rf, Haney lf.

There weren't many black people around Beatty and Bly. More than Indians lived on the reservation. There were blacks. There were a few Mexican families. One Mexican family was large—had so many kids, about ten or twelve. And they lived up close to where Pee Wee [Idella (Patterson) Williams] and her son David Allen lived. Not too far from them.

Beatty was a small town. I guess you can call it a town. It had a grocery store with one gas pump in the front and it had the long porch. I remember this chief's son had this beautiful black stallion. He got drunk and rode that horse right up to that store. I don't think I'll ever forget that one. The man called his dad. His dad came down there. But his dad was a mean, mean man. He came down there with a bull whip, and he whooped the boy. He wasn't a boy; he was a young man.

I remember a little friend in Bly, this Indian girl. Her name was Henrietta. We were in the third grade in Bly. And she asked me why was my hands brown on the outside and it was the same color as hers on the inside. And I told her I didn't know. And I really didn't. I did not know why. We would stop at my house because you always had to take care of your school clothes. So we go to my house, [and I] put on my play clothes. Then go to her house, and she put on her play clothes. And we go play.

I said, "When we get to my house, I'll ask my mom."

So I asked my mama. I said, "Mama, why is my hand the same color as Henrietta's on the inside, but it's brown on the outside?" And she told me it was because I was a Negro. I must have been about nine or ten years old. I was in the third grade.

After we left Beatty and Bly, my mom moved us to Stockton when I was twelve. So when we moved to Stockton, this might sound strange, but we had never been around a lot of black children. So when we started school there, it was kind of frightening because we had never lived around that many black people in our life. It took some getting used to. It was a city.

The black kids said that we talked funny. What they meant by that I don't know. "Why do you talk like that? You sound funny." They used to say we talked like white people. They didn't tease us about anything else I can remember. Always talking about how we talked.

And then she was moving us back and forth from Stockton to Oregon. I graduated from middle school in Redding, California. I was there for a while. Then we went back to Bly to live. We lived in Klamath Falls for a while. And then my mom decided she was going to go home to Stockton, so she took us. Since Aunt Isoria was there, that was home for my mom.

My friend David Allen Williams's mother, who everybody called Pee Wee, used to sell alcohol to Indians on the reservation. Yep, when we lived on the reservation up in Beatty. They'd just come into the house. "I want a shot." You get a shot glass and pour them a shot. I remember that.

This house was like on a little knoll and a pasture there. And coming into Beatty on the right-hand side was the cemetery. They put their people on—I forgot what you call them, off the ground. And then they burned them. They didn't bury them. Yeah, they burned them. They would be up there for about a week. The funeral would be so long. They would have their drums, and they would dance.

❖   ❖   ❖

My father finally left Oregon and came to Sacramento. I remember he worked at one of the Air Force bases around Sacramento, McClellan or Mather. My dad was living in Sacramento, and my mom and the three of us kids was living in Stockton. Next thing I know we were moving to Sacramento in 1949 to live with my father. We lived on T Street. On Third and T.

I remember we used to take the bus to go to school to Sac High [Sacramento High School]. There was a fountain, and it was called "Kay's Fountain." And we'd go there after school and play the jukebox and dance and have an ice cream or, you know. And the owner was Japanese. Her name was Kay. I remember she was telling me about having to live in an internment camp and how they took her dad's land and property and stuff. I cried. She was just a little girl when they put her in there.

Our whole family wound up in California. Aunt Isoria and Uncle Adam moved to Stockton. Grandma had a sister Augusta living in Sacramento. Her husband's first name was Leon.

Around 1958, Grandpa Lonnie came down to Grass Valley, California, from Wallowa to work, but he left my grandmother up there temporarily. Mr. Amos and his family had moved to Grass Valley at the same time. Grandpa came down and lived in Sacramento with us on the weekends. He'd stay with us and then go to Grass Valley during the week to work.

Grandpa didn't work up there long. He brought Grandma Carrie from Wallowa, and they both moved to Sacramento. Uncle Adam, Aunt Isoria, and Uncle Lester retired in Stockton. They are buried there. Grandpa Lonnie and Grandma Carrie are buried in Sacramento. My parents are both buried in Sacramento. I lost my brother in 2013. I lost my sister in 2011. They are buried in Sacramento. So now I am the only one living.

Courtesy Kerry King
Carrie Blinks Powell, b. 1899 in Arkansas.

99

JAMES LESTER LANE

James Lester Lane was born in La Grande, Oregon, the son of Dorothy (Kent) and Lester Lane. He attended Greenwood Elementary School in La Grande. After his mother's unexpected death, he went to live with his grandparents, Albert and Ollie Marsh, in Louisiana. He graduated from Chatham High School.

James served in the US Army and was honorably discharged. He loved moved to Stockton, California, and worked in community social services with at-risk youth until his retirement.

He married Willette Loretta Maynard on July 7, 1977, in Reno, Nevada.

My name is James Lane. I was born January 6, 1941, in Saint Joseph Hospital in La Grande. My mother's second marriage was to Alvie Marsh, and I remember him because he was a big, strong, strapping guy. I remember [when I was] a kid, he'd be walking down the street, and people would stop him and want to feel his muscles. He was big. All of the Marshes were big, the brothers.

What I remember most about La Grande, it was very, very cold. In the wintertime, we had to walk to school, and your clothes would actually freeze on you. So we would have to stand by the radiator and thaw ourselves out. It was amazingly cold. I remember Alvie would be driving us in the car, and it would be like a whiteout. You couldn't even see the road. You'd have to have sticks on the side of the road so you'd know where you were going. So you drive in front of the sticks, and you knew you were on the road. Wintertime we would play in the snow, make snowballs, slide down the hill.

Courtesy Seretha Lane Jefferson
Lane Family L-R: Rhonda Jeanette, Dorothy Kent, Seretha Mae (baby), Lester and James. C. 1943.

Most of my friends were within the Hilliards and Andersons and Lawsons. I didn't have that many white friends. We used to fight with them all the time down by the river. Throw rocks at them or snowballs in the wintertime.

I had my sisters, Dorothy, Jeanette, Seretha, and Ollie and Oredia. Well, Oredia died when she was a small child.

We went to Greenwood Elementary School there in La Grande until my mother died. When she died, Alvie took us to live with his mother and father in Louisiana and all that, more later on.

My earliest memory of a logger is Alvie. As I was saying, he was a large man. Very strong. And they used to go away to work in the woods. And my grandfather, Lonnie

Powell, who was Carrie Powell's—my grandmother's—husband, was a logger too. They used to go logging together in the woods. Then they would come home, like on the weekend. But sometimes they'd stay up there for weeks working in the logging. Cutting logs was very dangerous work because he had to go all the way up to the top of the tree and chop it. And I guess you could fall or get hurt.

For fun, they had a big old place where they put these ashes from the stove. Well, I had this friend, Cecil, who I played with. And I remember me and my friend Cecil, we'd go out and play in the ashes. We'd throw ashes up in the air. By the time we got home, we looked like ghosts with all this ash all over us.

I went to, like I said, Greenwood Elementary School. And I didn't go there very long. That was just prior to when my mother died and we left for Louisiana. I enjoyed my childhood in Oregon. I was too young to really understand segregation and all that. But I didn't play with the white kids. We knew they were there.

We used to have to walk down the road to catch the bus to go to school. And it was like, white kids, they used to ride on the bus with us, you know. While we were on the bus, they was friendly. And then we'd get to their stop or our stop and [go] our separate ways.

For me, Oregon was fun as a kid because we'd go out into the woods and get crab apples off the trees, and it was just fun.

I remember the logging trucks. I always remember them coming down the hills loaded with logs, and they had this place they called Minam Grade. Yeah. They had runaways with the trucks, and loggers got killed if trucks turned over. But I enjoyed Oregon as much as I remember as a kid. It was fun.

Courtesy Linda Bauck

Minam grade runs up the Wallowa River canyon on its way to Elgin and then La Grande. This is part of High-way 82 was traveled by those going from Maxville and Wallowa to La Grande. It is the primary way in and out of Wallowa County. Truck wrecks most often occur at the curve at the top of the hill.

101

Well, seemed like there were two churches that the black people went to in La Grande. There was a Church of God in Christ, and there was a Baptist church, which most of the blacks went to. They didn't mix when they went to church, the white and the black. I don't remember the names of the white churches. My mother, she was really into the church, so we had to go every Sunday.

In La Grande in the theater, we had to sit in the back. It was a different way of life, but I wasn't fearful of anything. I just played with my little group, and that was about it. So I don't have any really bad memories of childhood. Everything was fun. It was fun because we'd find things to do.

I remember up in Oregon, what really made a big impression is the Indians. I used to watch them. But I guess they had their own government where if they did something, the chief would take care of it. The sheriff in town wouldn't do anything. It was like the chief, he had the say-so and would do the punishment or whatever.

I remember they used to really—well, I'm not stereotyping Indians, but they like alcohol. And they would walk right up into your house because they believed that they owned everything. They just walk up in and sit down. You be in the house, and they would just walk in. I always thought that was kind of strange, but I guess that's the way it was. The land belonged to them at one time or the other. They figured it still belonged to them. That always amazed me how the Indians would walk into your house and stuff.

I had quite a culture shock when I moved from Oregon to Louisiana. We had an all-white school, and I went to Louisiana to Jasper Henderson High, which was all black. It was a lot more fun being with all black kids because they had their sayings and little things they did, you know. And I can remember other kids coming on the school busses. They be out there making fun of them, you know.

I really enjoyed living in Louisiana. To me, it was a lot of fun. I didn't stay there very long before I moved to California with my dad, Lester Lane. But in just a little time, it made an impression on me.

I remember your grandmother Ollie. That was the strongest black woman I probably ever knew. I was a kid, and I figured I could run fast, but that old lady, she could leave you in the dust. She wasn't afraid of nothing. She was very, very strong.

I remember they had an old mule. And you'd be walking, and it would walk up behind you and bite you. I remember Grandmother would be in bed, "Have you seen ol' Jim today?" Talking about that old mule. He was mean. If you see him in time, you yell at him, and he run off.

As a kid, we go off into the woods and play. They had rattlesnakes. You see the trails, and we hear a rabbit or something making a noise, we'd run off and beat the snake and take the rabbit. And try to raise it, and he'd die by tomorrow. We weren't afraid of anything. We'd go off in the woods and never got bitten.

We went up to La Grande in 2001, my sister Seretha and my wife, Willette. We drove up there to visit Mother's grave. It was like time had stood still. They remember Mother and everyone, these older white women my mother had worked for. I guess she was like a housekeeper for them. They remembered her. That was about it for La Grande. Hadn't really changed or anything. Kind of like it stood still.

SERETHA LANE MARSH JEFFERSON

Seretha Mae Lane was born in 1943 in La Grande, Oregon. Her parents were Alvie Marsh and Dorothy (Kent) Marsh. She had four sisters—Dorothy, Jeanette, Oredia, and Ollie—and one brother, James Lester.

Seretha grew up in La Grande and attended Greenwood Elementary School. After her mother died, the family moved to Louisiana, where she attended Olive Grove Community and Jasper Henderson Elementary Schools and graduated from Jasper Henderson High School. She attended Southern University and A&M College in Baton Rouge, Louisiana, and later transferred to Grambling State University, where she graduated with a bachelor of science degree in English education. After graduation, she relocated to Fairfield, California, where she currently resides.

Courtesy Seretha Jefferson
Alvie Marsh

Seretha worked as a substitute teacher, a teacher for youth at risk, an employment and training consultant, a coordinator of youth programs and special projects, and an education consultant for the California Department of Education. After retiring in 2004, she helped form a nonprofit corporation whose mission focused on youth development. She served as chairman of the board and executive director for eleven years.

Seretha was married briefly to James Jefferson. She has two sons, Terrence and Aquil, who later changed his name to Damon. She is the nana of six amazing grandchildren: Volencia, Najah, Vraughn, Taliya, Ishmael, and Jamison.

Seretha's interests lie in serving others, particularly in providing scholarship assistance to graduating high school seniors and providing clothing and other assistance to women who are re-entering the community from prison or from homelessness.

Seretha credits having a personal relationship with God as the most important thing in her life. She had a praying mother, grandmother, and aunt who were women of strength and modeled this to her throughout her life. For over thirty years, she has been an active member of Mount Calvary Baptist Church in Fairfield and Suisun City, California.

My name is Seretha Jefferson. I was born in La Grande, Oregon, in 1943. My father was Alvie Marsh, who came from Louisiana, and my mother was Dorothy (Kent) Marsh. Our family lived in La Grande, and my father lived and worked during the week in Wallowa. My older sisters are Dorothy Lee Lane and Rhoda Jeanette Lane, and my older brother is James Lester Lane. Marian Oredia Lane, my younger sister, was born in 1945 and died in 1947. My youngest sister is Ollie Marie Marsh.

My remembrance of La Grande is very limited, and I don't remember Wallowa or Maxville. I don't have a lot of memory about my dad as a logger. I just know he was gone during the week and came home on weekends. My mother ruled the roost. My dad did not intervene when she disciplined.

I don't remember doing too much playing because our mother worked, and we basically had to stay in the house while she was working. I don't remember playing with a lot of different kids.

I remember going to church. The church was right across the street from where we lived. Sometimes at night, our mother would go to church and tell us not to be in the window trying to see what was going on in the church. We would hear tambourines going, so we thought she was really engaged. We would look out the window not knowing she could see we were looking out the window. She'd come home and say, "Who was looking out the window?" Each one of us replied, "Not me." Everyone would get a whipping. To protect us from the rowdy environment in La Grande, my mom used the extension cord. That was your protection.

My mother died in 1953, and my sister Oredia also died in La Grande in 1947. I was just nine years old. I think I was traumatized by the death of my mother and sister. As a result I blocked out a lot of memories. My memories aren't good about Oregon.

After burying my mother and sister in the Wallowa cemetery, my father packed all of us children in the car and took us to Louisiana, which added to the trauma. My Uncle Amos and his family caravanned with us. When we got to Louisiana, we lived with my grandparents, Albert and Ollie (Elmore) Marsh. My dad went back to Oregon to work. Three of my siblings were separated from my baby sister, Ollie, and me, which added more trauma.

Though I was nine when we left La Grande, I don't remember a lot about school in Oregon. My memories of going to school are in Louisiana. When I arrived, it was a culture shock because I went to school in Oregon with white kids. When I got to Louisiana, I went to a one-room school that had six grades. My aunt was the teacher, and all the kids were black.

Having come from Oregon, I pronounced some words differently than the other kids and my aunt. In fact, my aunt whipped me a couple of times because I corrected her. I was stubborn because I knew this is the way you pronounced some of the words.

In school in Louisiana, I enjoyed and excelled in reading, math, and science. That was my educational experience in Louisiana. I went to segregated schools from about third grade to graduation from college.

In Louisiana, we lived in the country. So there wasn't a lot to do for fun. My best childhood memory of growing up in Louisiana was going to segregated schools, having my aunt as my first teacher, and having other teachers who instilled in us a

Newt Ashby Collection, Wallowa County Museum
One of the big Shay engines out on the tracks in the winter. The men look dressed for cold weather.

strong work ethic and a sense of accomplishment.

Going to the grocery store with my grandmother, who was in her eighties, and watching her endure discrimination yet not have hatred was a valuable lesson passed onto us. We endured racism. We could not go to the swimming pool or movie except on certain days. We had separate days to go to the state fair. We couldn't go to the library.

Courtesy Linda Bauck

Wallowa Cemetery, Wallowa, Oregon.

We had to go to the back of a doctor's office.

Through all of that, I never saw my grandmother or my aunt show hatred or talk negatively about white people. We were being prepared to live in a larger world with acceptance. They always knew that we were going to have to go out into the bigger world, and we would achieve much more than they had. We were raised by the village. That's my best memory.

We went back to Wallowa in 2001 to put a headstone on the grave of my mother and visit my sister's grave.

NADINE MARIE (PATTERSON) KELLY

Nadine Marie Patterson was born in 1935 in McNary, Arizona. Her parents were Joseph, Jr., and Helen (Millard) Patterson. Her grandparents, Joseph, Sr., and Arie (Spears) Patterson, moved to Wallowa County in 1937. Nadine and her parents followed soon after.

Nadine started school in Wallowa, then attended in Beatty, Klamath Falls, and Bly, Oregon, before moving to La Grande. She left La Grande when she and her husband, Otha Willingham, got married. She was fifteen and he was eighteen. Otha came to Oregon from Mississippi and lived in Pendleton. He worked at the Olin Howard Car Wash. After the wedding, they moved to Pendleton and lived with his brother and sister-in-law. They left Pendleton in 1971.

Nadine was a full-time housewife and mother, though she did some day work in the early years of her family. Later she went to work for the State of Oregon in the Pendleton Mental Hospital, where she attended to patients.

Nadine and Otha had seven children: Doris Jean, Barbara Ann, Laverne, Otha, Jr., (1), E. J., Deborah, and Otha, Jr., (2). Barbara Ann and Otha, Jr., (1) died tragically in a house fire in Pendleton. The fire started in the kitchen.

Otha died of cancer and left Nadine to care for her family alone. Nadine married twice after Otha's death, first to Eldridge Freeman and then to the late Charles Kelly.

Nadine is a Christian and began worshiping in the Boyd Memorial Baptist Church in La Grande. She now belongs to Mount Olivet Baptist Church in Portland.

Nadine's favorite hobby was fishing. She and Charles purchased a mobile home and traveled around Oregon fishing in bountiful lakes. She also enjoys cooking.

My name is Nadine Marie Kelly. I currently live in Portland, Oregon. My maiden surname is Patterson. I was born in McNary, Arizona, on February 14, 1937. My parents were Joseph Valley Patterson, Jr., and Audrey Helen Patterson. They were working in McNary when I was born. My father worked at the sawmill. My grandfather, Joseph Patterson, Sr., and my grandmother Arie (Spears) Patterson were living there too. They also were a sawmill family.

We called my paternal grandfather Papa. He was a Baptist preacher, though he didn't have a church. My parents and I were Baptist too, as far as I know. But we weren't that religious that I can remember.

My mother's maiden name was Millard, accent on second syllable. They pronounce it that way instead of Millard, accent on first syllable. She was born in Shreveport, Louisiana. My father, Joseph, Jr., also was born in Louisiana, but I'm not sure of the town.

We left Arizona when I was three months old and came to Maxville in Wallowa County, Oregon. We came on the train. I'm really not sure whether they took the train just to La Grande or all the way to Maxville. My mother and I came together. Dad was already there. I don't know exactly when he came. He never said. I guess it was barely before we came. In Maxville, my father was a log cutter. Mother was just a housewife.

My maternal grandparents came to Oregon after my parents and I moved from Arizona. They lived in Bly after Mother and I moved to Bly. His name was Claude Millard, and his wife was Josephine (Humphrey) Millard. He worked for the sawmill. When we lived in Bly, we didn't live with them. We had our own place. It was a row of company houses. They had one bedroom. These were like the loggers' houses in Wallowa where my cousins lived.

My grandfather was working at the sawmill when he got hurt. He had to have his leg amputated.

My mother and I moved around a lot. We never stayed in one place very long. Sometimes it was just a short stay with family. Sometimes my father was with us, and sometimes they were separated. Over the first twelve years of my life, we lived in Maxville, Water Canyon, Wallowa, and La Grande. We also lived in Beatty, Bly, Klamath Falls, and Sacramento, California.

Remembering Maxville, I know I ran around and played with the kids up there in the woods. The kids I remember most were my cousins, Amos, Jr., Frank Wayne, and David Allen, and a girl named Addy. Addy's the only girl I can remember. I remember Kerry King and her family, but that was way after. Plus I remember them in Sacramento.

My grandparents didn't live in Maxville. They lived at Water Canyon down by the Wallowa River. They were called Ma and Pa Pat by everyone and were the sweetest, most loving grandparents you ever wanted to have. They were that way from the beginning until the end of their lives. The most special thing between my grandfather and me was the nickname he always called me. He called me "Nade."

I thought Papa was just so handsome. He was a short, fat man, and he was just so jolly. He reminded you of Santa Claus. He'd always be hugging you and stuff. He was a logger. You could hear him in the yard after work filing those crosscut saws back in those days. It would be in the evening. And he let us all file with him sometimes.

Courtesy Vearl Lewis
Nadine Patterson Kelly at Maxville, c.1937.
Nadine moved to Maxville as a baby in 1937.

Grandma Pat was the sweetest woman, you know. I just can't praise her enough. She were just so kind and good and loving.

We lived in Water Canyon where my grandparents lived before I started school. I had a pet snake. I called him my worm. Mother said every time they would feed me, I said, "I got to go out and feed my worm." So they assumed it was imaginary. Mother said they finally went out to see about the worm, and it was a snake. I guess he would be there all the time when I fed him. Must have been a water snake or garter snake or something. Mother said she almost fainted.

This was down in Water Canyon. At that time, Water Canyon had all these little houses on it for working families where the Ashbys lived. Old Man Ashby was the superintendent for Bowman-Hicks Lumber Company where all the men worked. The Ashbys had really nice houses. Water Canyon is still there, you know. We lived up on the hill. I can't remember exactly what the black people's houses looked like. I just remember that they were there, and I guess they were all the same, little shacks.

Of course, I went fishing with Papa and Grandma. Sometimes, Papa and I would go by ourselves to crawfish. I remember one time especially, it was in Water Canyon, and I jumped in the water because I thought I could catch the fish with my hands. I was just a little kid. Mother said she thought, "My husband will kill me." So they got me out of there, thank God. I thought you could just dive in and get the fish.

I went to school in most of the places we lived. As far back as I can remember, I started school in 1943 in Beatty. I remember not wanting to wear dresses because I was brought up wearing overalls or jeans. We went from Beatty to Klamath Falls, and I went to school there for a short while. And then from there we went back to La Grande. I went to school in Wallowa too. Bly, also. That's out from Klamath Falls. We moved around a lot.

I went to school in Wallowa for a year. It was during the time or shortly after those kids got killed by a Japanese bomb attached to an air balloon. I was supposed to go on a field trip with my class, but then I don't know what happened. I was sick or something.

At that time, a group of Oregon school kids were on an outing with their teacher. The schools always took kids on a field trip. They ran up on one of those Japanese bombs that came down in balloons. The Japanese made them back in the wartime. So they ran up on one, and it blew up and killed them. I think it's documented. Mother told me about it.

I went to different schools, and I liked school. I didn't have a favorite teacher. I had one that I didn't like. This was a teacher in California when I was there. Her name was Mrs. Blackwell. I never will forget her. Mrs. Blackwell. Oh, my gosh. Now, I guess she was okay. Know I just acted up so bad. I remember we were lined up to go to recess or somewhere. And I put my hands over my ears and screamed as loud as I could. She came back there and slapped me. And that created a war. Mother went to that school. Boy, I think she turned it out. That was in Sacramento when we lived across the street from the school.

I have many memories spent with my grandparents during visits and short stays in Wallowa. As a little girl, I dipped snuff together with Grandma. She dipped Red Seal and Garrett. I tasted it. It was horrible. So she made me some snuff. She mixed cinnamon and cocoa and put it in one of her empty snuff boxes. When she dipped, I dipped. When she spit, I would spit. And we would crochet. I had such a good time when I was there with them.

Spending the day with my grandmother, Ma Pat, was always special. She had me do whatever she was doing. She would have me crochet with her when she was making these doilies. Mine always turned out to be a little hat or something instead of a doily. I remember crocheting in circles, and it wouldn't stay flat. It would keep coming up. And pretty quick I'd have a hat or thimble. And she thought that was the cutest thing.

I remember being in Wallowa when I was around ten or eleven. I would make biscuits for Papa and put them in a little pan. I forget what kind of pan I put them in. They

Joseph Valley Patterson, Jr., father of Nadine Kelly and Lillie May "Macy" (Andrews) Hadnot.

Aaron Patterson, son of Joseph Valley Patterson.

were real biscuits because Mama always had me in the kitchen cooking for her even at an early age. We didn't have any electricity. I had to cook on a woodstove. In spite of cooking at an early age, I never really learned how to cook the way you are supposed to. Everything was such a mess.

I cooked the biscuits from start to finish. I made them the way they are supposed to be made with flour and everything—milk, baking powder, and everything. Everybody said they were the nastiest biscuits. But Papa would eat them anyway and say they were so good. And he would tell that story all the time.

I have a good memory from one time when we moved to La Grande. It's about birds. I don't know what kind of birds they were, but I know we used to eat them because I'd catch them for Mother, and she'd cook them. Mama had this thing she called a "downball," some kind of trap. It's made of boards you prop up with sticks. You put a piece of rope on it, and when the birds get under there, you pull it and it falls down and gets the birds. So I'd pull the string and, you know, get the birds so Mother could cook them. I don't know what kind of birds. My favorite food was chicken—always been my favorite food. Fried chicken. But these were wild birds.

We were in La Grande when I found this porcupine under the porch. So I went and told Mother. And oh, my goodness, you would have thought it was Christmas or New Year's. I thought to myself they would try to kill the thing and get rid of him. Mother cooked that thing after they caught him. How they caught him, I have no idea. I forget because I didn't want to know. It scared me. I remember this piece of meat looked like a black piece of meat to me on the stove. They told me to eat it. Nope. I never will forget that. But they ate it. Porcupine is good, they say.

I know Grandma ate 'coon, but I don't remember porcupine. Grandma would eat anything. That's the way they were brought up, I guess. They ate 'coons and porcupines and probably snakes and everything else. I don't know about snakes, though. They'd have squirrels and stuff like that. Oh my goodness. And stuff I wouldn't even think about eating now.

We always had a lot of food for Christmas. I mean, they'd start baking cakes and pies days before. They put them in what they called a pie safe until it was time. Then they'd bring them out, and we'd have this big spread of food. We always had plenty of food, good Christmas stuff. You know, we might not have had much other than food, but we had food.

Courtesy Arie Patterson

Front row L-R: Nova Jean Henderson and David Allen Williams. Row 2: Arie Spears Patterson, Helen Wisdom, Irene "Weedie" Williams and Adolf Williams. Row 3: Ona May Hug, Unkown, Nadine Kelly. Photo taken at Maxville. David and Aldof are not related.

Through all of our moving around, I remember my Marsh relatives from Wallowa County very well. After living in Maxville, Uncle Amos and Aunt Mary, and my cousins, Amos, Jr., Frank Wayne, Penny Merle, Pearl Alice, and Kay Frances, lived in Wallowa.

Aunt Mary used to do my hair all the time for school. She was a religious woman. She would teach us from the Bible. I went to church with her there in Wallowa at the Assembly of God Church.

Aunt Mary cooked strange things sometimes. I remember one time somebody told her about garbanzo beans. I remember this very well. Someone said, "Well, you may use garbanzo beans instead of chicken" (protein, I guess). And so she had us eat those beans. I thought that was the worst thing ever. It was so funny. It was before I turned twelve, so that would have been around 1948. I thought, Those didn't taste like chicken and dumplings to me. I wouldn't dare say that out loud to her, though. That would hurt her feelings. So I didn't say anything. I just said, "Aunt Mary, that is so good." I just remember lying about that. I'll never forget that one. Nobody dared say to her it wasn't good. Who was eating garbanzo beans back then, even? I don't know, but I'll never forget that.

My Aunt Mary, Uncle Amos, and grandparents were wonderful people to me. I thought Uncle Amos was so handsome. Yeah, he was, you know. He was tall and dark, and he was always happy. All the time, I thought.

My parents had a volatile marriage, and my mother and I moved around a lot without my father. They must have first separated when we left Maxville. We moved back and forth between La Grande, Beatty, Bly, Klamath Falls, and Sacramento.

My mom went back and forth to Sacramento several times beginning when I was a baby. I know we were there more than once after she would leave Dad. She didn't have family in Sacramento, and I don't know who we stayed with. But I know I was still a baby the first time. She did housework to earn a living. She would clean and cook, and she'd take me with her.

Mama told me about a time that we were at the theater and they had this movie on. I forget the name of the movie. But this guy was in the gorilla suit. And I guess he came and got me, and I wasn't afraid of him.

Two parts of one photo recombined
Ma and Pa Pat - Arie and Joseph Valley "Pa Pat" Patterson, Sr.

We were living in Sacramento when I was about five years old. On my birthday, I remember there was a knock on the door. So Mother went downstairs to see who it was. And when she came back upstairs, she was bleeding all over, like when you get a head cut. My dad had cut her. Cut her across her eye over her forehead, and she was just bleeding all over. And of course that traumatized me and everyone else. I don't remember what happened after that. Or I'm sure she had to go to the doctor and all that. But I remember that very vividly.

My mother never officially remarried after separating from my dad. She was always a Patterson until she passed. But she had two sons after my parents separated: George Allen Fletcher, Jr., and Donald Lee Fletcher. George, Jr., was born in 1944 and Donald Lee in 1945. Their father was George Benjamin Fletcher, who my mother met in Sacramento. He was in the military. Both of my brothers were born in Sacramento.

We were living back in La Grande when I turned twelve. Mother was living with a man named Jeffrey Ford. He was a violent man. That was just a terrible time. Jeff worked at the Bowman-Hicks sawmill in Wallowa.

Mother and I were up visiting Wallowa. It was evening, and all of adults were partying and having a good time. I don't know where my grandparents and auntie and uncle were. They were not rowdy people like that. This happened there in Wallowa where the black families lived in the little row of company houses.

Anyway, Jeff got angry with Mother and started beating her. I can't remember whose house it was in front of. All I know is there seemed to be a lot of people there, and they were all just standing outside while he was doing that to my mother.

No one was helping her, so I ran over to my cousin's house and got Aunt Mary's gun. They weren't home, but I knew she kept the gun in her trunk. Uncle Amos had given it to her years ago when she drove from Arizona to Maxville after he had come out and got a job. So I went back over there where he was beating Mother, and I shot him.

I didn't kill him, but I shot him. When I aimed for Jeff's head, George Trice grabbed the gun and knocked down my hand. I'm only twelve years old, you know. And the bullet went through Jeff's leg.

So someone called the police. It was a gunshot, you know. And Jeff had to go to the hospital in Enterprise. Mother had to go to the hospital also. And she was in there for a good while.

The authorities didn't arrest me after it was explained what happened. They gave me a floater. I was only twelve years old. My Aunt Pee Wee from Sacramento was there, so the next day, she took me California with her. The police didn't do anything to me. They just thought it would be a good idea for me to go with Aunt Pee Wee to get away from there for a while.

I had to go through those changes to try to help my mother. And all those people were there. They were all at their homes. And I guess these were all honky-tonk people that were out in the yard where my mother and Jeff were.

Uncle Amos and Papa were angry when they heard I shot Jeff. They were very upset, but not with me. They were angry with Jeff. Papa was talking that Louisiana "deedon" language or whatever he was saying when he got really angry. I don't know what he was saying, but he was pretty angry.

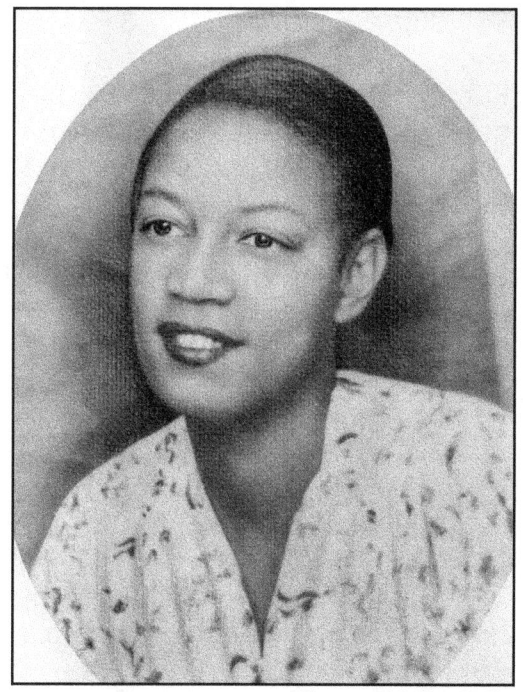
Courtesy Nadine Kelly
Helen Millard Patterson, Nadine's mother.

I stayed in Sacramento about a year after that incident. My cousin Dave Allen was there. Aunt Pee Wee was his mother. He was my only cousin in California at the time. That would have been in '49.

Dave Allen and I were close. And I was happy in Sacramento. I had friends there. I had my friends Sally and Dorothy Lee. All of my friends were older than me. I always ran around with people older than I was for some reason. So then after a year, I went back to Oregon. I went back to live with my mother, who had moved to La Grande.

Life was okay in La Grande. She was still with the same guy, which I couldn't understand. And they fought. So I left and stayed at Aunt Ethel and Uncle Ester Wilfong's house. I was fourteen. They were a very kind couple who knew my family from Arizona. Uncle Ester worked in the sawmill in Arizona. But in La Grande, he worked for the government.

I was living with the Wilfongs when I got married at fifteen. I got married in Walla Walla, Washington. I married Otha Willingham.

Meeting him was a story in itself. Him and his brother-in-law, well, they were in Pendleton because that's where his brother was with his family. So they heard there were some girls in La Grande. So they drove down, and they came to my house. And we lived upstairs at the time. And I was upstairs looking out and seeing them out there. Mother would tell me, don't open the door. I went upstairs and yelled. Mother wasn't there. They just knocked and knocked and knocked. So they got in their car and left. So they came back after a while, and that's when I had left Mother's house. I was up living up with Uncle Ester Wilfong and Aunt Ethel. Otha came back, and the rest is history.

Otha came to their house. That's where he met me. They made him welcome and everything and whatever. They'd let me go with him. And, you know, he took me to Wallowa to see Mama and Papa and stuff. So we decided to get married. He asked me, and I didn't know—I didn't know nothing. So Mother agreed, you know, because—I always thought Mother thought I was pregnant or something, you know. Who lets their daughter marry at fifteen, you know? But I wasn't. We were married over a year before I got pregnant. He was eighteen. Yeah, he was young too.

He came here from Mississippi. I think he came to Oregon by himself on the train. He said they'd keep waking him up. So finally he cussed them out. Said he didn't give a you-know-what about where he was. He said he was trying to sleep going over those mountains. He never saw any mountains. He was scared, coming all the way from Mississippi to La Grande, Oregon. Anyway, that's how he got there.

After we got married, we lived in Pendleton. That's where he was living with his brother and sister-in-law. So I moved to Pendleton. I lived there until 1971.

Then I remember going fishing with Papa in Wallowa after I was married and pregnant. We'd always go to Wallowa back then. I remember running with me being pregnant once on a fishing trip. And I had to get over a fence because I saw a snake. I thought the snake was after me. So I'm running from the snake, and I fell over or got through this barbed wire fence somehow. Back in those days, we had those maternity skirts with the belly cut out. Anyway, when I got to where I was going to safety, my skirt was split all the way from the bottom up and wouldn't go around my stomach. I don't know if I ever went fishing with Papa again because I was so scared of the snake.

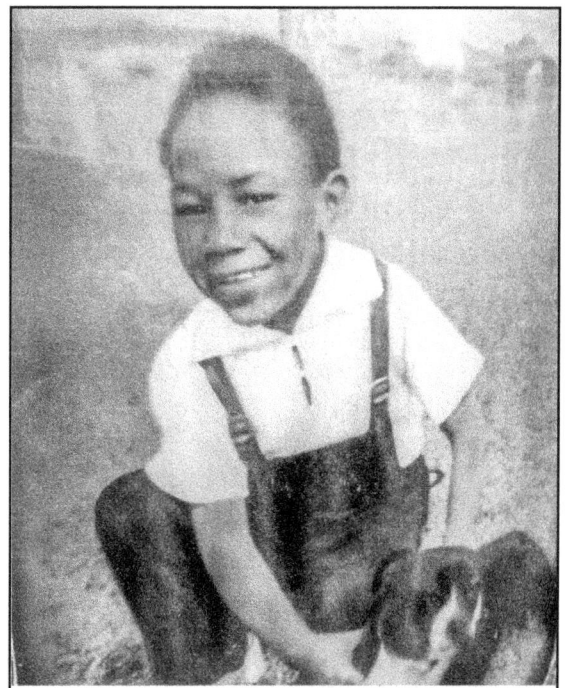

Courtesy Nadine Kelly & Pearl Alice Marsh
David Allen Williams, beloved cousin of Nadine Kelly and loved by all, in Maxville, who knew him.

I started cooking for my mother when I

was young. But I really learned to cook after I got married. My mother used to cook all the time, but I never took the time to learn to cook with her.

I remember Papa [Pa Pat], Daddy, and Uncle Amos going hunting, yes, I do. But the most I remember is after I was married because we used to go back to Wallowa for hunting season all the time. And Papa would load us with meat, yeah. I've been there to help him wrap because they'd butcher, and we would wrap the meat.

So these are my memories of my Oregon childhood beginning in Maxville. In spite of the hardships and pain, I have great memories of being in Maxville, Water Canyon, and Wallowa as a child. I survived some troubled times, but I survived.

AMOS MARSH, JR., REMEMBERED
(1939–1992)

Amos Marsh, Jr., was born on May 7, 1939, in Williams, Arizona. He was the first child born to Amos, Sr., and Mary (Patterson) Marsh. He died on November 2, 1992, in San Jose, California, at the age of fifty-three.

Amos attended Wallowa Elementary School and graduated from Wallowa High School in 1957. In high school, he excelled in football and track, which earned him a scholarship to Oregon State University, where he continued to rack up championships in those two sports. While at Oregon State, he majored in history.

After college, Amos was recruited to play professional football for the Dallas Cowboys after the 1961 draft because they were impressed

AMOS MARSH JR.
  "Mush"
"Most great men are dead or dying, and I don't feel so good myself."
Cougar Staff 4; Letterman 2, 3, 4; Football 1, 2, 3, 4; Captain 4; Basketball 1, 2, 3, 4; Track 1, 2, 3, 4; Chorus 1, 3.

Courtesy Wallowa History Center
Recap of Amos's high school career.
From the 1957 Wallowa High School Annual.

Courtesy Wallowa History Center
High School Senior Photo
Amos Marsh, Jr.

by his speed. He also was a powerful player, earning the nicknames "Moose" and "Forward Marsh." While living in Dallas, he met and married Helen Bradford. They have four children: De Wayne, Amos LaDon, Tonja Marie, and Rhonda Kay.

Courtesy Pearl Alice Marsh
Amos as an infant in Maxville.

He played as a wide receiver special teams player. He was eventually moved to fullback because of his size and speed, and he led the team in kickoff and punt returns. He set franchise records with a 71-yard run from scrimmage and a 79-yard kickoff return. In 1962 he ranked seventh in the NFL, with 802 yards and a 5.6-yard average per carry. That year he set a franchise record with an 85-yard touchdown reception against the Los Angeles Rams and also broke his franchise record for the longest kickoff return with 101 yards in a play against the Philadelphia Eagles.

Playing as a fullback in 1965, he led the Detroit Lions in rushing (405 yards) and touchdowns (8). On August 19, 1968, he was traded to the Atlanta Falcons.

After retiring from professional football, Amos and his family moved to San Jose, California. He first worked in management at the Ford Motor Company and then became a sales representative for a regional business. He went on to own his own optometry business.

Courtesy Pearl Alice Marsh

Amos, Jr, 1st row, far right, with his Boy Scout troop.

His passion was politics and government. He served on the Santa Clara County Grand Jury and was an influential member of the Democratic Party.

Amos grew up in the Assembly of God Church and then, following his mother, became a member of the Seventh-day Adventist Church.

❖   ❖   ❖

Amos Marsh, Jr., was born at home on May 7, 1939, in Williams, Coconino County, Arizona, to Amos, Sr., and Mary (Patterson) Marsh. The family moved from Arizona to Maxville, Oregon, the year he was born, after his father, a logger and sawmill worker, was acquitted of selling whiskey to White Mountain Apache men on the Apache Reservation. The grandparents of Amos, Jr., Joseph and Arlie (Spears) Patterson were already living at Wade Siding outside of Wallowa, which was later named Water Canyon by Henry Newton Ashby, superintendent of the Bowman-Hicks Lumber Company.

Amos grew up in Wallowa and gradu-

Courtesy Wallowa History Center

Amos Marsh, Center, Wallowa High School basketball team.

ated from Wallowa High School in 1957. He was very popular with schoolmates and friends throughout the region and was an iconic figure among the youth of Wallowa County. He was extremely charismatic, and he had a melodic tenor voice and an artistic hand with pencil drawing, among many other talents. But he was best known for his athletic prowess in football, basketball, and track. His high school sports career reached a high at the East-West Shriners' Tournament, where he scored a 98-yard touchdown to put the East over the top.

Courtesy Pearl Alice Marsh

Amos, Jr. with Walter Mondale.

As a sprinter and long jumper in track, Amos helped Wallowa win the 1957 State Class "B" title. During those years, he developed a famous rivalry with Jim Puckett from Cove High School.

After graduating from high school, Amos accepted a track and field scholarship to Oregon State College (OSC), where he majored in history and planned to be a teacher. His athleticism made him a star in both track and football at Oregon State. He ran a 9.5-second 100-yard dash and was an outstanding running back for the OSC Beavers. He also competed as a hurdler and long jumper.

Amos's power and speed landed him a professional contract with the Dallas Cowboys in the National Football League, where he played from 1961–64. For years he held the record for the longest kickoff return by a Cowboy: 101 yards against the Philadelphia Eagles in 1962. He next played for the Detroit Lions, where he was the leading rusher in 1965, carrying the ball 131 times for 495 years. His last team was the Atlanta Falcons, where he was waived in 1969.

Amos married Helen Bradford in 1962, and they have four children: De Wayne, Amos LaDon, Tonja Marie, and Rhonda Kay.

After retiring, Amos became a political activist in San Jose, California, and served as an effective campaign director for several Democratic politicians. In the 1970s, Amos served on the Santa Clara County Grand Jury.

Courtesy Wallowa History Center

First Grade Class, graduates of 1957. Mrs. Hattie Fisher teacher.
Row 1, L-R: Beth Bechtel, Sandra Henderson, Nancy Brooks, Gail Davidson, Charlotte Evans, Jesse Lee "Rabbit" Langford, Jr., Donna Mae Silvers, Clifford Lindsey, Melvin Houser, Amos Marsh, Verna Graham, Anne Couch.
Row 2: Janice Henry, John Burns, Janis Dailey, unknown, Vernon Bennett, Gary Lively, Gary Skelton, Keith Jewell, Unknown, Unknown.
Row 3: Don Silvers, Jim Burns, Harold Pearce, Darrell Prince, Lola Prince, Lonnie Armon, Lowell Prince, Melvin Van Arsdale.

BY GAIL DAVIDSON FINEBERG

Gail Davidson Fineberg is the granddaughter of Henry Newton Ashby, from whom she learned that we are all one, with one another and our natural world.

Courtesy Wallowa History Center
Gail Davidson Fineberg, senior photo.

Amos Marsh, Jr., was funny. He had an infectious, irrepressible laugh that had a habit of escaping from behind his hand clapped to his mouth as he lounged in the back of a high school classroom, where he and his buddies rocked their small desk chairs against a chalk board behind them. In sports competitions or in class, he was even-keeled—consistently friendly and warm, never angry that I saw, nor moody. Already an amazing athlete who could outrun nearly everybody else on the field or gym floor, he never acted like a big shot. A lot smarter than he ever let on in class, Amos succeeded at "fitting in." He and his little brother Frank were just part of our gang—our graduating class of 1957, which with 40 kids was the biggest in WHS history, I think. We were all together for 12 years.

118

By the time Amos got into junior high and high school, he was one of the big guys, who comprised Wallowa's B-league champion football, basketball and track teams. To comprehend just how big they were, a person has to understand how important football and basketball were in a tiny mill town without much else going on. On Friday afternoons in the fall, the town of Wallowa shut down for football. The pharmacist, the hardware store owner, the grocers all came to the games, as did siblings, moms and dads, if they could get away from work on farms or in the woods or the mill. Even my 70+ year-old grandmother drove her ungainly Lincoln five miles to the games and

Courtesy Wallowa History Center and 1967 Wallowa High School annual

1956-57 WHS Track Team: L-R: Jerry Roberts, Darrell Prince, Amos Marsh, Jim Reeves, Roger Burchett. Standing, Gary Lively.

We the students of Wallowa High are proud to recognize the following boys; Jerry Roberts, Darrel Prince, Amos Marsh, Jim Reeves, Roger Burchett, and Gary Lively for the new records and honors they made in the state track meet held at Springfield May 8, 1956.

Jerry Roberts, Darrel Prince, Amos Marsh and Roger Burchett took first place honors in the 880 relay failing by one second of tying the state record.

Darrel Prince took second place in the 440, Amos Marsh second place in the 220. Amos also tied the state record in the 100 yd. dash of 10.2 seconds. Jim Reeves ran the mile run setting a new record of 4 min. 32.8 sec. breaking his old record of 4 min. 37.5 sec. set the previous year. He also set a new 880 state record of 2 min. 1.5 sec.

parked on the 40-yard line, where she joined all the other fans who raced up and down the field with the teams and the referee carrying the 10-yard chain to mark progression of the ball. Amos, our hero, usually was in one of two places—streaking ahead of the pack for Wallowa's goal line, or at the bottom of a heap, clutching the ball to his chest.

Quarterback John Burns, at our 50th class reunion, reminisced about one game, I think against Enterprise, our arch enemy. Amos had been bugging John to pass him the ball so he could demonstrate his receiving and running prowess, but John had other plans. The score was close, and John didn't want to risk an interception. He told Amos, "No way, you s.o.b. You're going to have to carry the ball." He did. Thirty yards down a wide open field for a touchdown. That's how I picture Amos in an all-star game played in Pendleton at the conclusion of our senior year: In my mind I see one lone figure, running erect, legs pumping like pistons, aiming for goal posts a few yards away. Way behind him and the 50-yard line is a jumble of bodies beginning to sort themselves out, wondering where the ball is.

John and his twin, Jim, talked frankly about race never being an issue that got in the way of their friendship with Amos. "He often spent the night with us," John recalled. "We lived with our grandparents in their little house, and there wasn't much room so we had to share our bed with Amos. His skin felt just like ours."

Courtesy Pearl Alice Marsh

Amos, with his arch rival Jim Puckett, on the podium at the 1956 State track meet, where they won 1st and 2nd place in the 100 yard dash.

John, Jim and Amos were no dummies. But no guy in our junior high or high school would ever admit to being smart and enjoying learning. The girls, on the other hand, were as competitive about grades as the boys were about sports; we knew how smart they really were. They'd all sit in the back of the room, snicker and write notes. With his wicked sense of humor, Amos could crack up our class at will, as well as our teachers, who could not keep a straight face with all the rest of us giggling.

At the end of the day, scholarship won. The first one in his family to go to college, Amos went off to Oregon State University with a scholarship in hand - to run in the track program and to study. Amos's first love, how-

Courtesy Pearl Alice Marsh

Amos Marsh running the 100 yard dash at Oregon State University.

ever, was football. He prevailed.

Oregon State Beavers and University of Oregon Ducks were fierce rivals, with nasty Beavers dumping green paint on Oregon's beloved bronze statue of the Pioneer Mother, which happened to reside outside my freshman dormitory. Amos, always a gentleman, came to call on football game days, and I was always happy to see him. Over the years, we'd hang out in my dorm or sorority and talk until game time. He was, after all, my very first friend; we met at his grandma's house when we were 4 years old.

In fact, we had been friends for so long by the time we got to high school, it seemed perfectly normal to invite him along with the rest of our class to my house for a tape-recording session in preparation for our senior prom. On this particular night, my parents were on their way to Las Vegas for a much needed vacation from sub-zero winters in Water Canyon. My uncle was left in charge of us during the recording session. Dad was carrying suitcases down steps from the kitchen to the garage, and Amos was coming up the same stairs with a case of Coke. The two locked eyes but neither spoke, turned aside or turned back. I went down to the car to tell my father good-by but he compressed his lips and gripped the wheel. He said nothing, but I got the message. And I still grin when I think of that night or see the snapshot of Amos stretched out on our living room floor listening to our favorite dance music on 45 rpms with the rest of our friends. It wasn't Selma, but we made our stand.

We kids were protective of Amos in a way. We knew instinctively what was right and what was not, and we knew that social lines had been drawn, not by us but by some of our elders. I enjoined my first battle with my parents at age 5, when I wanted Amos and Frank, the only kids I knew and the only friends I had, to come to my first birthday party. In response to my mother's "No," I boycotted the event. That, still, remains my proudest moment, other than the 2017 Women's March in DC and the time I sued my boss for equal pay. Ignoring her father's angry glares, a girlfriend of mine, a tall, beautiful blonde, laughed and smiled while dancing in the gym with Amos after basketball games. We didn't talk about this stuff; we just circled the wagons.

Amos called to talk to me shortly before he died. I think I was working in Washington, DC, but my husband was thrilled to take the call from a real football hero, a Dallas Cowboy. I still feel sad that we didn't have one last visit. But memories are the next best thing. I have enjoyed this time with you, my friend, Amos.

BY DALE JOHNSON

Courtesy La Grande Observer
Halfback Amos Marsh of Wallowa is supported by two East players after his 98-yard run for the second East touchdown in the Shrine All-star game played at Pendleton Saturday night.... The east their first victory since 1953.... Over 8,000 fans watched....

I had a couple stories about Amos Marsh that I thought were interesting. And one of them relates to the time he was on the Shriners' football [team].

Jerry Burton, who was a coach, I think, at Linfield, won the state championship. Well, the two coaches who won the championship were the coaches of the Shriners' team the next year, and Gary Burton had a pretty good halfback that played for him at Linfield. When they had the Shriners' game and Amos was on that team, Burton started his own player at halfback. He thought he was a pretty good player, and he was a good player.

Oregon State was very interested in Amos Marsh as a football and track prospect. So they sent a friend of mine, John Thomas—who told me this story—up to scout Marsh in the Shriners' game. Tommy Pro-Prothro, Oregon State's coach, said, "I want to have a good report on Marsh. We're interested in him." So Thomas drove up to Pendleton from Corvallis to watch the ball game. But the first half Amos didn't play. Burton played his own player.

Wallowa County Chieftain, Mar. 10, 1977, "Out of the Past, 20 Years Ago", March 14, 1957 "Two football players from Wallowa County were named this week to the Shrine all-star team and two other players were selected as alternates. Amos Marsh of Wallowa and Perry Davis of Enterprise were placed on the first team backfield. Vern Walker of Wallowa was named as an alternate tackle and Woody Colpitts of Joseph was selected as an alternate back." Amos Marsh's family was from Maxville, Colpitts was a Promise homestead family.

The coach at Eastern Oregon was the honorary trainer for the team and had coached Burton at Eastern Oregon. He said, "Burton, if you want to win this ball game, you better get Marsh in that ball game, or you're not gonna win it." Thomas went to the coaches and said, "Are you gonna play Marsh?" Burton said, "I don't think I'll play him very much because I think my back is better."

So Thomas got in his car. He was interested in getting back to Corvallis from Pendleton. So he got in his car and took off to go back to Corvallis because Marsh wasn't gonna play.

He turns on his radio as he drives out of town, and Marsh starts the second half, and he just goes crazy. He's running 90 yards; he's returning kickoffs; he's gaining 200 yards the second half. Thomas, who's supposed to be there scouting him for Prothro, is on the road toward Hood River. And he's thinking, "What am I gonna tell Prothro when he asks me about Marsh?"

So from the radio broadcast that he got, he made up a report for Prothro. Prothro called him in and said, "What do you think about Marsh?" Thomas said, "Get him a scholarship. He's the guy we need." And he didn't even watch him play in the ball game for the second half. That's a pretty true coverage of what happened in that ball game that night.

And the other story about Amos. I was living in Corvallis at the time he was going to college, so I'd see him occasionally. I refereed football there at spring games and training sessions at Oregon State. Prothro played Marsh most of the time. Then he was kicking extra points and kickoffs and things like that. But he wasn't using him as a running back.

When he graduated, the Cowboys came up. They drafted and signed Amos, and people asked the Cowboys why they picked Amos as one of their first picks when he wasn't a full-time running back starter. And Gill Brant, who was the head coach of the Cowboys, said that was the biggest waste of football talent he'd ever seen.

Of course, Prothro was a pretty good football coach, but he and Amos sometimes had their differences. And I don't think he used him like Brant thought. When he went to Dallas, they started him as their number-one running back, and he wasn't a running back at Oregon State. But Brant said it was a biggest waste of football talent he'd ever seen. I always thought that was a good story on Amos.

La Grande Observer, "East Speed, Spirit Wins Game 19-12."

Posterity could possess no finer game in the annals than that Shrine game witnessed by 8,500 fans Saturday night at the Pendleton Roundup stadium, for this grid classic, which the East won 19-12 by scoring all of it's points in the last quarter, will certainly go down in the books as one of the greatest ever seen as far as sheer "desire to win" is concerned.

The East, which trained here at the college field, was trailing 12-0 at the beginning of the fourth period when that "will to win" caught fire and on the first play of the period Pat Walchi of Stanford drove over for the first East score.

On the first play and standing behind the goal line, game hero Amos Marsh of Wallowa, cut through a nice hole in the center of the West line, saw daylight, and dashed 98-yards, leaving the West secondary far behind as he went over for the tying and game winning score. Perry Davis, Enterprise fullback, plunged for the extra point to give East the lead, 13-12.

A moment later, with the West trying desperately to score again, linebacker Jerry Dougherty from Heppner intercepted on the West's 35 and ran the ball to the West's 20.

Then Marsh, quaterback Lou Miller of Moro, and Walchi carried the ball to the eight and Marsh carried it the final eight yards on one gallup to add the final tally.

The game had a storybook finish and left the largest crowd in the history deliriously happy at the ending - most were from east of the Cascades.

Coach Franz Haun and his assistants Beryl Bethke and Buck Culver, could certainly be proud.

BY "COACH" DONALD WILSON

The girl in Enterprise, she and Amos were friends. I don't know how close friends. Don't know anything about it. But I do know that after one basketball game, they had a milkshake bet. She bet on Enterprise, and Amos on Wallowa. And they played the ball game down here, and Wallowa won the ball game. So they went down to Burrows,' Cafe and they were sitting at the counter having a milkshake.

I was cleaning up the gym after the kids left. I came home [and] got a phone call. I

Burrows Cafe where Amos and the girl from Enterprise paid of their milkshade bet. The owners of the cafe got a couple of negative comments which they ignored and did not appreciate.

think I got two or three women calling up and told me I had to talk to Amos because he was down there with a white girl.

I says, "Well, Amos told me." I said, "She's paying off a milkshake bet with her friend."

"Well, you ought to talk to him. He shouldn't be down there with a white girl."

I says, "What do you mean?"

They wouldn't identify themselves. But it really irritated me.

They had a bet made, and the girl was paying it off. They were friends, which I says I think is perfectly legal. I says, "If we had a kid that had been in trouble, and he had a bet with her—a white kid who was the trouble— would you call me up and chew me out and say I shouldn't let that white guy who was in trouble with the law have a milkshake with a—"

"That is different." Oh, yeah I'm sure it's different.

You know, I've never been prejudiced. I can't understand what the hell is wrong with them.

Anyway, I thought there was a lot of prejudiced people when they first came to the Wallowa area because there was a lot of southern whites moved up here, and I was

1966-67 Wallowa High School Basketball team. Frank Marsh 2nd from left front row, Amos 2nd from left back row and Don Wilson, coach, last right back row.

flabbergasted with that.

FRANK WAYNE MARSH

Frank Wayne Marsh was born on June 19, 1940, in La Grande, Oregon. His father was Amos, Sr., and his mother was Mary (Patterson) Marsh. He married Joyce Elaine Taylor on March 28, 1970, in Reno, Nevada. They have three adult children by birth, Francine, Alece, and Frank Akeem, and three adult foster children, Taylor, Devory, and Tatiana Wilson, who they raised from toddlers. Frank and Joyce are the proud grandparents of three girls, Aliyah, India, and Jayda Davis, the daughters of Francine and Auston Davis; and one boy, Jordan Marsh Simon, the son of Alece Marsh and Paul Simon.

After graduating from Wallowa High School in 1958, Frank enrolled in Linfield College, McMinnville, Oregon, for two years and then transferred to Oregon State College in Corvallis, where he earned a bachelor's degree in sociology.

Courtesy Pearl Alice Marsh
Frank Wayne Marsh in his Army dress uniform.

Frank had a short career in professional football. He played the 1967 AFL season for the San Diego Chargers as a defensive back. In the 1968 AFL expansion draft, he was selected by the Cincinnati Bengals and was tried at running back.

Frank served in the US Army for two years. He was stationed in Fort Ord and Okinawa, from where he was honorably discharged. When he came out of the army, Frank started his professional career working for the Job Corps at their conservation and urban centers in Pollack Pines, California. Finding the area too remote, he moved to San Jose, where he worked in retail briefly before working as an insurance agent for Century and Aetna. His final career move was to the Santa Clara County Juvenile Probation Division, where he worked until he retired.

Frank's main interest is in the well-being of his four grandchildren, on whom he dotes generously. He also enjoys investing in real estate rental property and manages his own portfolio. One of his main goals in life is wealth building

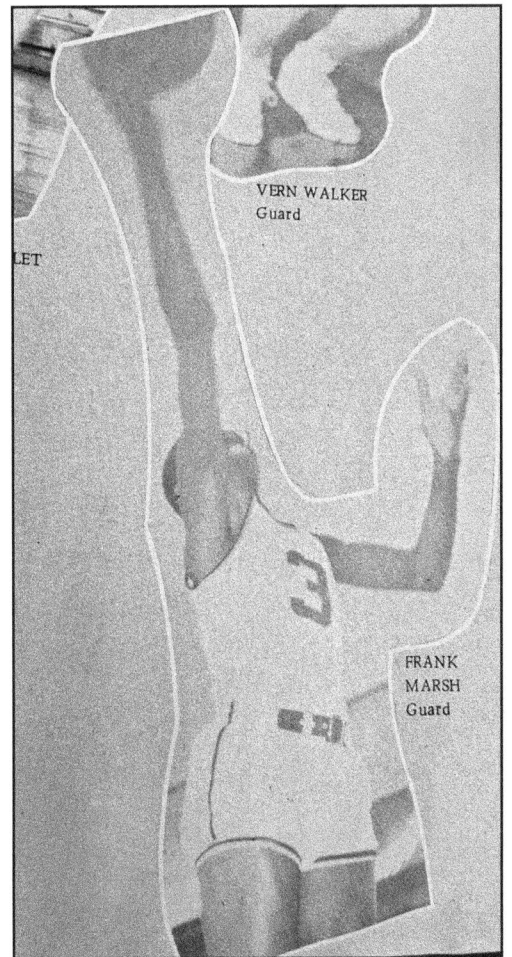

VERN WALKER
Guard

FRANK
MARSH
Guard

Courtesy Wallowa History Center
Frank Marsh, guard, Wallowa High School basketball team.

for his grandchildren. He also likes fine cars and has collected several over the years.

❖   ❖   ❖

My name is Frank Wayne Marsh. I was born in La Grande, Oregon, on June 19, 1940, at the Grande Ronde Hospital. I grew up in Maxville and Wallowa in Wallowa County, Oregon. My parents were Amos Marsh, Sr., and Mary (Patterson) Marsh. My grandparents were Joseph Valley and Arie (Spears) Patterson, Sr. We called them Papa and Grandma. Everybody called them Pa and Ma Pat.

I am my parents' second child. The first child was Amos, Jr. We were born thirteen months and twelve days apart. In the end, there were five kids in the family. I was the second child. Amos, Jr., was the first. Penny Merle was the third, Pearl Alice was the fourth, and Kay Frances the fifth. Everybody understands our place in the pecking order.

I was born premature. A friend named Robert Terry took breast milk from my mom in Wallowa back to the hospital so that I could eat. My dad's friend, Uncle Smokey, used to tell me, "Hey, I saw you out in the incubator." I felt special to him. He cut logs with my dad.

I wasn't supposed to make it, but I did. My mother used to laugh when telling the story about how "white" I looked with straight hair. Dad said he was going to stick around for a while to see if I turned dark. If I didn't, he was going to leave. Then one day, she said I started getting a little curl in my hair and turning toasty brown. Dad never left.

Both of my parents were born in Louisiana. Mom was born in DeRidder but lived in Alexandria as a child. Dad came from a settlement area called Olive Grove between Eros and Cartwright in Jackson Parish.

My grandparents were already in Oregon when my parents came. They came in 1937, and my parents came in 1939. Papa was born in Rapides Parish, Louisiana, and Grandma was born in Woodville, Texas. Papa worked as a logger like my Dad, and Grandma took in laundry for a few people.

We were one of a few black logging families that migrated to Wallowa County in the 1920s, 1930s, and 1940s. The first town we lived in was Maxville, a sawmill town owned by Bowman-Hicks Lumber Company. We lived there until I was five and then moved to Wallowa, an all-white town save a few black logging families. The black families didn't stay long except ours. After the Langford family moved to La Grande, we were the only black family with children left in Wallowa.

Amos and I graduated from Wallowa High School in 1957 and 1958. Pearl and

Courtesy Pearl Alice Marsh

Amos and Frank Marsh.

Courtesy Pearl Alice Marsh

Amos, Mary, Frank, Arie and Penny.

Kay were in elementary school when we moved to California in 1958. Penny never attended school because of a severe handicap. So I grew up with just my immediate family and maternal grandparents. We had cousins who came to visit once in a while. But that was basically it.

The house we grew up in was basically a three-room company house. We had a living room, which had a wood-burning heater. We had our kitchen with a big woodstove, cupboards, and big pans for washing dishes. And Mom and Dad's bedroom. Amos and I slept in the living room in the big bed across from the sofa and chair. Our sisters slept together in a twin bed in our parents' bedroom. We had water from an outdoor well, of course. And the bathroom was the regular old outhouse. And that was tough. It was difficult. In today's world, it's repulsive. But at the time, that was the only thing we had. So we used it.

For the winter, we had wood and coal delivered for the cooking stove and heater. The wood would come from the Landis family. He would bring the wood. I don't remember where the coal came from. Maybe from a guy named Fred Josey. The coal, of course, had to be shipped in on the train. But I don't know where they loaded it. Maybe La Grande. But then they'd ship a load of coal to Wallowa County, and that would last all winter.

My dad, Papa, and uncle were all log cutters in Maxville. Logging was one of our most hazardous occupations, even now. At that time, they pulled a crosscut saw. The crosscut was a piece of steel that had sharp teeth. You had two men on each end, and they would pull it back and forth. That was a crosscut. Dad was physically strong and had to be mentally tough to be able to put up with all the challenges of cutting logs.

Crosscut partners worked well together for a while, but sometimes even brothers would get where they couldn't work with each other. Dad ended up working with Uncle Smokey. I don't know the specifics of it. I know Dad and Uncle Alvie sometimes had little run-ins, but they didn't last long. They were the best log cutters in the woods and needed each other. And they were very close as brothers.

You see, when the logging started in the South, they were pulling the crosscut. They said they tried to have Indians do it, but they couldn't stand up to it. They didn't do it. So, the blacks logged. That was part of the history of the logging industry.

When the logging industry went big-time was when they came up with the chainsaw and hauling trucks instead of trains. The chainsaw, you didn't have to manually pull it. All you had to do was carry a little engine, turn it, and cut a tree down. So when they started to harvest the forest in a more industrial scale, that's when the logging began to decimate the forests. Now you don't have any big, virgin trees in Califor-

Courtesy Wallowa History Center

Flora, Oregon homesteaders Virgil and Lou Ghormley using a crosscut saw, of the type used by the log cutters, to cut blocks to split for firewood or maybe make fence rails. There is a log rolling tool leaning against the logs in the log deck on the left of the photo.

nia or in Oregon. When Dad first got to Oregon, you had trees, eight, ten feet on the stump. When we left, only three or four feet on the stump.

The workday would start somewhere around four thirty or five. That would be the time they would get up. Mom and Grandma always cooked a big breakfast. It was oatmeal, pancakes, eggs, bacon or ham, grits, biscuits, and homemade jelly. Mom would make a lunch for Dad. Dad would leave home somewhere around six, six thirty. It would take an hour to get out to the woods and get set up. And then work would start. They had to get out of the labor truck that brought you to the woods. Then they'd have to walk up to the area where they were cutting logs.

Everyone had a strip going, say, maybe 150 to 200 yards long and 20 to 30 yards wide. It was all marked straight so that you didn't go over somebody else's lines. Everyone tried to get the same amount of timber going up the hill or where you're going to cut out. After you cut out that strip, you could move over to another and start again. But it would take you probably an hour to drive to where you worked. Maybe five or ten minutes sometimes to walk up through the logging to get to where your strip was.

Then you work the day. And usually by two thirty or three, Dad would be on his way home. Take him an hour to get home, maybe four [o'clock]. Then when he got home, he would have to file the chains on his saw, check his equipment, and check his gas. They had to file the saws at night. Sometimes they'd take a blowtorch and temper the teeth, make it harder.

Mama would have cooked. Then he'd get cleaned up, eat supper—we ate family meals together with Dad—visit friends for a while, maybe go up to Earl's pool hall, come home, go to bed, and repeat the cycle all over the next day.

I worked with Dad probably four or five years. I started up in Oregon. Amos and I both worked with Dad. Then when Amos left to go to Oregon State, I worked with Dad the last two weeks before high school started for me. Then when I graduated from high school in 1958, we left Wallowa. And I started working with Dad full-time in the summer months down in Grass Valley and worked on Highway 80, Soda Springs. I worked with Dad every summer until I graduated from college.

After we moved to Wallowa from Maxville, my father drove the candy wagon. It was the labor truck they called "candy wagon." Basically it's just a big truck. They'd put a little housing over a bed where people could sit in the truck along the sides and with your chainsaws and other equipment in the middle. They would take all the men, maybe five or six, out to the area where they were going to start logging.

They had a little tin heater in there. It was somehow nailed to the floor so it couldn't move around. They'd build a little fire and keep warm because sometimes in the winter months it would be well below zero. Once you got out, there would be a lot of bark to build a little fire coming back home. I really couldn't tell you why my father drove the candy wagon instead of someone else. I guess Ed Holloran recognized him as responsible and a leader.

Papa had trouble with his chainsaw sometimes, but no more trouble than I think anyone else had with their equipment.

Like most black men, if they were the head of the family, they didn't have too much time to sit down and play with the kids. Dad would go to work sometimes before we got up, and by the time he'd come back, it was almost dark. So we spent most of the time with Mom.

My mom was a housewife. She took care of the whole family. She washed, cooked, cleaned house, bathed kids, canned food for the winter, and made quilts for bedding. And she nurtured her children, physically, spiritually, and morally. She also made sure we had fun even if she often had to discipline us.

I remember Maxville but very little. Some of it I don't know if it's actually an accurate memory. I don't know if sometimes I run two memories together and come out with one. But I remember Maxville a little bit. Maxville was set high up the mountain from Wallowa, a small sawmill town that served as the area's industrial center for the local logging industry.

We had big pigs. I remember the pigs. I remember walking in the tall grass. I remember Maxville at nighttime, when the lights went out or sun went down, it was black. It was dark. It was unbelievably dark, and Mom used to always say, "The devil will come and get you if you don't act right." So I stayed in a constant state of fear when I was a little kid. At nighttime, I was in constant fear of the devil. "Oh, the devil looked like this, with big horns, a long

Courtesy Ronee Riggle Stone
This is the front of the Don Riggle house at Maxville. Bishop Meadow is in the background. Bishop Meadow and the west side of the meadow was the setting for Maxville. The superintendent's lodge was next door to the right. Don Riggle was woods boss for Bowman-Hicks. This is his son Jack. The Riggles lived at Maxville until the early 1940s.

tail, and a pitchfork." I said, "Oh, man. I hope I don't see him tonight."

I was just a little preschool boy in Maxville. My brother and I had an adventurous early childhood in Maxville. The Maxville I remember was a little black community, and I played with Amos more than anybody else. I can't remember any of the white families in Maxville. I remember some of the black children there. I remember more than anybody else my cousins Dorothy, Jeanette, and James Lester. I remember my other cousins, Rosie and Robert, but they stayed in Water Canyon.

Maxville was just a place where Mom and Dad, Amos, Jr., and I lived. We felt secure because Mom and Dad were taking care of us. So it was just a normal life. It was no consciousness of Maxville as a company town, per se. I didn't know anything to compare it with. It was just Mom and Dad and our security.

Sometimes Amos, Jr., and I would find frogs and throw rocks and sticks at them. This was the early 1940s when we didn't have television and video games and could only get a radio station every now and then. We didn't play cowboys and Indians because we didn't have the movies. The Indians we knew were from the Nez Perce reservation, and all the white men worked in the sawmill, farms, ranches, and woods like Daddy.

Papa and Grandma lived at Water Canyon on the Wallowa River, where the company boss lived. My Uncle Joe, Aunt Helen, and Cousin Nadine lived there too for a while. Mama and Daddy took us to visit them on weekends.

I remember moving from Maxville to Wallowa. We stayed somewhere uptown at first, though I can't remember the exact location. We stayed somewhere down where the road turns the corner past Shorty's store. I remember when Bowman-Hicks built the little house that we ended up being raised in. But I couldn't tell you exactly where uptown we lived. It was near the corner down where you would go into the mill before you get to Shorty's. Somewhere down in that area. That's what I remember.

They built our house. Now, they might have moved Grandma's house. I don't know. But I know they built the one we lived in. And that was the only one I can remember them building. Grandma lived next door to us, facing the house on the right-hand side. I remember when they pulled the train caboose for someone else to live in. That was the one that Robert Minor's family stayed in. On the other side, over time, a variety of people stayed there. Uncle Walter stayed there for a while. I think Helen and Jeff stayed there for a while too. There was a big house near the road. I recall Ester and Ethel Wilfong stayed in it, or it might have been Robert and Susie Mack. Jesse Langford and his family stayed in it for a while. And then we moved in.

Grandma's house was to the right of our house if I'm facing the house. These other

Courtesy Pearl Alice Marsh

A couple of old out houses in Wallowa.

people were on the other side between our house and the big house. There was only one house between our house and the big house up by the common pump.

Uncle Alvie's family didn't live in Wallowa. They moved to La Grande. He had a small trailer up in Wallowa on the other side of the truck route from where we lived. So he would go back to La Grande where his family lived on the weekend.

Our parents and grandparents were the nurturing adults in our lives. Dad was the strong provider and Mama the housekeeper and primary caretaker and disciplinarian. Papa was jolly, and my Grandma was the heart of everybody. She was great. She was the heart of me. I really enjoy thinking about them.

Amos and I were busy little boys. If discipline ever broke down, if we did something that Mom said don't do, Mom was gonna get you. You know, kids playing. We might be doing something right today, and the next minute we weren't. Maybe we didn't bring the water in when Mom

Courtesy Pearl Alice Marsh
Amos Marsh, Sr., Amos Jr. and Frank Marsh at Oregon State College, 1959.

told us to. She would get mad and come after us. But if we could get to Grandma, she would take care of us. She was the ultimate protector, I guess. So it could happen any time.

Mom never whipped us. She would spank us. Today they might call it child abuse, but it was all right back then. It wasn't that she was brutalizing us. If there was something we had to do and we didn't do it, there were consequences.

I followed Amos, Jr., anyplace. If Mom said, "I'm gonna get you boys," Junior would say, "Come on, Frank." I'd say, "No, Mama's gonna get us." Next thing you know, the belt would be smoking. I'd be hollering and say, "I ain't gonna do this no more." Until the next time.

Sometimes, Dad protected us from Mom because she would put the belt or a switch on you. If I could run and get to Dad, sometimes he'd say, "Don't whoop this boy."

One time, Dad almost got us. We were in Maxville, and Amos would always get us whooped. This time, it was serious. Amos got some matches and took me around behind the house and started trying to light the Montgomery Ward catalog. But the pages were too tight together, so it wouldn't burn. Dad came out and found the matches. Mom had to keep him off of us at that time. We learned later his sister had set their house on fire when he was a kid and the family lost everything.

Most of the time I got spanked, it boiled around Amos and me. We were best of friends and buddies. And sometimes the worst of friends and buddies. If we were supposed to be doing something Mama told us to do, we would end up doing something else, and Mom would come out and rectify whatever was wrong and then mete out the consequences she felt were right. She'd send us to go get wood because we used a woodstove, and sometimes we didn't respond as quickly as she thought we should.

Papa was a lot of fun. When we were little boys, Papa would call us and say, "Hey, boy, pull my finger." And we'd pull his finger and then break our necks to get away while Papa would cut a big one. We'd just fall out laughing, and Grandma would be so angry. We thought it was fun. That was Papa.

Papa made the best nutmeg cake and sarsaparilla tea. I started drinking coffee with my grandmother. I could get coffee and jelly cake. I would go to her house every morning for coffee and jelly cake.

La Grande was a place we went to meet black friends. It was a city. The big train station was in La Grande, so you had more people coming and going from all parts. When we moved to California, La Grande wasn't a city to us anymore. Only had maybe 4,000 people. We went to Boise, Idaho, a couple times visiting and to Portland maybe once or twice. Then we came down to Sacramento a couple of times while growing up. But mainly La Grande to me was a city, and we always had a good time. Enterprise was the biggest town in Wallowa County. La Grande was the biggest town in Union County. And Pendleton was the biggest town in Umatilla.

In Wallowa to shop, we only had one "major" store. That was Shell's. Shell's had clothing, housewares, food, and so on. Then Shorty McKenzie had a store. That was where we used to get our groceries. It was located about a half mile from our house on the truck route. It was quicker to go to Shorty's than up to Shell's. So there's where we got most of our groceries. We got our gas at Jake Silver's. There were two more gas stations in town, but we usually did most of our business with Jake. If our car got low on

Courtesy Dan McKenzie
Orville "Shorty", Kathryn, Ted and Aura McKenzie. Shorty and Aura had the Wallowa Cash Market on the north side of Wallowa. It was a popular place to shop for groceries.

gas uptown, we might go and get gas at Texaco or Shell. Generally didn't go to the Shell station because it was on the far end of town going toward Lostine and Enterprise. So we never would go down there. Well, I wouldn't say never, but just happened if we would be down that area and out of gas. We would get enough to get to where we were going. Then, a mile and a half, we'd get back to Jake's.

We bought most stuff we needed at the stores in Wallowa and Enterprise. But back then there also were door-to-door salesmen who came by. Some lived in the community. I remember one. I can't think of his name. But he used to come out. They'd come out, and they'd have a lot of different stuff to sell. They'd mostly sell snake oil, that kind of BS. Well, that's a little harsh. It wasn't snake oil, per se, but that type of stuff that promised more than it delivered. Then Grover Johnson sold shoes.

Courtesy Vearl Lewis, Silver's Colletction
Jake Silvers service station.

Jesse Langford, one of our neighbors, could measure you up for a suit. He'd take in your length of your arms, your legs and your waist. You could order a brand-new suit. Then, there was the Watkins man, but I can't remember his name.

In La Grande, we played out in the street. When we got to La Grande, we would find the kids our age and go play with them. We would shoot dice, shoot marbles, have foot races, and run from street to street. Some of the kids we played with were Rabbit and Man, who moved from Wallowa, Jimmy, and Donald Lee. Will and Frankie Anderson had some kids we'd play with. There also were the Lawsons, whose sons were about our age—Jimmy, Leonard, and Maurice. And there was Robert Minor. Aunt Dorothy and Uncle Alvie and James Lester, in the group. That was about it.

If we were shooting marbles, we would find a place with dirt, draw a circle, and shoot marbles. Sometimes we would run races. Victory went back and forth. Sometimes I could outrun you. And other times, you could outrun me. We did that out in the street. We also would go over to the railroad tracks, but we didn't run on them because if the train was coming, that was bad. You can get injured or killed.

La Grande had lots of kids, including pretty girls. I thought Dorothy Lee, Mattie Ruth, and Mayola were the prettiest girls in the world. But that was the three girls, Mattie Ruth, Dorothy Lee, and Mayola. And a little boy about seven, eight I was, and they were about fifteen, sixteen. Oh wow.

Mom would give us a dollar, at that time big money. We'd go over to Granada Theater for about ten cents and get a bag of popcorn and have extra money in our pocket. Then Amos would go over and go down to the Hilliards' café. They had the music going, and he would get a fish sandwich. Those were good times. When you don't have anything, a little bit is everything. Now you might have a whole lot and still have nothing.

La Grande had the Granada Theater and then one other theater where you could buy popcorn and watch a big-screen movie. You had more black kids there—the Andersons, the Lawsons, the Hilliards, the Minors. The Hilliards had a little restaurant that sold fish sandwiches. Across the tracks from where the black folks lived was the train station.

There was an old woman name Mother Wadie. The Lawsons were somehow related to her. She was their grandmother, I think. But you know how black families were. Relationships crossed families and unrelated friends.

Courtesy Pearl Alice Marsh

Joseph Patterson, "Pa Pat," was a minister. This is his license for Arizona.

One guy I was afraid of was Fred Warrior. He had a leg missing. I was afraid of him. At that time as a child, anything that was out of ordinary bothered me. I was sensitive to why his leg was missing. I didn't know why. So I didn't know whether he was happy or sad, but I figure he would be sad. It wasn't something that I would see every day. No one explained why his leg was missing; I assumed it had something to do with the military or work. But I couldn't be sure.

Daddy and Papa belonged to the Masonic Temple in La Grande. I knew it was a fraternal organization—how you kept your equipment in shape and in order. Dad and Papa didn't discuss their civic activity like the Masons and Eastern Stars. I know they were supposed to have been doing things in the community, whether it was scholarships or helping some family or project along. But I really couldn't tell you, other than they had meetings in La Grande about once a month. If it was something major, they went to Portland.

The black churches were there too. On Sundays, the music would be going at each one. It was almost like a festival. The Baptist church was led by the Banks brothers, D. D. Banks and R. R. Banks. They were circuit preachers from Walla Walla and would travel to their churches in Walla Walla, La Grande, Pocatello, and Hermiston to preach to black people. The Church of God in Christ, or the sanctified church, was pastored by Reverend Paul Lowe. On Sundays, he would get to playing that guitar, and we'd come running.

Courtesy Wallowa History Center

Main street Wallowa, Oregon in the 1950s. Black families got gas at the Texaco and another service station, Silver Service, back up the street.

I remember another church but not the denomination.

Papa was a Baptist preacher. My dad's family were Baptists too, but he didn't go to church. Papa used to preach over at the Baptist church. Every once in a while, he'd practice his preaching on us. He'd tell my sister Pearl, "When I say, 'Are you going to heaven?' I want you to shout." He would say it, and Pearl would get up and shout. Then he might say, "All little girls going to hell, stand up and shake your head." Pearl would get up and shake her head. That's what my Papa would do.

We practiced religion same as most people. We went to the all-white Assembly of God Church in Wallowa. Mom made sure we went to Sunday school, midweek service, and Bible school in the summer. We said grace at meals and prayers at night. We were taught to pray and thank God for everything. I think I stopped going to church probably around fourteen, fifteen. About once a month or so, we would go to La Grande and visit the African American churches. The music and preaching were black, and the pews were full of people who looked like us.

Our parents and grandparents came from the South, but our only exposure to segregation came when Aunt Dorothy died in 1953, and Uncle Alvie drove his family to Louisiana in his big green Mercury. We followed in our Oldsmobile. It took us three days and two nights to get there.

When we got to Louisiana, Dad never took us into Monroe and Ruston. It wasn't up until maybe two or three years ago I thought about it. What Dad was doing was protecting us because when we went to Enterprise, we would run into any of those little white stores and do whatever we wanted to do. And I started thinking. That's why my dad didn't take us into Monroe, because we didn't know how to act according to Jim Crow laws. If something had happened, he would have shot and killed all of them. He would have shot all of Louisiana up. But it was only this year or maybe last year I thought about it like that.

I said, "Oh, man. My dad was thinking about me. I didn't know how to act." When we would go

Courtesy Pearl Alice Marsh

Frank Wayne Marsh, First grade, Wallowa Elementary

135

to Enterprise, open that car door and didn't even shut it. We'd go to those stores, a little black kid coming in and looking at this and that. La Grande, the same way. Everybody did that. No fear. Just the way of life.

So that was the reason. And sometimes even now, I'm overprotective of my kids because I know what's out there in this cruel world. Kids don't know. That's good. But I know. And so that would be the protection my mom and dad had for me. That was tremendous. I think about it. I think about that.

We grew up hunting and fishing like all the other kids in Wallowa. Mom would take us fishing in the summer on Saturdays when the men would be off from work. Dad never fished. I never saw him with a fishing pole in his hand. But Papa would go with us. I learned fishing a little bit from Papa.

When we went to the sloughs, we caught mostly catfish, perch, bass, and carp. That was mostly slow-moving water. The Wallowa River was different. It was clean, clear, and fast-moving water. When we went with Papa, we'd catch rainbow trout and sometimes German brown trout. We kept everything that could bite the hook unless it was under legal size. I think Mom caught a salmon once. I know she caught a twenty-one-inch steelhead.

I didn't enjoy fishing. It was boring to me. But everyone else loved it. They would talk to each other while fishing. Amos, Jr., and I would throw rocks and try to catch squirrels, maybe catch a frog or something. Sometimes I had to help clean the fish. Yeah, I had to learn how to clean fish. It wasn't that difficult, just stinky and messy. You had to wash it, gut it, take the eyes out, and scale it. Then wash it real good inside and out. We skinned catfish. They'd pour hot water on the catfish, which would take the slime off and loosen some of the skin. Then you took the tail, gut it out, head off, wash it real good, fry it in cornmeal, and eat it.

My dad's outdoor sports activity that Junior and I did with him was hunting. Dad hunted every season. That was a food source. When we were real young, we didn't go hunting because it's kind of dangerous out in the woods. And Dad would have to watch us and look for deer and see that we didn't fall or get bitten by snakes. Everything was out there. So we really didn't start hunting with my Dad until we got around thirteen or fourteen years old, at which time he bought us guns.

First of all, we had to go out and learn how to shoot guns. When we were young, we shot a .22 in the backyard. Then we learned how to hunt ducks, pheasant, and small animals. We did that because all the little boys first had to learn how to shoot a .22. That's not that big.

As far as actually bringing some birds home that I shot, instead I scared a hell of a lot of them. Maybe brought one or two but not a lot. I remember duck hunting with William Crow. I went duck hunting with him quite a bit. And I went hunting with Stan Goulet. I remember hunting with him. I think Dan Lively and Mel Houser was there. Gary Myers might have been there.

But when we got big enough, Dad bought us each a .270 Winchester. We learned how to use the bigger guns out in the woods. Then we learned how to go hunting with Dad. We went out a couple times with friends hunting the big game, deer hunting.

We scared a lot of deer, and I actually killed one. I thought I killed two, but my Papa

Courtesy Wallowa History Center, Wallowa High School 1956-57 annual.
Letterman's Club, Wallowa High School, 1956-57. Front Row L-R: Frank Marsh, Greg Johnson, ? ,Gary Lively, John Burns, Amos Marsh, Larry Snook, John Edgmand. Back Row Sitting: Duane Berry, Alvin Gorham, Gayle Lively, Roger Burchett, Mel Houser, Stan Goulet, Keith Hescock, ? , Dale Lindsey. Back Row Standing: John Allen, Dale Hulse, Vernon Bennett, ? .

said he shot the one. So he took credit for it. But I thought I had killed that one deer. Dad thought I shot it too, but hey, no big deal. Papa made a big fuss about it. It was his deer. I felt pretty good about myself until Papa said, "No, I got that one." If one happened to fall, he'd claim it. It was all good.

After hunting successfully all day, we came home with the deer. And it's amazing now to think back. We killed the deer in the morning and gut and cleaned it out, put the liver back in the cavity, and left it in the woods all day. Intestines, the lungs, everything was cleaned out of it. And since we killed chicken and hogs, cleaning deer was just like anything else.

When we came home, we'd build a fire because it'd be getting kind of dark. We hung the deer by the horns and skinned it from the neck down. We'd start off cutting the skin around the neck and legs and pulled the skin right off. Then we'd take it down and cut it into quarters. Then Mom, Grandma, and the other women would start working on it, cleaning the meat and cutting into cooking pieces. I can't say they cut it all that night. They might have cut some during the next day. Sometimes they might cut it into quarters, take it up to the locker freezer at Shell's. And they might end up letting the butcher at Shell's butcher it up, making it into stew meat, roast, steaks, and so on. But a lot of the times they just cut it themselves. Usually when we first killed it, the first thing we ate was the liver cooked with onions. We'd eat it with syrup and biscuits.

I started school at Wallowa Elementary School after we moved down from Maxville. My first three grades were in the high school building that all the older kids were in.

And then the gym burned down, and they built the new school for the first through fourth grades. I went to the fourth grade in the new white building.

To me, school was kind of tough because, like a free-range chicken, I was used to running around and making up games and adventures to do all day. The first time I had structure where you had to sit down and listen to the teacher and get assignments to do was when I started school. So I didn't really enjoy it. As a little kid, I didn't understand the benefits of education. After I got the hang of school, I always liked science. I always liked nature.

There were good people and bad people in Wallowa. I was cautious of everyone as a child, just my nature. But Mary Marsh said, "You're going to go to school and learn something." So that was one of the big things I did. After a while I adjusted to it, and I got a chance to see a lot of the different kids at school and make friends. So it became more enjoyable as time went on.

I don't know if I had a favorite teacher. Probably Ms. Guillory in the fourth grade. She was one of my favorite teachers. And then in high school, it was Anne McDaniels because I think she had a good understanding of kids and education. Don Wilson was my coach. He was always important too. He was a good friend after I left high school [and] went to college on up until he passed a few years ago.

I can remember some of my friends from elementary school. William Crow was a pretty good friend because he stayed right across the road from us. So I saw him all the time, [and] he was back and forth all the time. A couple other friends would come down, like John Edgmand. But you know, mostly kids didn't go up into anybody's house. That was just one of the things you didn't do. Kids played outside. In elementary school I only saw most of the kids during the weekday because they lived and worked out on the farms.

Before starting school, I also played with Rabbit and Man Langford. They were black kids who lived near us. We would walk to the store together.

We didn't encounter a lot of racism in Wallowa. There were a few redneck families, but most were pretty decent. I remember this white kid, Willard Horton. He would

Courtesy Wallowa History Center

Frank with his 1957-58 football team. Frank played a sport each quarter. Football was in the fall. Frank is 4th from the left, Row 1. Head coach, Don Wilson is at the end on the right.

come out, throw rocks at us, and use the n-word. I told Mom, and she said, "Pick up a rock and throw it back at him."

One time, Rabbit threw a rock and knocked him on the head. It went bing, and he went running to his mom and cried. She came down, talked to Mom. "Mary, your boys are throwing rocks." Mom said, "Your boys been throwing rocks at my kids all the time."

I remember a boy named Raymond pinched me at church, and I said, "Mom, he pinched me." She said, "If he pinched you, you pull a plug out of his behind." So I couldn't wait for him to do it again so I could tear his butt up. If Mom told me to do something, I did it. No one ever jumped on us or said anything because they looked at my old man's guns too. That's the way it was.

Melvin Houser and I were always pretty close. I used to go over to his house and over to Earl Berry's. I used to go to their house and play over there for a while and that kind of thing, and they would come to mine. As we got a little bit older, my good friends included John Edgmand and Stan Goulet. By the time I got to high school, I had many, many friends. Mostly a lot of that centered around sports because we'd play sports together, and that made for real comradery with a little more bonding. And then I had a lot of friends from church because we went to the Assembly of God. I remember the Landis family. Pullins—both Pullins families—and the Reels.

I was known up there in Wallowa for being good at sports. Amos was the number one in all the school sports until he left. Then I went from being number two to being number one.

In the fall of the year, I played football. In the winter months, I played basketball. And in spring I ran track. There was no baseball season because school was out in the summer, and most kids had to work on their farms. Each season I was ready for one season to end and the other season to start.

"Coaching Amos and Frank was a great experience on my part because I had never coached any African Americans before. They were kids, and they were great kids, and their folks were great parents."

In football, I played the same position as my brother. We both played halfback. He was always a little better than I was. In basketball we could play together because we both played guard. We ran track together but different events. I ran the hurdles; Amos ran the hundreds.

In track, it was the hurdles for me. I won State in track. That was in 1958. That was when I got a scholarship to run track in Linfield College. And from there I went to Oregon State. I ran the high hurdles. Then I got out, graduated from Oregon State with a bach-

Courtesy Kay Frances Marsh
Mary Marsh and her father, Pa Pat.

139

elor's degree in sociology.

After graduating, through my brother, I had the opportunity to try to play professional football. And I went to Detroit. Stayed over there one year. Then I went to San Diego, and I was activated for a couple days. And that was the end of my professional football career. Then I came home and married Joyce. That's the way it went.

We made stilts in Wallowa. That was basically taking a long two-by-four and building a platform with a block on it parallel on both sides. If you took a rubber strap cut from an inner tube, you could nail it over the platform block to make a strip to stick your foot in it. Then you step on it, get your balance, and you could walk on the stilts. It took a little bit of practice. You'd fall a couple times. But after that you learn how to walk.

I don't recall exactly how high we would make the stilts, but they were high we had to learn how to step on them from the porch. It might have been two or three feet at the most. But it would be high enough.

Christmas in our house was always a fun time because it was something you build anticipation for, building up to the climax on Christmas Day. Mom made Christmas extra fun. We always had turkey and dressing, gravy, potato salad, candied yams, cranberry sauce, sweet potato pie, apples, oranges—everything that little boys or girls would want. You could eat as much as you want, even candy and drinks. Papa used to make eggnog. We didn't get as much of that as we wanted, but we got some.

Christmas was just a climax of all the happiness and joy energizing us for a two-week period. School's out. You can sleep late. Everything was just great at Christmas. And it wasn't just about receiving gifts. It wasn't like Christmas is commercialized now. Mom would let us look in the catalog and see something and order it for us. We got a few toys. I remember a couple trucks. I remember getting one special gift for Amos and me. We got a sled. We had to share it, but it was okay. We would take it up to the hill and ride it down and take it back up. And we took turns.

Christmas was about enjoying everyone. Enjoying Mama, Dad, Papa, Grandma, my brother and sisters and friends—everyone, just enjoying everyone. That was Christmas.

After we finished opening gifts and eating, we used to go over to William Crow's. He'd have an electric train. We would play with it just like he played with it. So it was all about sharing. That part was good. I remember Amos used to get a chemistry set and a wood-burning kit. It was an enjoyable time for me.

They always had the Christmas programs at church. The theme was all about the birth of Christ. So that was special too. We each had different Christmas poems to recite, and then they give us a little bag of candy. Same way in school. We also would go down to the movie theater and watch nothing but cartoons. We would go down somewhere around noon or one, march down from school to the theater down town, and they'd run cartoons until about four. Then we would go back to the school and go home. It was all about entertaining kids. Yeah. That was Christmas.

One thing that was always important, Mom made sure we always felt proud of who we are. We were black and taught to be proud that we were black. She taught us to be happy that we were black.

After I got older, I remember she said, "Only you can make yourself feel inferior." So I always felt pretty damn good about myself.

Mom told me, "Whatever you want to do, you can do." When Amos went to high school, he said, "I'm going to play professional ball." "No," they said. "He can't do it." He did it. When Amos went to college, some wanted him to go to Eastern Oregon College in La Grande. He said, "I'm going to Oregon State." He did it.

We were empowered by Mama, by her saying, "Whatever you want to do or whatever you want to be, you can." So I took that to heart. And I might hear an n-word from some white person, and I'd look at them and say, "Hey, that's your loss. I'm doing great!"

I remember one incident where a kid went to the preacher and said something about, "He's black." And the preacher said, "Well, he can't help it." And that pissed me off more than it hurt me.

"He can't help it." That was saying somehow that I was less than he was, and that bothered me. But I felt because I could always be on top of whatever he was, I was okay with it.

Overall, I had a good childhood in Wallowa. From my infancy all the way up to high school and college. And I cherish every moment I had with my family and friends. A lot of times at night, I lie awake and think about the wonderful times and experiences that I had as a kid growing up.

Junior and I had the admiration and love for each other that I think is normal for brothers. And we had our disagreements also. I would say overall, our childhood was positive. It was just normal, growing up with family relationships.

If there is anything about my growing up that I would like to tell my children and grandchildren, or leave them with a lesson learned or some values, it is to live each day to its fullest. Enjoy life while you're young. And while you think it's awfully difficult when you're young, when you get older you'll find out that the younger days were the most enjoyable days that you've had because you didn't have any responsibility. So enjoy the days that you have while you're young.

Courtesy Pearl Alice Marsh
Frank Wayne Marsh

PEARL ALICE MARSH

Courtesy Pearl Alice Marsh
Pearl Alice Marsh, 6 years old.

Pearl Alice Marsh was born in La Grande, Oregon, in 1946. Her parents were Amos Marsh, Sr., and Mary (Patterson) Marsh. She had two brothers, Amos, Jr., and Frank Wayne, and two sisters, Penny Merle and Kay Frances.

After leaving Wallowa at the age of twelve, Pearl Alice moved with her family to Grass Valley, California, where she attended and graduated from Nevada Union Senior High. She went to Sacramento State College, where she earned a bachelor of arts degree in social welfare and worked in the antipoverty program as a community organizer. She next enrolled at the University of California at Berkeley and earned a master's degree in public health and a doctorate in political science.

Pearl Alice has been a committed activist in US social movements since the 1960s and has fifty years of professional experience in planning, grassroots organizing, community and national politics, public policy, academia, and government. She served as an appointed and elected commissioner in the City of Berkeley, California, and on a number of volunteer advisory and governing boards.

Pearl Alice traveled and worked throughout sub-Saharan Africa to help strengthen democratic institutions and promote popular participation in governance. Her distinguished professional career in public policy has covered a wide range of issues, including health care, mental health, international trade, domestic violence, grassroots economic development, education, and interethnic relations.

Pearl Alice never married but has loved and mentored a host of nieces, nephews, and students during her lifetime.

She has retired but continues her historical research and writing and engagement in politics.

My name is Pearl Alice Marsh. I was born on September 6, 1946, at the Grande Ronde Hospital in La Grande, Oregon. I lived in Wallowa, Oregon, with my family until 1958, when we moved to Grass Valley, California. I finished the sixth grade at Wallowa Elementary School.

My father, Amos Marsh, Sr., was a log cutter for Bowman-Hicks Lumber Company when he and Mama first moved to Maxville in 1939. He later worked for Ed Holloran and Son. Mama was the family housekeeper and manager. Country and small-town women like Mama worked by a different standard than city women. She and her neighbors worked hard. There was no cushy life.

My grandparents were Joseph Valley and Arie Elizabeth (Spears) Patterson. They came to Wallowa County from Arizona in 1937. Papa worked for Bowman-Hicks, and Grandma kept house and took in ironing for a few whites. They lived at Water Canyon before moving to Wallowa.

I am the next to the last child. I had two older brothers, Amos, Jr., and Frank Wayne, an older sister, Penny Merle, and a younger sister, Kay Frances. My brothers both graduated from Wallowa High School in 1957 and 1958 respectively and went on to Oregon State College. Amos, Jr., went on to play professional football for the Dallas Cowboys and Detroit Lions. Frank graduated from Oregon State with a bachelor's degree in sociology and signed as a defensive back with the San Diego Chargers but never played. My sister Penny Merle was totally handicapped and never walked or talked. She died in 1962 in Grass Valley at the age of sixteen. Kay Frances attended San Jose State College after graduating from Nevada Union Senior High School in Grass Valley.

Wallowa doesn't look any different today than it did back then. It's a small town with a highway that runs through it. No stoplights. No stop signs on the highway, only the side streets and roads that intersect.

We passed Shorty's grocery store on the way to school. Shorty was a butcher, and Margaret Dougherty was the clerk along with Shorty's wife, Aura. Uptown was Jake Silvers's gas station, the hardware store, Shell's Mercantile, the bank, the drugstore, the post office, and Lawyer Chrisman's office. There were more, but these are the ones we frequented. When I was very young, we had a movie theater and candy store.

And then there was Ms. Hauprich's candy shop and Baird's Tavern where the men went. Dad went up to Earl Haney's pool hall, and that's where he'd played poker. Wallowa was just a nice little town, and it still is.

Our family lived in a three-room house owned by Bowman-Hicks in Wallowa until I was about five years old. Mama paid the rent to Lawyer Chrisman. After I started the first grade, we moved to a big five-bedroom house left by the Langfords. None of our houses had indoor plumbing.

Our small house was two doors down from the Langfords. They had at least five kids. Their father, Jesse, Sr., cut logs with Daddy and Papa. Jessie also measured and sold mail-order suits to the men as needed. His wife, Mattie, took care of the children and home. Jesse gave all of their kids nicknames. The first five were about our ages. So Amos, Jr., was close to Rabbit. Frank Wayne was close to Man. Penny Merle was close to Peaches. I was close to Shorty, a girl. And Kay Frances was close to Beemo, another girl.

My mother hated nicknames, except for Amos, Jr., who was called "Junior" so he wouldn't be called "Amos" like his father. She didn't like calling us by just our first name either. "I gave you two names," she would say. So the rest of us were called by our full names—Frank Wayne, Penny Merle, Pearl Alice, and Kay Frances. She lost a little boy in childbirth after Kay Frances. His name was Keith DeRay. Two names.

Dad's closest friend was Lonnie Powell, who we called Uncle Smokey. He was born in March 1897 in Pennsylvania. His hobby was carpentry. He built a little carpenter shop next to the house he shared with his wife, Ms. Carrie. Dad would go down there, and they'd spend a lot of time talking about work, people, "old times," and "hoorah" one another. Uncle Smokey built Dad's gun cabinet. My brother Frank still has it.

Ms. Carrie was walleyed in one of her eyes. But she was very sweet. I used to go down to her

Courtesy Pearl Alice Marsh
Berdiene Landis, who lived in Wallowa, and Pearl Alice.

house, and she'd let me use her powder puff to put powder on my face. She would let me dab her some sweet cologne, Evening in Paris or something like it.

Ms. Lucy and Hosea Lowry lived next door to us. Ms. Lucy was gentle and would spend time with me and let me talk to her. I called her "Ms. Nucy."

By the time I was born, no one in our extended family lived in Wallowa except Grandma and Papa—Ma and Pa Pat—who lived right next door. Any time we wanted to visit Grandma and Papa, we just ran in.

Grandma was a great cook and spoiled us. She wasn't political. She was just a sweet grandma. In most ways, she was a passive woman, not an assertive woman like my mom. Papa didn't boss her around, but he "wore the pants in the family." Mama used to get mad at Grandma because Papa wouldn't let her handle money. Mama handled all our family's money Dad brought home. Papa bought everything for their house. He did all the grocery shopping, clothes shopping, animal purchases, and feed. I remember one time Mama yelled at Grandma saying, "You even let Papa buy your drawers," meaning her underwear. I don't know if that's a plus or a minus to have a husband who does everything for you. But Grandma wasn't complaining. Mama was complaining.

Papa was fat and jolly and spoiled us too. Our other relatives, who had left Wallowa, lived in La Grande, Pendleton, and Bly, Oregon, and would come for Sunday visits and Grandma's cooking from time to time.

Papa's mother, Clementine (Valley) Patterson, came out one time from Louisiana. She moved to Oakland, California, with her other son, Aaron.

My father's mother, Ollie (Elmore) Marsh, and sister Willie came out one time from Louisiana for a week. His father, Papa Albert, died of kidney disease. Grandma Ollie died many years later. She didn't look sweet like Grandma Pat to me as a child because she was skinny. I always associate sweetness with plump. But she was very, very kind. Every year, she sent a huge box of raw peanuts from her garden. Amos, Jr., was in charge of oven roasting them, and we ate them while they were still warm.

Both my parents were born in Louisiana. Daddy was born in Eros, Jackson Parish, and Mama in DeRidder, Beauregard Parish. They met as adults in Arizona in the 1930s. Daddy's Louisiana roots were stable. He came from a large family of aunts and uncles, each of whom had inherited 80 acres of farmland from their father, Louis Marsh, Sr. After emancipation from slavery, Louis purchased a total of 360 acres in Jackson Parish. So they lived and farmed for generations in a stable, rural community known as Olive Grove. Because of Jim Crow practices against Afri-

Courtesy Pearl Alice Marsh
Marriage License of Joe Patterson and Arie Tooke, Pa Pat and Ma Pat.

can American landowners, they never became wealthy, just made a living. The family did send their two youngest children to college.

Mama's family was less rooted. Her mother was born in Texas to a large farming family. They owned their land but not nearly as much as the Marshes. I'm not sure how or when she got to Louisiana, but Mama was born in 1914. Grandma was married to a man named Rutledge who died when Mama was a young girl. Grandma was married twice and had two daughters, Mama and Aunt Idella, before she married Papa. Both previous husbands died.

Papa was a sawmill worker in Rapides Parish, Louisiana, when they met. He and his first wife had four boys before she died. Her name was Stella (Morton) Patterson. When Papa and Grandma met, his boys needed a mother, and Grandma's daughters needed a father and provider. He and Grandma married in 1923 in Alexandria, Louisiana. Mama was nine years old.

Dad was a log cutter in Wallowa County but started out working in Louisiana sawmills when he wasn't working the fields in the off-season with his family. After he left home, he worked in a sawmill in east Texas for a while. But in 1931, he went to McNary, Arizona, and that's where he met Mama and Papa and Grandma. And that's where Mama and Daddy got married. Then they came on out to Oregon in 1939, where Daddy became a log cutter. He was good too. They still tell stories about how able he was with his brother on the crosscut and then by himself on the single chain power saw.

Mama didn't work outside the house. She had her hands full with five children with one being handicapped. That was Penny Merle. It was very hard. I don't know how she did it. We didn't have indoor plumbing. So she and Grandma had to pack water from the communal water pump to wash all of our clothes and bedding; to cook, mop floors, and bathe everyone. She had to iron all of our clothes. It's just amazing how hard she worked.

Mama taught us women's crafts like patching clothes. Money was tight all the time. But Mama managed funds really well. We never went without. Mama had a little gimmick, though, with us kids. She convinced us that material stuff didn't matter. So we never had a big craving for material things beyond our means. We did order school clothes, but she made some of our clothes. I don't remember feeling like we went without. They did have a charge account up there at Shorty's. And poor Shorty McKenzie. I think he carried the whole town on credit during the winter when the snow kept the men out of the woods. So we, like everyone else, ran up a pretty good tab there.

Mama and Grandma prepared and cooked wild meat; Daddy and Papa would hunt and kill deer. So in addition to the little store-bought meat we got, we always had meat in the freezer to cook. And we grew big gardens. So we always had home-canned greens and beans and other garden varieties to eat. So I don't remember feeling like we were poor, though we clearly were.

We always had a good car. Daddy would never buy a used car. His father bought a car once, and when he took it in to get it checked, some white guy—this is in Louisiana—some white guy had bought the same model and was having trouble with it. And they switched out the cars on Papa Albert. And the car never ran right. So my dad had nothing to do with used cars. So we always had new cars.

I think we did okay as a family. We were working poor, but we were good.

❖ ❖ ❖

Mama raised us in the church. Dad didn't object, but he wasn't going to be caught dead in a church. We were Pentecostal Christians and believed in "the end of times." The apocalypse was always right around the corner. It's been right around the corner since I was a little kid. I can remember going to church and being terrified when they talked about the end of times when the Lord was going to come, and you were going to go to hell if you had been doing bad things. And they'd always look out at the world and see something that was a predictor of the end of times—bad weather, people were growing more sinful. And that was scary.

Now we still got the same thing going on, maybe worse. It's the end of times. I think it would be convenient if God ended time and took us on off to glory. But he's going to make us stick around here a while and clean up the mess we made of the earth he gave us. So I don't think the end of times is coming too soon.

Courtesy Pearl Alice Marsh
Idella (Took/Patterson) Williams, sister of Mary Marsh.

We certainly came from poor circumstances. But we never went without necessities and a few luxuries. The important things we had. One thing I hated growing up was using empty jelly and mayonnaise jars to drink Kool-Aid water. If Mama bought regular drinking glasses, we'd break them. So we wound up drinking out of jelly jars. Back then jelly and all kind of food came in glass jars. So that's what we used for our glasses.

I am six and seven years younger than my brothers and was in their way a lot. Amos, Jr., had patience, but Frank Wayne didn't. One time the boys went to Boy Scout camp. I was about four years old and too young to know I couldn't go and pitched a fit when Mama said I had to stay home. To placate me, Mama made a cot with a sleeping bag in the garage where I could sleep outdoors safely and see the night sky. I slept out by myself the whole night. Of course, Mama checked on me every fifteen minutes.

Frank Wayne could be unpleasant. He was just somewhat crabby with me most of the time. He was skinny, so I thought he envied my plumpness. But Amos, Jr., was a lot of fun and a great big brother who played with and protected us when he wasn't off with his buddies.

We used to go fishing a lot as a family. And

Courtesy Pearl Alice Marsh
Mary Marsh, mother of Amos, Frank, Penny, Pearl Alice and Kay.

of course fishing was fun. We would run up and down the banks checking on Grandma, Mama, Papa, and anyone else fishing. I was allowed to fish too but never caught any. One day while we were fishing at Willow Creek between Elgin and Imbler, Frank Wayne distracted me, and Amos, Jr., caught a little perch and put it on my hook. When I turned around and picked up my pole, they said, "Baby, where's your bobber?" My bobber had gone under water, which meant I had hooked a fish. I grabbed my pole and yanked the fish

Courtesy Pearl Alice Marsh
Assembly of God Sunday School class. Black girls (left) Betty Lou Langford, (right) Pearl Alice Marsh.

out of the water. After we got home, I wouldn't let anyone take it off. I packed the fish around all week until it dried up and fell off.

I remember playing baseball for a minute with my brother and my first home run. The Langford boys, Amos, Jr., Frank Wayne, William Crow from across the highway, and a few others played baseball in this big open space in front of our houses. I always wanted to play with them, but I was too little. So given a chance, I would run out onto the field and Amos, Jr., would pick me up and take me back to the porch. I'd run out as soon as the game got good, and he would pick me up and take me back. Finally he asked me if I wanted to bat. I was shocked but very excited. I got up to bat, swung, hit the ball, and ran all the bases, never dropping the bat. When I got to first base, Rabbit or Man was playing. Someone threw him the ball, and he fell down and dropped it. When I got to second and third bases, the baseman fell down, and I came on home. I was so satisfied with myself I quit the game and didn't play anymore. After I got older, I realized that my brother had rigged the game and let me hit that home run and got me out of their way.

My sister Kay Frances and I were real best buddies. We are just twenty-one months apart in age. So that was close enough where we could be real friends but not so close as to be competitive. As little girls, we split everything fifty-fifty. We figured that out on our own. So when we were still drinking out of a bottle, if Mama made me a bottle, I'd drink half and go find Kay and give the other half to her. If Mama made Kay a bottle, she'd drink half and bring it to me.

We used to go down away from the house to what looked like a long way away. We would go in the warm sunshine, pick flowers, and watch butterflies. Buttercups were an early favorite. We had lupine and dandelions. We would bring those back home and put them in little baby food jars for vases. We would make mud pies in a jar lids and set them by the house so that the sun could bake them. It was learning how to cook.

Kay was always meticulous. I wasn't. We used to make a "two girl" train and crawl in and out underneath the beds. Beds were high back then. One time we were crawling under the bed, and Kay tore my dress. She said, "Uh-oh, Pearl, I tore your dress." And I looked back and said, "Oh, that's okay. Let's go," and just kept going. Kay was horrified. But it didn't bother me that my dress was torn.

One more Kay story. So as an older sister you're obligated to pick on them a little. So I would always tell Kay in the dark that there was a bogeyman who was going to get her. And oh, boy, Kay would get so scared. I would just be tickled to death. "The bogeyman is going to get you." So then Kay wouldn't go anywhere by herself. And if Mama sent her—even into the bedroom when the light was out and it was dark—Mama would make me go with her. I would be so mad. Mama said, "Well, you scared her about the bogeyman, so you just get in there with her." So that taught me a lesson about the bogeyman.

I loved my sister and felt responsible for her. I remember to this day a selfish decision I made. We always went to school and came home for lunch. One day Mama gave me money so that Kay and I could eat up at the drugstore. They had a lunch counter. We were going to go with my school friends. Well, Mama made me drag Kay along because she had to go wherever I went. I was just annoyed that she was tagging along.

After we had been walking around with my friends, looking at store items, Kay finally looked at me and said, "Pearl, I'm hungry." I was horrified that I had let my little sister get hungry and had been so preoccupied with my friends that I hadn't paid her any attention. So I stopped right then, and we went to the lunch counter, and I fed my sister. I just regretted that my whole life. And I never would do it again.

I don't remember being teased or bullied by classmates in Wallowa because I was black when coming up in grade school. But I do remember racial incidents in my childhood. White kids in Enterprise or Joseph always stared at us. Kids would scamper down the aisle to their mother, eyes bugged wide open, and point in our direction. Usually the mother would avert her eyes and hustle them off to another aisle.

I remember one incident well. We were the only black family in town, and we belonged to the Assembly of God Church. We had a church full of white families and friends. I had church friends, including a little boy who was one day younger than I. That made a big difference in my mind, made me older. But entering the first grade and going to school meant uptown kids and farm kids whom I didn't know.

Mama always drove by the school on her way to the store. [She] was driving by one day and saw me off playing with a ball by myself. She stopped the car and called me over to ask why I was playing alone. I said, "Because the other kids don't want to play with me." She was not going to stand for that. She gnarled her brow and told me emphatically that I was going to "get over there and play right now!" I had a choice. I could either go home and get my butt whipped for not playing, or I could go over and put myself in the game. I chose the latter.

I was athletic like my brother Amos, Jr. So when I started playing, I became a playground winner and good at everything. A classmate said nobody wanted to face me in tetherball. My left hand was powerful. I could almost knock the ball off the rope. And I would swing extra high and jump out of the seat on the swing set at the highest point. We all did that.

But there were limits. The one thing I couldn't do was swing on the monkey bars. I'm sure it was because I was too fat, and my arms would give out. Those skinny girls like Kay Landreth, Gwen Lyman, and Sue Ann McGraw could go back and forth on the monkey bars several times and never hit the ground. I'd get about three bars over and clunk. Gravity.

In terms of belonging to groups, some mothers organized a Brownie troop in the second grade. I was ambivalent about joining because you had to have the meetings at your house, and we didn't have an indoor bathroom. But Grandma gave me fifty cents so that I could go join. When I went to join after school, I was hanging out at the door looking in. I made eye contact with the organizer, or so I remember. And she never invited me in. So I left, and this was the beginning of my eating disorders. I stopped by Shorty's, bought fifty cents worth of candy, and ate it before I got home. I told Grandma I had changed my mind about joining.

A little friend told me when they asked why I wasn't in Brownies, the adult said she didn't think any of them would want me in Brownies, which wasn't true. My friend quit.

I did belong to 4-H. The leader was Zana Peterson. When she organized girls' 4-H, she came down to our house and explicitly asked Mama if I could join. And of course Mama said yes. She told the white mothers if they didn't want their daughters in 4-H with me, they could keep them out. And if I was the only girl in 4-H, I was going to be in 4-H. So I was in sewing 4-H for a year. I think I still have the little scarf I made, a pink scarf with a fringe. I wasn't good with domestic stuff like my sister Kay. So I got out of that.

Once Mama became a Seventh-day Adventist, I joined Pathfinders. That was their church youth adventure group. We used to go to both winter and summer camp. I even went to summer camp at Payette Lake, Idaho, one year. I sold "World's Finest Chocolate" candy bars all winter to the diabetic women in town and paid my way to camp. So though Brownies didn't work out and I had no talent for 4-H, eventually there was a nice group for children that I got involved [in] and was active.

We went to Louisiana to visit Dad's parents one summer. He had left the harsh realities and painful memories of Jim Crow behind for a better life in Oregon. We drove in a two-car caravan with my uncle Alvie and his family in his Mercury and our family in our Oldsmobile. It was a long ride, too long. The car broke down once, and Kay got at least one spanking. The only way we could get a respite was to invoke the "I have to pee" card, which only got a brief roadside pause.

Returning to Louisiana for my father was a triumphant moment over "peckerwoods" who thought they could keep him and his brothers down. It also was a moment to show the relatives and friends how he was thriving in Oregon—healthy kids, pretty wife, new car, money, and joy. But since it was Louisiana, my brothers were kept under strict supervision, not because they were mischievous but because the South was cruel to young, black men.

The sights, earthy smells, and wild sounds of rural Louisiana were delightful. But Grandma Ollie had this huge, horrible old mule named Jim who just seemed evil to me. He would hide around the corner of the house and wait to chase Kay Frances because he figured out she was the scariest. Grandma would pick up a stick and boss him around and he'd take off. But boy, he kept us going.

My father's youngest sister was the local schoolteacher in the one-room schoolhouse. She had this large presence in our lives, though we only met her once as children. Mama and Dad told stories about Aunt Willie being educated, and occasionally there was the short phone call to Louisiana when we all got to say hello. She was inspirational. I wanted to be like Aunt Willie. She was responsible for many children getting on the right track in life, both family and her community school children.

I have to tell a special story about Aunt Willie. I was so excited to start the first grade in Wallowa. Before starting school, I used to ask Amos, Jr., and Frank Wayne to read to me, and they would get tired. So I couldn't wait to go to school and learn to read myself. That was big. I excelled in school right off. But I had one little problem. For some reason, I could not remember how to spell my first name. I could spell "Alice" and "Marsh," but I could not remember how to spell "Pearl." After a few months, it precipitated anxiety. When I had to spell my first name in class, I had minor panic attacks.

In Louisiana, Aunt Willie sat with me and calmly taught me how to remember to spell my first name. When we came back to Wallowa and went to school, Mrs. Fisher was pleasantly surprised that I could, and I was so proud and relieved.

Education, reading, and learning were staple values in our household. I loved school. Our house was about a mile from the school, so we walked every day and came home for lunch.

Mrs. Hattie Fisher, who taught every child in Wallowa for about fifty years, was my first teacher. I was a good student. I didn't miss a question on an exam until the fourth grade and Mrs. Brown marked me wrong on one question. I felt permanently damaged and don't think I recovered after that. But I was a good student and loved class.

Mrs. Fisher marked me "wrong" on one question in the first grade but corrected it. The question was, "Does the sun always shine?" I answered yes. I had older brothers in science classes. Some of the kids differed, invoking nighttime and cloudy days when it rained. I held my ground. Ms. Fisher smiled and acknowledged to me privately that I was right.

My second-grade teacher was Mrs. Olive. She lived in Lostine, and every now and then we stopped by her house on the way to Enterprise so she and Mama could visit. My third-grade teacher was Mrs. Johnson. She was nice, but Mrs. Fisher and Mrs. Olive had spoiled me. I got in trouble once with Mrs. Johnson.

It was around Christmas, and she left the classroom. The kids decided to discuss Santa Claus and what he was going to bring. Mama didn't teach us there was a Santa Claus. When she was young, she used to make a long list for Santa Claus. And of course, she never got any of it except a doll because they were poor. So she didn't want us to be that disappointed. She wanted us to know our parents bought us the gifts they could afford. We did look through the Montgomery Ward catalog and pick out dolls and a few other toys she ordered. But we knew the source of our bounty.

After Mrs. Johnson went out, I announced to the whole class there was no Santa Claus and started a big uproar. I'll never forget this little guy's face turning purple-red as he burst into tears and shouted at me. I held my ground and said their parents were buying all their gifts. Mrs. Johnson came back to the classroom and saw the uproar. She found out what was going on and took me out to the hall and said, "Pearl Alice, your mother taught you there is no Santa Claus, and we know that. But these children's parents told them there is a Santa Claus, so you let them believe it." So I said okay and went back into the classroom feeling more mature than the rest. And that was the end of that.

Mrs. Brown, fourth grade, she had this crackly voice, a big mole on her face, and was stern. Papa had a garden by her house, and she would come out and exchange pleasantries with him. I saw her differently for a brief moment, but then it was back to the fourth-grade classroom.

It was okay for girls to be smart when I was going to school in Wallowa. I was smart. Sue Ann McGraw was smart. Gwen Lyman was smart. A bunch of us girls and a few boys were smart.

We had a boy in our fourth-grade class who was somewhat slow. He usually missed most of the test questions. Mrs. Brown would give us a quiz and then have us pass your paper to the person behind you. She would call out the answers, and the person behind would correct your quiz. Then you'd get your grade, A, B, C, D, and F. I don't think this boy ever got better than a D. But he finally figured it out.

One day Mrs. Brown gave us a quiz and told us to pass our papers back. Well, he wouldn't pass his back. He kept his paper and marked the answers as she read them. The next thing you know, he turned his paper in and got a perfect score. We all knew he had cheated, but we also knew he turned out to be smart.

I finished the sixth grade in Wallowa. Dad's job played out. So Mike Holloran, for whom he worked, moved his operation to northern California. While my brothers graduated from Wallowa High School, my sister and I moved to Grass Valley, California, and enrolled at Hennessy School.

Every Christmas the Chamber of Commerce sponsored cartoons at the theater along with bags of free candy and fruit for the kids. Some kids went to churches that wouldn't let their kids go to the movie theater. We were glad our mom wasn't that strict. We came from a more tolerant household. Mama was a very devout Christian, but she didn't go overboard on simple things that weren't in the Bible like cartoons at the picture show.

Holidays were great. There was all that cooking. Mama and Grandma were excellent cooks. They mastered the art of cooking on those big old woodstoves. I remember when we were little kids, Mama cooked thirty-five-pound turkeys for the holidays in a woodstove. She'd put the turkey on the night before and keep the fire burning. We'd smell turkey all night long. Oh, gosh, it was so good. Then she cooked the cornbread dressing and the potato salad and the green beans, collard greens, candied yams, rolls, pies, and cakes, and it was just wonderful.

We had a tradition that when Mama boiled the giblets to make gravy, my oldest brother, Amos, Jr., got the turkey neck. For some reason he loved the turkey neck, so we all deferred to him. It was like an honor to save the neck for him. If my memory serves me, I think Frank Wayne got a drumstick.

Then of course for Christmas, we turned around and cooked a big turkey again. The union gave us a big turkey at Christmas.

Daddy would pick out a Christmas tree and bring it down from the woods. Mama built the base for it and set it up, and then we'd decorate the tree. She put a lot of

Courtesy Pearl Alice Marsh

First grade, Wallowa Elementary, graduating class of 1964.
  Back Row L-R: Raymond Miller, Sandra Collins, Maridee Conner, Connie Weaver, Kay Landreth, Jennie Wade, Linda Keeler, Jonathin Johnson, Weldon Carper, Steven Horten, Gary Bradley, Douglas Berry.
  Middle Row: Larry Henry, Sue Ann McGraw, Mike Wort, Lynda Nell Leverenz, Fred Murphy, Maxine Fanning, and Stirlon Talbot.
  Front Row: Gene Werst, Dick Pullen, Sharon Vanasche, Pearl Alice Marsh, Gary Miller, Donald Schaffer, Gwen Lyman, Dallas Armon, Janet Kessler, Diane Makin, Patty Haney, and Darlene Davis.

nuts and oranges and candy and apples under the tree. I remember filberts, almonds, walnuts, pecans, and Brazil nuts. She would buy the chocolate drops that had different colors and flavors inside. Some of them we liked, and some we didn't. As kids we had a bad habit of going under the tree and biting the top off the chocolate drops to see which ones we liked. And if we didn't like them we'd sneak them back.

Mama also gave us a little money to Christmas shop. I think it was five dollars each. She took us up town and dropped us off. We'd go into the shops and buy gifts for the family. I would always get Dad handkerchiefs. And I was always pissed off because he never acted enthused about them. Later in life I thought, well, it was somewhat predictable. He would be lying in bed with his eyes closed, and I'd take his handkerchief in and give it to him. And he'd say, "Yeah," and lay it on the bed. He wouldn't even look at it. Of course, it always was the standard white linen handkerchief. But I wanted him to appreciate it each year.

Now that I'm old, I realize my father was an orderly person inside. And so to have all these noisy, boisterous kids, five kids. And Mama trained us well in terms of faith, personal discipline, and hard work. But she wasn't a real disciplinarian. So we were a wild bunch. And my poor Dad had to live with that. My goodness. But anyways, that would be Christmas.

Getting ready for the Christmas program at the church was one of the fun things about Christmas. We went to the Assembly of God Church when we were little. Weeks before, Mama would get the Montgomery Ward catalog and let Kay and me pick out our Christmas matching dresses. It was a collaborative effort. We would look at the colors and styles of dresses and negotiate which we both liked the best. We had to agree on a dress. I wore one for chubby girls, a size 12 or 14. Kay forever wore a 6X. One dress was a beautiful turquoise taffeta that shimmered in the light. We dressed alike for both Christmas and Easter.

Mama taught us all how to crochet because she loved crochet. And we learned how to quilt. And we learned how to patch clothes. She and Grandma had to patch Dad's and Papa's clothes. They'd be torn in the woods, or sparks would burn a hole. So we learned how to trim a hole and how to tuck it to make a nice, beautiful patch on their clothes. I did not take the cooking very well. I don't know if I was slow or they didn't have patience with me. But I just didn't learn the cooking thing. Kay did.

We did handwork with Mama and Grandma. I tried to knit, but I'm naturally left handed, so I would loop my thread the wrong way and just get it all tied up in knots. So I can knit now, but that didn't catch me. We used to make doll dresses. We always had access to Mama and Grandma's scraps of material. And we even had access to the linen drawers where they kept new things to embroider. They would buy pillowcases and scarves, chair sets, and other pieces. Mama would keep hers in the bottom drawer of her dresser. She would let us pick something out if we felt like doing some embroidery.

One day, I wanted to embroider. So she let me go and pick something out. She had just gotten this nice linen table scarf. And I picked it out. Mama's heart sank, but she let me have it. So I embroidered and finished it. Mama had a rule that you had to finish what you start.

When we wanted to quit something, she would say, "When a task is once begun; never leave it 'til it's done. Be the task great or small, do it well or not at all."

And then she bragged on me, "Oh, Pearl, that is so beautiful. But do you mind if I take out this flower and redo it?" Now, I didn't mind. So she took that flower out and redid it. "Oh, do you mind if I take this flower out and redo it?" So pretty quick I caught on that she was taking out all of my work. So when it got down to these two brown lines that connected the flowers on one end of the scarf to the other end and [she] said, "Oh, Pearl, do you mind if I take these out?" I said, "No, you can't take out any more." So I have that scarf today, and it has my little long brown stitches connecting Mama's beautiful flowers.

My strong political beliefs came from Mom and Dad. They were New Deal Roosevelt Democrats. I can remember when I was a little kid hearing them talk about Russia and Joseph Stalin and what was going on there. And I can remember them talking about the Sacco and Vanzetti trial. They always voted. So that's where I learned my political values, from Mom and Dad. I don't think Papa and Grandma had any politics, but they voted. But Mama and Dad talked politics.

So I enjoyed growing up in Wallowa. I have renewed childhood friendships and visit once a year. I'm a member of the Wallowa History Center and hope to contribute the historic African American community to their work.

I spent the first twelve years of my life growing up in Wallowa. We were the only African American family in town after the Langford family moved to La Grande. That was around 1953. I lived with my parents, Amos and Mary Marsh, Sr., and brothers and sisters, Amos Jr., Frank Wayne, Penny Merle and Kay Frances. Next door lived our grandparents Joseph and Arie Patterson. Everyone called them "Ma and Pa Pat."

We lived in a small three-room company house, owned by Bowman-Hicks Lumber Company. Every month, Mama went to town with money from Dad and paid our rent to Cecil Chrisman, the lawyer in town who collected rent for the Company. When the Langfords moved, we moved to the big house with five bedrooms and a large kitchen and living room.

In the winter, Kay Frances and I shared one of the bedrooms upstairs and my brothers shared the other. In the summer when it was way too hot, we moved to the bedrooms at the back of the house where it was cooler.

We didn't have indoor plumbing and Mama had to do all of her cooking, clothes washing, and cleaning with water packed from the communal pump. It was very hard for her, but like all women, she did her job. My sister and I learned "women's work" from Mama and Grandma. Kay was able in the kitchen, but I wasn't and didn't grow to like it.

Courtesy Pearl Alice Marsh
Pearl Alice with United Nations peacekeepers in Guinea, West Africa.

KAY FRANCES MARSH WYRICK

Kay Frances Marsh was born on June 5, 1948, in La Grande, Oregon. Her father is Amos, Sr., and her mother, Mary Patterson. Kay's grandparents were Joseph V. and Arie (Patterson), Sr. They were part of the Louisiana families that migrated through Arizona to Oregon.

Kay's family moved from Wallowa to Grass Valley, California, when she was ten years old. She attended Hennessy Elementary School and graduated from Nevada Union High School in 1966. After graduation, she attended San Jose State College in San Jose, California, where she majored in political science.

In her early career, Kay worked with Head Start children in San Jose. She went on to work in customer services for the Pacific Gas and Electric Company for nineteen years and Johnson and Johnson Pharmaceutical Company for twelve years. She retired in 2011.

Kay Frances married Joseph Henry Wyrick, Sr., on August 1, 1999, in Las Vegas, Clark County, Nevada. They couple remained married until his death in 2008 in San Jose, California.

Kay Frances

Courtesy Pearl Alice Marsh

Throughout Kay Frances's life, she has been an avid textile crafter, which she learned from her mother and grandmother. She sews in all genres—clothes, accessories, quilts, and craft projects. She loves the challenge of unique and advanced sewing techniques. While her work is much admired, she has not been tempted to start a business but instead shares her work generously with family and friends.

Her second leisure activity is bowling. She bowls in both winter and summer leagues in Modesto, California, and has developed a "respectable average" for a bowler her age.

And, finally, she volunteers in political campaigns, believing it is her civic responsibility as part of keeping our democracy strong.

Kay Frances's religious path followed her mother's, including the Assembly of God Church and Seventh-day Adventist Church in Wallowa. In her later years, she adopted an ecumenical form of worship and is comfortable celebrating in all faiths and religions.

Kay Frances retired to the California Central Valley, where she now resides.

I was born June 5, 1948, in La Grande, Oregon. I don't know the name of the hospital. I don't remember. I know it was not the hospital that my second oldest brother was born in, because I think that hospital closed sometime between his birth and that of some older siblings of mine.

My parents were Amos and Mary Marsh. On my mother's side, my grandparents were Arie and Joe Patterson. They lived in Wallowa next door to us. On my dad's side, my grandmother was Ollie and grandfather Albert Marsh. They lived in Choudrant, Louisiana.

I grew up in Oregon next door to my paternal grandparents for the first ten years of my life. In 1958, we moved about 700 miles away to Grass Valley, a small town in northern California in the mother lode where there had been a lot of gold mining.

Moving was exciting, going into a whole new, unknown place. But I also felt bad for leaving my grandparents behind. I don't remember the move being a traumatic experience. But there was a traumatic event associated with the move for me.

About a week before we left, there was this awful thunderstorm up in the mountains near Wallowa. And oh, it was just an awful night with lightning all about and thunder crashing down. I was a pretty skittish child. So I remember that more so than I do the move to northern California.

Thunderstorms were frequent in Wallowa. During the late summer, thunderstorms would roll up. This one was particularly bad. If a storm came up during the daytime, of course, it was daylight. But this storm came at night. Maybe that was part of the frightening aspect of this storm. This one happened at night when it was dark. So there was no electricity, no lights were on.

I was born in the era where if there was thunder and lightning, you turned off everything. Nowadays, you leave all power on; TV stays on; radio stays on; lights stay on. So with everything lit up, it's not quite as frightening as when it was all dark and the only light I could see was the lightning flash across the sky.

Mother, my two sisters, Pearl Alice and Penny Merle, and I were in the house. My brothers had gone to California with my dad to find a house. They were both in college. Papa and Grandma were in their house. I can't remember what anyone did to comfort me. I imagine Mother explained what was happening and to be calm.

I was a child then, but I still don't like being in total darkness. Hence I sleep with the light on in my bedroom. I always say you could shine a spotlight in my eyes, and it wouldn't prevent me from going to sleep. I could still sleep. When I wake up, I like light to be there.

My parents were from Louisiana. I don't remember much about my mother's childhood. I know there were stories told about her growing up. I don't know if she was reared in Louisiana or in Arizona, where she and Dad met later on. But Dad grew up on a farm in Louisiana. I know there was talk about that. I didn't sit still when they were reminiscing [about] their childhood and things that happened in the past. I'm not sure what I was doing. But I probably just wasn't listening when they were told.

There were four of us kids. My oldest brother Amos, Jr. And then under him is Frank, Frank Wayne. Next would have been Penny Merle. She was the special child. And then there was Pearl Alice and me. Pearl and I are just two years apart, and so we had a real close relationship growing up. You know, with sisters growing up and playing house and being outside. A lot of picking wildflowers and just being outdoors. So we enjoyed those kinds of activities.

There's seven and eight years between my brothers and me. My oldest brother

Courtesy Pearl Alice Marsh

Kay Frances in Wallowa. The house is one of the houses Bowman-Hicks set up for their black loggers. Descendants remember living throughout the town of Wallowa before the lumber company moved in housing.

is eight years, and seven with Frank. So me being the baby, I did what most babies do. I whined and nagged a lot. My oldest brother had more patience and was kind. The next brother did a lot of teasing. I can remember that. But they were old enough so that most of my activity was spent with Pearl. My daytime activities were with Pearl, either in the house or out of the house. In the winter when you couldn't be out of the house a lot, Frank and Amos enjoyed comic books. So they were in their rooms doing what boys do, I guess.

I'm what they called a "Daddy's baby." My dad was a tall man, physically. He had lots of muscle and was strong. He could beat up the big, bad wolf. He could take care of everything. And he did. He provided for us financially.

He wasn't fat. And he was handsome. He was a very good-looking man. So just the aura of him as a strong man drew me to him. And being the last child and baby, he spent a lot of time with me. He couldn't get rid of me as a little kid. If I wanted his attention, I would just hang around until he'd stoop over and pick me up. Whereas, I'm told, if my siblings wanted Dad's attention, he would say, "Go to your mama." But when he would give me those instructions, that wasn't what I wanted. I wanted his attention. So I would stand there. I forced myself into his world. And so that's how I bonded and expressed my love for my father. I really can't explain it any more than that. There's just something about Dad that made me like being in his company.

I was prepared to follow my daddy into hell if he had asked me to. I specifically told Mama I would get his paycheck when we got to hell. My mother was a good, practicing Christian, and my dad wasn't. Since I went to Sunday school, I knew that Christians go to heaven. And I know that those who don't believe go to hell. It was pretty basic back in those years. Now I know a lot of churchgoers would probably end up in hell too. But as a small child, maybe four or five, I didn't have a concept of hell. My dad played poker up town at Earl Haney's pool hall, and I overheard a conversation that he was going to hell. So I decided I would to go to hell with my daddy because we could shoot pool and play poker together. I'd go with him. Hell didn't seem frightening, especially if I was there with my father. I would be safe. So that was why I say I would follow my daddy into hell and back.

I met my paternal grandparents on my dad's side of the family once. We went to

157

Louisiana when I was about five years old. We went with my dad's brother Alvie, who lived with his family about forty-eight miles away. He lost his wife. They had five children, so he took his children to Louisiana. Dad took the opportunity to take us along.

We caravanned together in two cars. Somewhere between Albuquerque, New Mexico, and Lubbock, Texas, we got separated. Dad was driving ninety miles an hour trying to catch Uncle Alvie. Mom told him to slow down because Uncle Alvie was behind us. Dad grumbled because he didn't believe her but slowed down anyway. Shortly after, Uncle Alvie came speeding by in his big dark-green Mercury. He had been trying to catch us. Dad grinned and we got back into our caravan.

I don't remember too much about the trip. I know it was long. And I certainly got tired of riding in a car all that distance. The car was crowded. Mother, Dad, and our sister Penny were in the front seat. Amos, Frank, Pearl, and I were all in the back. Even though we were small, it was still tight. I recall spending one evening somewhere in Albuquerque because one of the cars had trouble. There was a café nearby where we ate. It was some good food, down-home cooking. I remember the grits. I don't know much else about the meal. But it was a nice, comforting place because of the bad weather that was going on outside.

At one point, there was squabbling among us kids and Mama had to stop the car. I remember when we were coming back to Oregon, I was going from the front seat to the back seat, bouncing back and forth. I couldn't be still. And the car wasn't stopped. At some point, Dad's belt came off, and I felt it slapping me across the rear as I went across into the back seat. That caused me to sit still in my place for a while.

In Louisiana, my grandmother talked about giving Dad a whipping, and I had defended my father very aggressively. But after he hit me with the belt coming back home, I told him I wish I had let Grandmama whip his butt. Probably not in those terms, but I definitely let him know that.

When we got older, my father introduced me to gambling. When I turned twenty-one, our first trip was to Reno. And the gambling bug caught me too. I like gaming. I like the casinos, the bright lights and putting the coins in the slots.

Now, he had more discipline than I have about money, because I tend to go overboard with gambling. And Dad never did do that. And then he liked going to baseball games. So when he got older—or even when he was younger, with his grandchildren—he liked taking them down to see the Giants. And so I would always go along. Pearl too, when she was in town. But Pearl, being two years older than I am, went away to college. So during my high school life and early adulthood, I think I was more in Dad's company and doing things with his grandchildren.

It was just a pleasure to be able to do those things with Dad and for Dad. I really can't explain that love any differently than that. I felt safe when I was around Dad. He was always the protector. I had a car once that I had back in the '60s when the gas prices were high. People were running around and siphoning gas out of the cars. So I had this locking gas cap that I put on my car that I couldn't get off. I lost the key. But my dad actually twisted that cap off. Of course in the process he cut himself bad on something that was hanging. But he muscled it off.

So maybe that's what it was that I appreciated about Dad. I don't know if—my bromance with my Dad. Can I call it a bromance? I truly was in love with my father. And I loved my mother too. We moved to California, and that first winter Dad wanted to go back to Wallowa. And I wanted to go with my father. And so I did. Now, along the trip I really started to miss my mother. I can recall that when we finally got to Wallowa and went into the house, my grandmother had a niece from Texas who had moved to Wallowa to live with them. And she and my mother—same family, same genes—resembled each other. She looked so much like my mother to me. And that was such a comforting feeling when I walked in the house.

But it didn't keep me from leaving my mother in Grass Valley. And she probably reminded me of that when I mentioned how much I missed her and how much Macy reminded me of her. She told me all that love didn't keep me from leaving and going to Oregon with my dad. That was a wonderful trip. We went to see our grandparents, and I went with Dad, and from there we left and came back through Corvallis where my older brother was going to college. And then from there we came home. It was bad weather and snowstorms. So I don't recall that.

My later years now—if I had been eighteen or nineteen, I don't think I would have ventured off. Especially not [with] my father driving in snow. Because driving was kind of scary at times. But as [I was] a ten-year-old, he knew what he was doing. And I didn't know that I was in harm's way. I was with my father.

While my father was the provider, my mother was a homemaker. She stayed home and raised children. That meant a lot of cooking, cleaning, washing, ironing, managing our lives, homework, school, all of those things. Our father was a log cutter. He worked seasonally. During the spring, summer, into the early fall, at least when snow was not on the ground, he logged. During the winter, the woods were idle. So he and Mama made ends meet until work came again.

Mama did a lot of handwork. She enjoyed quilting but also did it out of necessity with five kids and all those beds to maintain. She pieced a lot of quilts. She and my grandmother would piece the tops and then quilt them out.

In order to get the quilts to the bed quickly in time, some were what they call "tied out." You take long strands of either yarn or a doubled, thick crochet thread. And you make these long stitches across the quilt. Then you snip the stitches in the middle and tie the ends into a knot. They were tied-out quilts.

I know now that my mother didn't like scrap quilting. In her later years, she got away from the homespun type and started to make quilts with matching materials that were very beautiful. She began to make quilts that she thought were more appealing to the eye. Her favorite was the Texas stars, sometimes called the Star of David or Christmas star. The pattern even had a few Native American names. It's made with diamonds; eight points. And so that was her special quilt.

Later on she made a double wedding ring, which was a lot of little pieces to hand stitch together. She did a lot of hand piecing. I don't recall her ever sitting at the sewing machine to put those pieces together. This is why I developed a love for sewing.

We have a few of her quilts made from simple blocks that were sewn together and tied out. To get the material for the homespun quilt as we called them, Mom and Grandma took old, worn-out material from Grandfather, Dad, maybe some friends' old

Courtesy Pearl Alice Marsh
Kay and Frank at Chief Joseph Days.

clothes.

They hold special memories now and are probably appreciated by me more than the pretty double wedding ring quilt that she hand-made.

There was a social worker who used to stop by the house all the time. Her first name was Claire. She worked in social services in a neighboring town called Enterprise. She and Mother socialized together, always having fresh coffee. I don't recall there actually being a coffee thing going between them. But Mother being a gracious hostess would certainly have offered something, and Claire would accept.

Claire then would bring nice clothing that came into social services. I guess they would have had something like a community closet, where people donate clothing that was given out to people who need it. At some point, she started bringing Mother the nicer coats, wool coats, and fabric for quilts.

Other than that, regular quilting mate-rial would have come from old clothing from [my] grandfather, uncle, and aunts. Then we would get a chance to buy new clothing to make up for what you didn't have.

When Dad's clothes got torn at work, Mother patched his clothing as well as she could. She patched what made sense to patch. But if you put patches over patches, then that's extra work. She kept his clothes in good repair. I don't recall my dad wearing clothing with a knee or elbow out or a tear or a rip. She would patch them right away.

I remember how you patch. Wherever a hole or tear is in the clothing, for instance the knee, you cut out a patch of cloth of similar fabric one-half to three-quarters of an inch larger than the hole, all the way around. When you center it underneath the hole, it would have exceeded beyond the hole all the

Courtesy Pearl Alice Marsh
Amos and Pearl Alice at Chief Joseph Days.

way around. And so then at that, it's called appliqué. Kind of like needle turning. And then on the top part, which would have been the actual clothing article itself, you turn the edge around and stitch that down so it didn't fray in the washings. And then you do a running stitch to sew a rectangle around that hole where you turned under the edge. And

Courtesy Pearl Alice Marsh

Brothers Amos Marsh, Sr's Louis and Alvie

then in the back, if there was fabric extending beyond the running stitch, you trim it down a little bit. The running stitch also helped keep the piece from fraying along the edges or coming apart when it went through the laundry.

Mother used a scrub board sometimes, but in my years as a child she had purchased a washing machine, which had an old dasher. It could really work some clothes over when you were doing laundry. Not like this modern stuff.

I don't think I ever patched with Mother. I did make string blocks with my grandmother. That's where you take a sheet of paper, like a telephone book or newspaper, to cut a strip pattern. Then you lay one strip of cloth on it faced right side up. You lay a second strip onto that fabric with the right side down, matching the edges. And then you sew along the one edge. When you finished, you flip that piece open. So then you have two right sides up. And then you lay another piece down on that piece. And then you continue until you had covered the whole block.

This allowed for something like crazy quilting, except these were all strips, and they all went across the paper. It was one

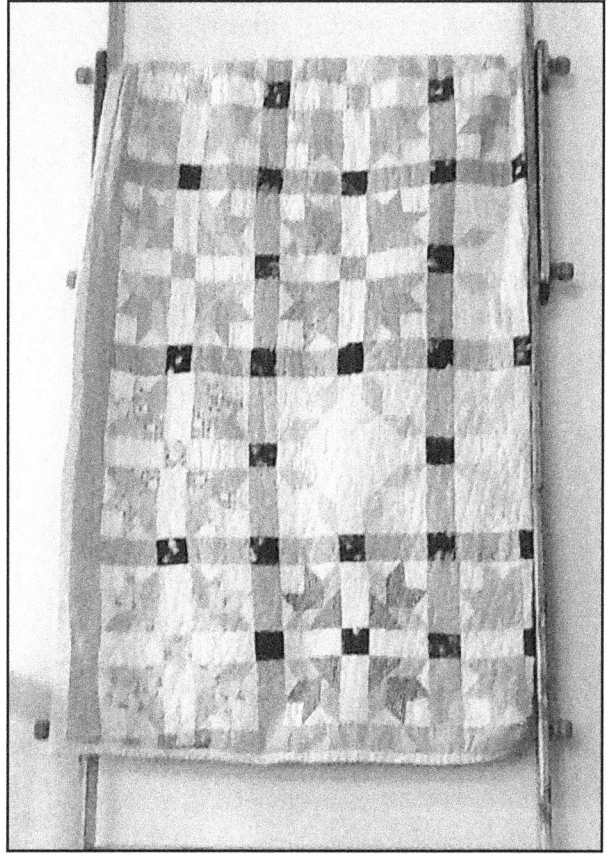

Courtesy Pearl Alice Marsh

One of the traditions of the pioneer women was to make a friendship quilt for beloved friends when they moved away. The women would piece the quilt and embroidery their names into the blocks.

This is a quilt made by the ladies of Mary's church for her when the Marsh family moved to California.

way to use up the scraps that you couldn't cut blocks out of or other geometric patterns.

Crazy quilting is done the same way except then it takes pieces of any kind of size, irregular pieces. You lay one piece on another and appliqué them down. Then you use a fancy embroidery stitch to hide some exposed seams that might be showing. When you're just trying to get quilts on the bed, string quilts is the way to go.

Pages from the telephone book were the backing for laying the pieces together. As I look back, I think it provided some stabilization for sewing the fabric. That way if you had some really stretchy fabric, you could still sew a piece against one that was not quite as stretchy and not have it stretch out of place. So they used pages out of the telephone book.

At the end, you could either tear the paper off, or you could leave the paper on as you put the blocks together. It provided some additional

Closeup of a quilt made by Kay.

thickness, like batting used a lot now in quilts. Back then I recall Mother purchasing some batting. But that was also an expense. We grew up with five children, and our Dad worked seasonally.

Mother could stretch a dollar better than anybody that I know. There wasn't a lot of money available to go out and buy batting, which was a real easy, simple thing to improvise. She used old sheets that were worn or older blankets inside as the batting between the quilt top and the quilt bottom. So that paper also added an extra layer of warmth.

Mother quilted at home. I don't remember in which room she quilted. She and my grandmother quilted together. Sometimes she would go down, and they would be in my grandmother's living room. And they would sew quilts. Now, we had an old treadle sewing machine. I know Mother used that for sewing. Exactly where it was set up in the house, I don't recall.

Mother made a few clothes. One year for a church program she made Pearl and me matching dresses that I thought were so pret-

A quilt block made by Kay.

ty. But she didn't make a lot of our clothes. Most were purchased. I don't remember the color of those dresses. But the material was kind of a sheer fabric and a floral print of some kind. It had a lot of gathering around the waist. So we needed a petticoat to make them stand out. I think petticoat might be the only name I can recall. We also called them "can-cans." Can-cans—yes, that's the name. Can-can skirts. So being the flirty type, I thought they were cute. The more fabric you had, the

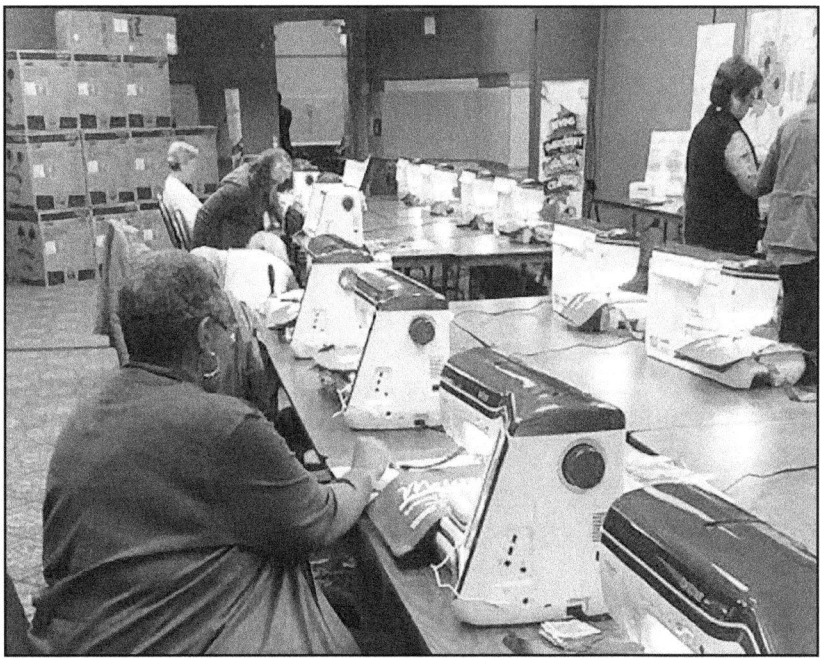

Courtesy Pearl Alice Marsh
Kay Marsh at the Pacific International Quilt show in Santa Clara, CA.

farther out your skirt stood. So that was the going fashion. Anyway, she made those dresses, and I can remember being very proud of my dress when we went for the Christmas program.

In my later years I developed a true love for sewing by being around my mother and grandmother. They allowed both Pearl and me to use scraps that they weren't going to use in quilts. Mother taught me how to make a set-in sleeve. You know, how to cut a pattern that had the sleeve cap and then how to set it into the opening, which they call the "armscye." And then, to make the skirts, you take a long rectangle and gather and stitch it that on to the bodice.

I cut out a few doll-clothes patterns under her tutelage and made them. Later on, in my teen years, she never denied me a pattern that I wanted to buy. She never said the fabric was too expensive for my sewing skills and capabilities or denied me my wishes and wants.

She allowed me, when I was maybe age fourteen and living in California, to make a dress and jacket out of some expensive brocade. I can't tell you the amount of money she paid for the fabric. But, probably back in those days in the early '60s, twenty dollars for fabric was more than most people would want to let a teenager cut up. But she believed in me. And she always inspired me to be the best and do the best that I could. So I made a very nice dress and jacket out of this pink brocade. And it was beautiful. I can't remember how long I had it. After some church social in Sacramento, I remember someone spilled punch on it. And then we just could never get the stain out of the dress. That was a very nice outfit that I made.

One other standout, [speaking of] can-cans, I made a dress to go to a school dance in eighth grade. And the dress had spaghetti straps, but they were probably about an inch wide. I don't know if that's really spaghetti straps. Probably lasagna straps without

Courtesy Pearl Alice Marsh
Kay ironing quilt pieces like her mother and grandmother would have done.

the curl! The dress was open in the back. And the panel piece in the back had this island of ruffles all the way down. But of course, I never took my sweater off because I was a shy girl at that point. And exposing your arms was more than I could handle. But I thought the dress was pretty cute anyway.

When Mother was teaching me how to set in a sleeve in this little doll dress—that's the part you called the "armscye"—she showed me how to cut out the bodice from a rectangle. On one corner you cut out the circle or quarter circle for the neck. And then on the opposite corner, you cut out an elongated piece for the armhole. And that's the armscye side. Then you place that rectangle on a fold so that when you cut it out, you have a half circle for the neck. And you have then the armscye for the front.

Now to the front, of course, you had to give it some shape. So you sew a dart along the bottom of that rectangle piece so you could bring it in for the waist. And you make a front and a back and put it together. Next, in order to have the poof on top of your shoulder, to make room for it, you had to cut the sleeve out to match that. And I can't really tell you the terminology for it now. I've had enough sewing classes at community college. I should know these terms.

I did all of this without a store-bought pattern. I made my own pattern for the doll. I would take a piece of paper, draw the pattern, and cut it out before pinning it to my cloth.

Patterns come in pieces. The top part of the pattern is the bodice. I took a rectangle-shape piece of material, cut areas for armholes and a neck. And then in order to give it some shape to the edge to be attached to the skirt and allow for a bust, I made a dart.

Mother taught me how to crochet with a needle. The needle has a hook on it. We started with a chain stitch and then hooked the end stitches together. She really loved crocheting, and I didn't. I learned how to crochet, but I didn't develop a love for it. Not like Mother did.

Our bedding was pretty because it had embroidery on all the pillowcases and edgings that were crocheted. And she made a lot of doilies to put on tabletops and three-piece sets to put on the back and arms of the sofa or chair. That was something that she liked doing.

She even made tablecloths. I remember a tablecloth that she made and sold it somewhere, I want to say for over $300. I wouldn't have made it. It's just way too much time as far as I'm concerned. But it was a very nice tablecloth.

It was swell to take a pattern and start making a little circle and then crocheting around it to make it larger. But I never developed a love for crocheting. For some reason I wanted to knit, and Mother didn't know how to knit. I joined 4-H at about eight years old. And then I learned how to knit. I appreciated knitting more than I did crochet.

I loved to sew. My sewing started from age five. But other than the string quilting, I didn't do any sewing with Grandma. She made quilts, and I don't recall any quilting. My grandmother also had a passion for embroidery. So I learned how to embroider with her. That was something we did together. We embroidered pillowcases mainly. I enjoyed doing embroidery with Grandma. I enjoyed her company for sure.

My relationship with my grandmother was very special. She had a lot of patience with me. Being the last child, my sibling next to me, Pearl, went to school two years ahead of me. So I had a lot of time to be by myself. My grandmother certainly filled that void.

A housewife back in those days spent quite a bit of time in the kitchen after breakfast was done. During the summer, that was when she would have time between breakfast and dinner to do the handwork that she liked to do, the embroidery work.

My favorite time with her was when I would get up in the morning and go down to her house. She had a little black cast-iron skillet. And I loved eggs. She would let me scramble my own eggs for breakfast. I thought that was pretty special.

When she would bake cakes, I did a lot of watching and learning. She would let me beat the cake batter or pour some ingredients into the bowl. During the winter when my grandfather was home, of course, she cooked breakfast, lunch, and dinner. He had three meals. So she and I spent a lot of time in the kitchen to prepare those meals.

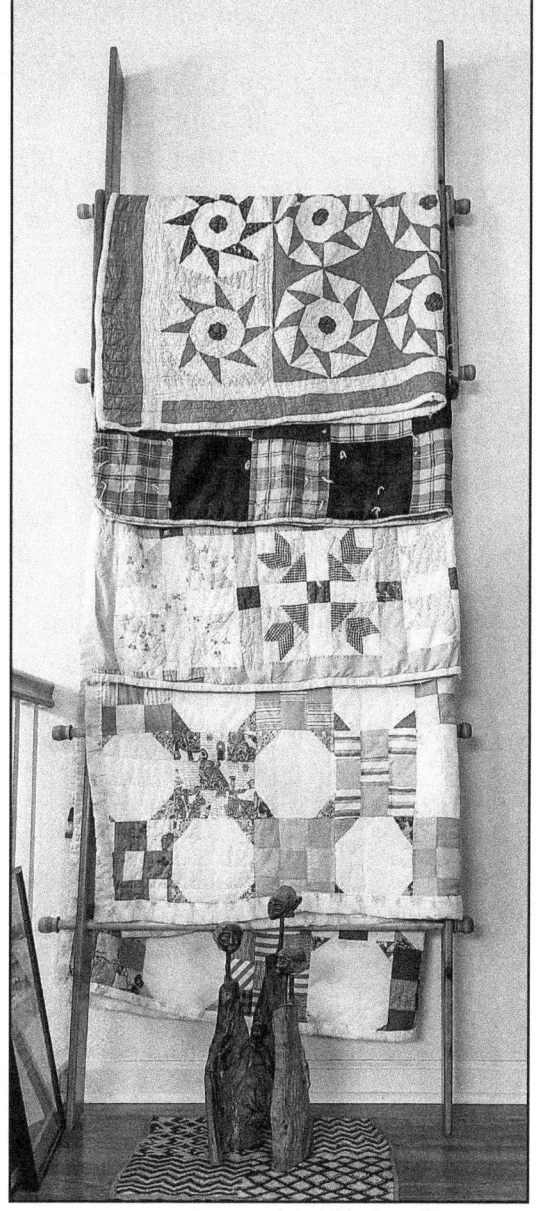

Courtesy Pearl Alice and Kay Marsh
A display of quilts made by Mary Marsh.

It was certainly a special time with my grandmother. I stayed down in her house in the evening. I would be down there after supper. And then, late at night, my father would be one or two doors away visiting a friend. When he headed home, he would give a yell out in front of grandmother's house. I remember going out to meet him. I'm sure Pearl was there sometimes too. We would go out, and he would walk us home to our house, which was maybe fifty yards away.

Once upon a time, there would have been a dwelling between our two houses. And at some point, that house was taken down. So as a child, it seemed like a wide expanse of darkness in which a lot of bogeymen would hang out and get a little girl if they wanted. So Dad walked us home. And sometimes he put us up on his shoulders. He was about six three. I felt like I was really on top of the world going home. It felt safe.

I was afraid of the bogeyman. Yes, I was. I was afraid of the bogeyman because my older sister, Pearl Alice, introduced me to the idea of the bogeyman. We didn't have an indoor toilet, so at night, I had to use a potty in the house. That potty was in the bedroom. At night, if we were in the living room and it was dark in the bedroom, I didn't want to go in there to go potty. Mother would say, "Girl, you better go to the bedroom and go potty." So during one of those exchanges, I said, "The bogeyman will get me if I go in there." And she asked, "How do you know about a bogeyman? Who told you about the bogeyman?" And I said, "Pearl told me about the bogeyman." So from then on, if I had to go potty, Pearl would have to go into the bedroom with me, which irritated her to no end. That was her punishment for introducing her scary sister to the bogeyman.

So at some point in time, maybe I would never have become frightened of the dark. I would have had a little more nerve in order to do that.

Growing up as siblings, Pearl taught me a lot of good things now along the way. When she went to school, she learned her ABCs. And she came home and taught me the alphabet, and I had some word recognition too. So I had a few skills when I entered first grade because Pearl shared her knowledge with me along the way. I don't know if she's ever had any regrets for the bogeyman experience. She might have enjoyed that I was frightened. Older sisters like to do that to the younger ones.

Mother and Grandma did a lot of cooking. I remember the fire and the cooking stove and a pot of beans on top. I don't remember spending time with Mother in the kitchen and actually cooking. She didn't have patience. My cooking happened at Grandmother's house. She would take time to explain what she was doing and allow me to assist. I loved to help her make cakes. Now, I don't recall any other preparation that went on.

Mother had a plate full. We had a sister Penny who could not walk or talk. The term that we used back in those days is not politically correct, but she was a spastic child. So Mother had a lot of things to do during the day taking care of Penny.

We left Oregon when I was ten. And by then, I knew how to do some cooking. I don't recall it being a hands-on teaching experience from that point on. It was more observation than anything. And I didn't observe enough because my mother made one of the best bread puddings in the world. And I never once stopped to try to figure out how she made it. I just know that it was very good, and I really enjoyed it. I regret that I didn't ask her more.

The only thing I asked her about making was Swiss steak. So I can make a pretty good Swiss steak. It's made with a cubed steak. The gravy is tomato based from a can of stewed tomatoes. So anyway, my later cooking skills came from observing Mother cooking.

One interesting thing I learned from Mother was how you make a cake by hand. You have to make sure all the ingredients are blended together well. So after creaming the butter and sugar and adding the flour, baking soda, some salt, and milk, you had to make sure you had a creamy, smooth batter. So she would beat it three times for three hundred beats each time. And she would count those out loud by tens. There is a term, but I can't remember. She would count from 1 all the way to 20. And when she got to 20, she would say "20." And then she would count 1, 2, 3, 4, 5, 6, 7, 8, 9. And then say "30." Then when she got to the next tens, she would call that number out, 30, 40, 50, and so on. I remember beating cakes that way.

Mother and Grandma cooked on woodstoves. Sunday meals were always big with fried or roasted chicken, stewed chicken, yams, some type of greens, and cornbread. And of course there would have been a cake.

Certainly the holidays, Christmas especially, was when we had the big turkey. Turkey is always impressive when it's roasted. Mother always nestled her turkey down in the dressing to cook. Grandmother cooked her turkey separately. She roasted her turkey. And then after it was done, she would put it down in the pan of dressing. It was a big thing to do at our house.

I marvel now in my older years thinking how Mother and Grandmother were able to cook those big meals on a woodstove, but they could do it. When the stove was roaring hot, if you put a pan on it, it goes from zero to burn your food up instantly. So you had to know your stove.

Courtesy Pearl Alice Marsh

Frank, Penny and Amos, Jr.

There were spots where you could bring a pot to a boil, if that was needed to get the cooking process started. And then move it over to a cooler spot to cook at a slower pace at a lower temperature. I would burn a meal if I had to cook one that way, because I wasn't very observant. My sister, Pearl, wasn't into that process either. I got burned more than once on the stove. I think we all did.

We also heated our home with wood. So we had a tin woodstove for heating.

Eventually, we all got a burn, but it only took one burn to teach you how to stay off the heater in order not to get burned. When the heater was roaring flames, there was a concern of safety too. I'm sure that we weren't allowed to open the oven and take something out of the oven.

We grew up where Mother and Grandma did a lot of canning. When you grow up in the country, certainly you can buy food at the store. But when you've got five children, like my mother and father, a garden comes in handy. Our food came from Papa's gardens. He loved gardening. He had two plots, one behind the house and one located uptown about a mile from home where someone allowed him to use some of their land. I remember going up to the garden with Papa and enjoying being out in nature with him. It's nice to see things grow.

I loved strawberries. And he always grew strawberries. And of course I had the urge to pick them too quickly when they were still green around the top where they were

Courtesy Linda Bauck

Old pioneer orchards were generously scattered throughout the area and were a favorite place for women to gather fruit, especially apples and plums for canning.

connected to the vines. So he would always have to say, "No, don't pick them." And corn. I loved picking and shucking corn. My mother and grandmother would can food from the garden for the winter.

Everybody canned. It wasn't just our mother. In our circle, there were friends who canned also. A lot of the women did canning. Canning was an involved process. I wasn't allowed to be in this process. But we watched when the greens were washed, cut up, and parboiled to go into the jars.

A lot of water was used. We didn't have indoor plumbing, so we would help Mama and Grandmother pack buckets and buckets of water from the outdoor pump.

The stove was kept roaring hot so boiling water could be used in a big container to sterilize jars. There were regular-mouth jars and wide-mouth jars.

A lot of water was needed to wash, cut up, and scald and parboil food. I remember tomatoes being put into a pot of scalding water to take off the skin. The same with peaches. And they would triple or quadruple wash the greens—mustard, collard, turnip—cut them up and parboil them to stuff in the jars.

Some of the fruit came from wild orchards. We picked apples, peaches, and plums. Mother made jelly. There was an orchard in the canyon across from the river, let's say seven or eight miles out of the town, that didn't seem to belong to anyone. But people could go and pick those apples. We call them crab apples. They were too tart for eating. But Mama would pick the apples and bring them home. She and Grandmother would can some apples and make jelly. Grandmother made preserves from strawberries. And of course preserves have whole fruit or whole chunks in them. I imagine Mother knew how to do it, but I remember Mother making more jellies, [in] which all the fruit pulp is pureed down and the juice is taken out for the jelly.

I imagine some of the fruit came from people who lived in the area or orchards in places like Hermiston and Walla Walla, which wasn't too far from us. So in the summer, a truck farmer would

Courtesy Linda Bauck

Jams made from plums gleaned from an old pioneer plum tree.

come through Wallowa with fruit.

My grandfather raised pigs to slaughter for meat. He and my dad hunted for deer also, so we had deer meat for the winter. Now, when the deer were shot and brought home, Mother and Grandmother were really involved. I can picture in my mind the deer being hung up and the hide being cut off. And then, after Dad and Papa finished cleaning it, Mother and Grandmother would cut up the meat to put it in usable pieces like steaks and roasts.

Once the pigs had been slaughtered, they didn't skin them. To take the hair off, they would fill a barrel with hot scalding water and submerge the dead pig, which made it easy to scrape the bristles off of the pig.

They hung the dead animals up

Photohrapher Hiram Merry, Wallowa History Center
Two men butchering hogs that they had raised. They are preparing to scald them and scrape off the hair. No part of a hog was wasted. This is similar to the way Kay's dad and Pa Pat would have prepared and butchered their pigs.
Hiram Merry, photographer, was a homesteader and amateur photographer of the area who did a superb job of recording the early way of life in the North end of Wallowa County.

in the yard from some pine trees. There were two tall trees in front of one of the small houses we lived in. I don't know who put the crossbar up between the trees, but a bar was anchored to the trees high up and then a pulley so they could get the deer or pig up off of the ground so he would be hanging by the legs with the head hanging down. Some of this had to do with— this sounds awful now that I think about it—draining blood out of these animals. They were hanged by their hind legs so they could cut and strip the skin off of the animal.

Deer liver. We always had liver that first evening when the deer was killed. It was a ritu-

Courtesy Wallowa History Center
Wallowa, Oregon in winter. The grader is plowing snow. Street lights were hanging over the center of the street. The Hardware store is first on the right, then Shell Mercantile is the second store on the right.

169

al. The liver was smothered in onions and eaten with biscuits and syrup. And then with pigs, our grandmother used to make something in a gravy with liver and what they call "lights," which was kind of spongy. She put it over rice. Most people enjoyed it. I remember picking out the spongy parts. Later on, I found out that spongy stuff was the pig's lungs. So I'm glad I picked it out.

Uptown there was a store that rented locker freezers. So after all the meat was cut up, it was taken up to the locker. Before we left Oregon, Papa bought Grandmother a big chest freezer that looked like a huge casket. Then the meat was kept at home instead of uptown. Some place uptown or in Enterprise, they would even cure meat for you, probably the pig hams for you. It was some of the best-tasting meat in the world.

Now I don't like wild meat because I think it taste gamey. Also, my social sensitivities stop me. It's not extreme animal rights, but I feel a bit more for animals now. I don't even eat as much meat as I would have eaten back in those days. I still like liver, but I gave it up these days because back then, calf liver was really delicious. But I'm leaning toward animal rights, so I don't eat calf liver anymore. Chicken liver is okay. And I do eat a little chicken. For some reason, it's easier for me to eat chicken than it is to know that a deer or cow has been killed for food. Maybe because I watched my Grandma wring her chickens' necks to kill them. I don't know.

All of this meat preparation took a lot of water, as with the fruits and vegetables for canning. Without indoor plumbing, water in buckets was packed to the work areas. Later, my grandfather had a pump at his house.

We knew Dad was the authority in the house even though my mother enforced that authority. She had the belt, and she was the disciplinarian. She was always telling us, "I'll tell your father about this." And we certainly didn't want her to tell Father about it. We didn't know whether he would or wouldn't act on it, but we felt he might. He didn't spank us, but we didn't want him to know we were bad children. So she kept us in control that way. We knew that Dad was the head.

When my father came home in the evening after work on paydays, he would have the check for Mother. He wore coveralls, so one of his suspenders would have been loosened already so he could go straight in and get clean. Logging was a dirty business.

Father used a gas chainsaw in the woods, and the chain would need to be sharpened almost every night. He used a file on the teeth and filed them one at a time, checking them with his finger, until they were ready for the woods.

Father drove the loggers' truck that was called the candy wagon, a truck with a little room over the chassis. All the men in the community rode the candy wagon when they went to the woods in the morning and came home at night. When it was really cold and freezing outside, Dad would build a fire in a little tin heater inside the wagon. Sometimes he would build a little fire underneath the truck in order to thaw the water in the radiator because it would be that cold in Wallowa.

In the summertime, this candy wagon would come home with some very good-tasting dirt on the back of it. Pearl and I would sneak around and lick the back before anyone could catch us. Some of that came from the fact that our grandmother was a snuff dipper. So Pearl and I probably tried pretending it was snuff. On the inhale with real snuff, if you did it wrong, you'd have a coughing seizure that told you that's not the route to take with powdered tobacco. Candy wagon dirt was different, and it tasted good. But we didn't let anybody catch us because dirt was dirty, and if Mama caught us, we'd get verbally chastised or a spanking. So Pearl and I had that secret ritual when the candy wagon came home.

Sometimes when Father came home, he'd go down and have supper with my grand-father and my grandmother at their house. The kids ate at home with Mother. I'm not sure why exactly. Maybe she gave us a meal a little bit earlier in the day because Father got home late. Or maybe he thought Grandmother was a better cook. And I tend to think she was

Courtesy Wallowa History Center
Wallowa Cash Market, popularily called "Shorty's." Shorty McKenzie was the owner.

too. Anyway, he would go down to Grandmother's house.

Mother could get food on the table, and it was tasty and would fill you up, but Grandmother put those little nuances to cooking that gave it a nice extra special flavor. She always had cake. With five kids at our house, cake didn't last too long, so Father didn't always get a piece. At Grandmother's house, she would have cake every day, and he was always assured a piece.

When Father didn't bring the check home directly on paydays, Mother would go to Ed Holloran's office and pick up his check. That was always a big deal if she let us go with her. On the way home, we'd stop at Shorty's store to cash the check and pay the grocery bill. She always bought at least one or two goodies for us kids on that stop at the store. I can really recall red or orange or rainbow popsicles. We'd get candy too. I loved Hershey bars. So we were allowed to get a candy bar or popsicle or ice cream cone. That was a fun time.

My father worked for Ed Holloran and Son logging company when I was growing up. The store where we did regular shopping we called Shorty's. I don't know if it had a more formal name or not. But the owner of the store, his nickname was Shorty; McKenzie was his last name. I don't even know Shorty's first name. But anyway, the store was called Shorty's. And that's where we predominantly did the shopping.

Now, about faith in our family. My dad was a believer; he just wasn't a religious person and didn't go to church. He was raised in the Olive Grove Baptist Church founded by his grandfather in Louisiana. He went to church when he was a child and didn't have a choice. But once he did, he never went again except for funerals. He left home about age thirteen or fourteen to work to help support the family. So that's when he ventured away from an organized church. But he was a religious person in his soul.

I remember him singing what they call "long meter" in the church. A leader starts a song off, slowly singing the first line, and the congregation sings the line back slowly in the same tone. This is done a cappella. Mama called this music "mournful." It sounded somber, almost gloomy, recalling hardships. The music softly tailed off at the end in a hush. The church was in a serious moment when the congregation sang long meter.

Mother was a churchgoing lady. My first recall of a church is Assembly of God church, a Pentecostal church. My mother didn't go to Sunday services every week. As I mentioned before, we had a sister who was handicapped. So it was a chore for Mother to take Penny out. If we were out in a public space and there was a lot of attention being paid to her, Penny would get agitated, and Mama had to take her home. Who likes to be stared at? And I don't know if people were staring. For that reason Mother mostly went to the church services when my grandmother would care for Penny.

My brothers, sister, and I went to Sunday school all the time. In the summer, we also had vacation Bible school. And that was fun because we learned crafts. There were four or five different churches in Wallowa, and each one had vacation Bible school. All of the kids were spread out between the different churches. In order to have a nice number of children, they ran it at different times so the kids could go to all the vacation Bible schools. You could call it the vacation Bible school circuit.

Our mother taught us about Jesus and scriptures at home. In the evening, she read Bible scriptures to us. She taught us the Lord's Prayer as our bedtime prayer when we were just young children. We didn't learn "Now I Lay Me Down to Sleep" for bedtime. I didn't learn it until my adolescence, in my early teens. The prayer we said at night before bed was the Lord's Prayer. Mother said if we were ever in trouble, we could call on the Lord's Prayer. That would be more helpful than "Now I Lay Me." And so she taught us that and the 23rd Psalm, "The Lord is my shepherd."

We learned other verses in the church too, especially for Easter and Christmas. Those were big times at our church for having special programs. Children always had to learn a verse for their part in the church pageant.

When I was about seven, my mother became a Seventh-day Adventist. So we went from going to church on Sundays to going to church on Saturdays, which was called Sabbath. Some of her church people in the Assembly of God stopped speaking to Mother because she switched. They seemed personally offended and just knew she was headed to hell.

But church was a big part of our life when we were young. We went to church a lot.

In 1958, when we moved to California, she joined the church in Grass Valley. Four years later, our sister Penny passed away. That really broke my mother's heart and my father's also. It was really an awful time, especially for the two of them. I know that I didn't experience the loss to the degree that they did. I don't think a child can experience a loss that a parent has for a child.

After Penny's death, Mother was very active in the church. She went to church on Saturday at Sabbath. Then she went back midweek for prayer service. I got out of prayer service because I had school the next day. She joined the Dorcas group, which was their community service group, made quilts for them, and aided families in the community. She was very actively involved in the church at that point in time. So religion and church have been a big part of my early life.

As we grew up, both of my brothers graduated from Wallowa High School. They were both athletes, especially Amos, Jr. So they had their friends. Pearl was my childhood playmate. I had brothers, but that was just it. They were just older brothers, and they didn't want to be bothered with little, young, sissy girls. And I don't blame them. Pearl was more of a tomboy and not scared of anything, so she could at least make them take her along sometimes.

I was truly a pain in the butt. If it didn't go my way, I didn't want to be involved. And my feelings got hurt very easily, and I cried a lot. I was your typical spoiled whiner. I whined and nagged all the time. So as far as a relationship with my brothers in terms of doing things with me, it didn't happen. I was being the last child, the baby in the family.

Pearl and I played outside year-round. I thought Pearl could do everything. Pearl taught me how to jump rope. We tied one end of the rope to a tree, and then the other would turn the rope. Pearl taught me my alphabet because she went to school first. So when she'd come home, she would teach me whatever she learned.

There was a field not too far from our house. I remember in the spring and summer, there were lots of wildflowers—bluebells, buttercups, dandelions, lupines, stickers with yellow flowers—they grew wild. I can remember running and playing down in that field. We did one thing that was kind of awful. There was one pine tree that had been a big gash. A bunch of ants lived in that tree. We used to kill grasshoppers with a stick. We would tap them on the top of the head enough to knock them out, place the dead grasshopper in the gash, and watch the ants dissect the grasshopper and pack away the pieces wherever they lived.

But mostly we did girl things like play house. We learned how to bake some really wonderful mud pies and mud cakes, all taught by Pearl.

I was a pain for Pearl too. When she got invited to parties I would cry my way into going. And then at the party, when they would play games, I wasn't very good. So I would win booby prizes and embarrass Pearl.

As we grew older, I began to hold my own a little bit. Except then she wanted to turn into the mother role.

I vaguely remember other African American households in Wallowa. I left Wallowa at age ten, so I don't have much memory moving back that far. During that time, my time was spent playing with Pearl and visiting Grandma and Papa.

I know a family, the Langfords, lived in Wallowa, but I remember them after they moved to La Grande when I was four or five years old. They would come from La Grande on a Sunday to visit, or at least they'd come out to eat Grandmother's cooking (like everybody did), and the children would come, and we would play. But I don't have any special dates that I remember.

There were families without children who lived in Wallowa. We all lived along the same row of company houses. There was a couple named Powell that we called Ms.

Carrie and Uncle Smokey, and another couple, Hosea and Lucy Lowry.

Uncle Smokey and Ms. Carrie left Wallowa in '58, the same time we did, to come down to California. Both families came to California because their job moved.

I remember our neighbor Ivany Sasnett's motorcycle. They called him "Lightning." He had an old Indian Chief motorcycle with a screen on the front. He would give us a ride down to the mouth of the canyon and back. Lightning had a skin disease [vitiligo] where his skin looked patchy. He had light spots on his face and hands. It was no concern to me, I was just curious.

One other man named Julius Coleman lived in Wallowa. I was fascinated by him because several of his fingers were cut off, probably from an accident in the woods. We called him "Coleman." He was what we called "batching." During the summer when they were logging, he stayed in a little Airstream teardrop trailer under the tree with the ants. He used to cook his meals. The only thing I ever recall him cooking was cream corn. I think everybody likes canned cream corn. And then he would roast wieners in a pan. That seemed to have been his supper four days a week, because he was there Monday through Thursday. On Friday when came out of the woods, he'd go to La Grande, where he lived.

We were very close to Grandma's household. But Mama also was good friends with Beulah Crow. The Crows were a Caucasian family that lived across the highway from us. Beulah and Mother became good friends. Her husband was nicknamed "Cotton." The Crows had four children. Patricia, their youngest daughter, was slightly older than Pearl, so she might have been three years older than I am. There was a lot of playtime together. We were always welcomed in Beulah's house and were in and out just like Patricia was in and out of ours.

Mother taught Beulah and Grandmother how to crochet. They didn't know how to read a pattern or start a new project. When there was something they wanted to crochet, a doily or a chair set, they'd either come over to our house or vice versa. Mother would have to start the pattern for them. But then they could read the rest of the pattern after that.

The Crows used to do a lot of camping in the summertime. I used to think, Gee, that would be fun to go camping. I really didn't want to go camping since I was afraid to be out in the wild. But it seemed like it was an exciting thing to do, to go camping. Because we lived up in the mountains, there were some wonderful wooded areas. The Wallowa River and Bear Creek River came through the valley—just beautiful places to go and pitch a tent and spend the weekend. My dad was not the camping type either. He worked in the woods and didn't want to spend his weekends laying on pine needles and eating outdoors. So we didn't go camping.

I remember Cotton. Cotton had a drinking problem. Well, he drank on the weekends. He got up every day Monday through Friday and went to the sawmill to work. He was kind of quiet. He didn't speak a lot. He would sit out on the porch in his spare time. That seemed to have been what he did. I don't remember any hobbies.

Now, they had a car, but Beulah didn't drive. She kind of knew how, but she just wasn't good behind the steering wheel. One day, she was upset and wanted to go and see her son William, who was in juvenile hall. It was a snowy evening. The highway was set up on a small ridge between our houses. So when you left our yard, you went down into a ditch and up on the highway and then down into another ditch and then up onto the land where their house was built. So she left in the family car and put the car in the ditch. Mother had to go over and maneuver the car out of the ditch. That was kind of funny for me as a kid.

They had some exciting happenings at their house. Their son William was always in trouble. He was a wild son and caused them lots of grief. He always tried to steal the car. It was grief for them but funny to see him trying to navigate the car. Unfortunately he ended up killing someone and ended up in a penitentiary for life. He died in 2002 in Texas.

I remember the Bate Sawmill. It was behind our house, separated by some land, the railroad tracks, and a creek that had water in it sometimes, enough to wet your ankles. So that separated us from the sawmill. The whistle would blow at lunchtime for the men to take a break. Then it blew again at ten to one and again at one.

I recall a man who worked at the sawmill who never said anything to me. But for some reason, there were bad vibes from my side to his. So when I would come home from school, I would always try to hurry past where the men from the sawmill broke to go home for lunch. He was one of them. I always wanted to be past that roadway where he came out of the mill. It was just awful. I had to be past that area when I heard the whistle blow. One day the whistle blew, and I had not made it to that juncture. So I turned around, and I didn't go home for lunch. I went back to this little lady's house. I can't recall her name. And she was very nice. She made me crocheted dresses for dolls back in those days. So I went back to her house, and that's where I stayed. I didn't come home, and of course Mother was in a panic. When lunchtime was over, I went back to school. That was back in the days when schoolteachers didn't mind taking a paddle and giving you a few. The school had been alerted, of course, that I hadn't come home for lunch. So everybody was on panic alert. Mother drove up to the school this time to save me from a spanking from Mrs. Pierce. I didn't get a spanking from Mother about it, but I certainly got a good talking to. She knew the situation. There was just something about this man that was frightening to me. So I always had to make the cutoff when the whistle blew. And I was 99.9 percent sure I did that every time except that one time.

Chief Joseph is buried at Wallowa Lake outside of the town named Joseph. The folklore I remember was, two tribes were coming together, Chief Joseph's son, I think, and a bride from another tribe. Anyway, out on the lake there was turbulence, and the canoe went down. And to my remembrance, they never found the bodies of the two.

I don't know if that was why the Nez Perce used to come up. Back then we called them Indians. Every year late July, they had a celebration called Chief Joseph Days. There would be a rodeo, a carnival, and lots of Native Americans in Joseph. We lived where the truck route and the highway came together, so we got a chance to see all of the traffic that went into Wallowa on their way to Joseph. One of our highlights was sitting on our front porch and counting the number of Nez Perce that went by a couple of days before the celebration got underway.

That was always a fun time because we would go up to Joseph. I loved the carnival with the merry-go-round and the cotton candy and a corndog and Kewpie dolls and lots of fun things that kids do at a carnival. Every summer we got to go up on the last day. I suspect Mother thought we would avoid the crowds.

They had a big rodeo up there too, with all the things that go along with rodeo—steers rope-tied, calves tied, wild bronco rides, bull rides, and all those kind of things. There was a lot of cattle where we grew up, and so there were a lot of cowboy types. Very interestingly, as far as I can remember, the queen of Chief Joseph was never Native American. She was one of the white ranchers' daughters.

I was always amazed by the regalia that the Nez Perce wore. Recently, I got a chance see it up close to see the beautiful handwork. I went two days and spent a lot of time during the evenings observing. At Tamkaliks, the annual friendship dance and powwow, all of the Nez Perce bands are in full regalia. They did a lot of dancing, with contests between the different bands of the tribe. And of course the fry bread. I bought the fry bread with honey on it, and my sister had the one with meat, cheese, and lots of sour cream—sweet versus savory.

Where we stayed, there was a coffee shop not too far from us. Every morning I went up there to meet old schoolmates for coffee. Each morning, there was this Native American also in there for coffee. He worked at a fishery. The Nez Perce have several fisheries in the area. So during the year he worked at this fishery. He had a caustic, but truth-telling, sense of humor. He took advantage to let the rest of the customers know that Native Americans don't just powwow nowadays but also go to school and are college educated. He did tell this one guy, who was talking about his education, that he went to college too. He talked about the work they did from a town called Pendleton, about a hundred miles from Wallowa. Every year, there's a group of horsemen in the Pendleton band who ride horseback all the way into Wallowa. For the big friendship dinner, they're supposed to bring wild game that they kill along the way. But this year there wasn't too much wild game caught.

So that's my story about growing up in Wallowa. It's a small story because I left

Courtesy Wallowa County Museum

Old Chief Joseph reburial ceremony just ready to begin, at the fool of Wallowa Lake. His remains were removed from his traditional summer camp close to Wallowa and moved to Wallowa Lake. A large crowd can be seen in the background on the east moraine. Photographed by Harley H. Richardson, La Grande, Oregon. 1926

when I was so young. But on my annual visits back, I enjoy getting to know my small school friends as retirees. And somehow, though many years spanned between when I left and when I've returned, there are enduring memories of friendship embedded in my mind that allow us to reconnect.

LUELLA ANDERSON MAZIQUE

Luella Anderson was born in La Grande, Oregon, on March 31, 1945, the daughter of Will Anderson and Frankie (Spikes) Anderson. She is one of thirteen children. Her father was born on September 9, 1895, in Waycross, Georgia. He died on August 19, 1957, in Portland, Oregon, at the age of sixty-two. Her mother was born on January 13, 1908, in Selsby, Texas. She died on June 6, 2000, also in Portland, at the age of ninety-two.

The Anderson family sojourn to Maxville, Oregon, brought them from the South to Arizona, where their first child, Will, was born but only lived a few hours. Their second child, a daughter named Bessie Mae, was born in 1928 in Arizona. When Bessie was two years old, the family migrated to Maxville, where Will worked as a log cutter for the Bowman-Hicks Lumber Company.

By 1940, the family had moved to La Grande and had eleven more children: Helen, Mayola, Leslie, Gladys, Harry, Robert, Jr., Mildred, Joyce, Janet, Luella, and Dickie. They moved to Portland in August 1955.

Luella attended Greenwood Elementary School in La Grande, and she graduated from Jefferson High School in Portland. After high school, Luella worked as a processing technician at Emanuel Hospital and Oregon Health & Science University until she retired.

Luella and Freddie Mazique were married on December 27, 1995, in Lincoln City, Oregon. They have one daughter, Dawn. Luella has three other children, John Massey, Jr., James Massey, and Anthony Massey. She has six grandchildren.

Luella has been a member of the Baptist faith all of her life. In La Grande, she attended Boyd Memorial Baptist Church, which remained her home church until 2014, when she became a member of Greater Faith Missionary Baptist Church.

Luella has a special interest in crossword puzzles, which keep her mind sharp; volunteering at local hospitals; and fishing. She has been a dedicated volunteer at church for many years. Her future plans include going back to school to study communications in order to help individuals develop their reading and writing skills.

My name is Luella Anderson. I'm the eighth daughter of Will and Frankie (Spikes) Anderson from La Grande, Oregon. I was born in La Grande in 1945. My father was born on September 9, 1895, in Waycross, Georgia. My mother was born on January 13, 1908, in Texas. My parents got married in Texas—July 1925, to be exact. And then they moved to Arizona. Then they left Arizona and moved to La Grande in the early '30s for Dad to start logging.

I don't remember my parents talking to me about moving up to Maxville, Oregon. I was the last of the girls to be born, and we lived in La Grande. But he did logging up there in Maxville when I was a child. I don't remember the name of the company. I heard it was Bowman-Hicks Lumber Company. But I actually forgot it.

My father was a sweet man. He was a hard worker until he got crippled from logging. They were out cutting logs. They had to use that old two-ended crosscut saw. And a tree fell and hit him on his hip and broke it. He was in his late forties, early fifties. They had to take him to Portland to get his hip repaired because they couldn't do it in La Grande. They didn't have a facility.

My father said cutting logs was hard work. He said you had to have a good partner that worked with you because if you didn't cut the tree correctly, it could fall and hurt the person on the other end. That's how he got hurt. I don't know who his partner was. You know, one would be on each end of the saw and be working across from each other. But I don't know who his partner was. I was just a baby when my father got injured.

My fondest memory of my father is when we would come home from school and my dad would be sitting on the front porch waiting for us. He was crippled then. So when we moved to Portland, he would always sit on the front porch and wait for us to come home. He would talk and play with us and try to help us with our homework. He would play with us outside and tickle our feet, just being silly.

My mother was sweet. And she loved her husband. She raised thirteen children and always let us know that she loved us. She was a homemaker. She didn't work outside the home in La Grande. Thir-

Courtesy Pearl Alice Marsh
The Anderson twins, Joyce and Janet, in a classroom photo, La Grande, Oregon.

teen kids was her job. Her close friends were Lucille Coleman, Obie Minor, Georgie Mays, and the Pattersons. All of them were friends. Mama was an excellent cook. I loved my mother's homemade biscuits, chicken and dumplings, turkey and dressing, just everything. She was an excellent cook.

My siblings in birth order were Bessie Mae, Helen, Mayola, Leslie, and Gladys; then it was Henry, Robert, Mildred, Joyce, Janet, Dickie and me, Luella. I'm the baby girl. Dickie was the baby boy. Mama never talked about how difficult it was for her raising so many children, especially after my father got injured. She didn't really discuss that; at least with me she didn't. Old people back then didn't really complain. I imagine it put quite a burden on her, though, until they got my father on his feet.

Mother was a churchgoing woman. She helped at the church all the time. Her church was Boyd Memorial Baptist Church in La Grande. They built it from the ground up. They raised money. They did bake sales and stuff to make money to build the church.

My mother was very fond of church. We went to church regularly. There was Bible study, and we had to get up every Sunday and go to Sunday school. Then there was an afternoon service. They'd do plays at special times. We had to attend unless we were ill. My mother was very religious. It made all of the children religious as well. All of her children really were into the church.

Boyd Memorial wasn't huge, but it was a Baptist church. I remember people getting ready for baptism. The pastors got us all ready for church. We didn't have a baptism pool, so they took us to the creek. They would put a white sheet on us and dip us in the water. I don't remember the exact location, but it would have been the Grande Ronde River, someplace down there. The river that runs through La Grande.

We all weren't baptized at once. I wasn't baptized until I was five or six years old. Mama didn't have her kids baptized like Catholics at six weeks or so. She didn't believe in that. We had to be a few years old before we got baptized. But all of us were baptized at a young age.

I was a baby when my father was still working in Wallowa County until he got injured. He worked up in Wallowa during the week and then came home on weekends. He'd leave La Grande for Wallowa on Sunday morning and leave Wallowa for La Grande on Friday night. Most of the men in La Grande did logging. Like my Dad, a bunch of them used to take off Sunday morning for Wallowa. Us kids would be asleep.

My father being gone during the week really didn't affect the family because we knew that was the livelihood to take care of his family. And we knew that he had to leave and go to work. Mom took care of us, got us up to go to school and everything.

We didn't go up to visit Wallowa when I was a kid. Not that many black people in La Grande had cars. We didn't have one, and there were too many of us to hitch a ride with someone.

Growing up in La Grande was the best time of my life. Everybody knew each other and got along—it was nice. I didn't have a whole lot to do in La Grande because it was very small. There were maybe eight or nine African American families living there, and they all lived real close together.

My fondest memory of La Grande is just being a child because it was safe and carefree. Kids could go outside and play, climb trees, ride bicycles, go fishing, do everything. We played ball. Soccer. And you could go and leave your windows and doors unlocked. It was safe.

La Grande was big enough that everybody had indoor plumbing. I didn't know what an outhouse was until I came to Portland. I was talking to people, and they were saying when they lived in Mississippi they had outhouses. You had to go outside to use the bathroom.

George Trice used to take us fishing by the

Courtesy Luella Anderson Mazique
Luella Anderson Masique

lake. We would throw rocks in the water. I fished a little bit. But it was more fun throwing rocks. We were children. They used to yell at us for throwing rocks and scaring the fish off and some other things besides that. Belly Moon, my niece Mary Sheryl, myself, Joyce, Janet, and Mildred would go fishing. They would take a bunch of us just to go fishing with them. That was George Trice. He lived in La Grande until his death.

We played with both black kids and white kids. All the kids had to get along and play together. I didn't even know about people being racist until I moved to Portland. In La Grande, black, white, and Indian fathers had to go logging together. The mothers had to take care of their families in the same neighborhood, so all the kids had to learn to get along together, and it was fine.

I didn't know the "nigger" word in terms of racism. I heard it in the neighborhood among African Americans, but I never even knew what it meant as a racist term until I moved to Portland. In La Grande, I had school friends of all races. It was fun. We would go out riding our bikes, go down to the train tracks and try to catch onto the end of the train to ride. And then we would get in trouble, because you weren't supposed to go down there to the train tracks. But kids will be kids.

Courtesy Irene Barklow Collection, Wallowa County Museum

After the debris settled from the wreck of the Bowman-Hicks train derailment there wasn't much to show why the train ran away. Train delrailments were not uncommon but it was not often that a train was so completely demolished. There was one fatality. Train wreck on Howard Creek in 1925. The railroad ran from on Bowman-Hicks land around Promise, Maxville and Grossman, through Vincent, down Howard creek to the Grande Ronde river, to the mill in Wallowa.

Most of the white people lived on one side of the tracks, and the African Americans lived on the other side of the tracks. But the whites would come over to ride bikes on our side. Yes, they did.

Mama taught a lot of the white women friends how to cook because they didn't know how. Mama would be fixing homemade biscuits and rice pudding and peach cobbler. They didn't know how to cook as good as Mama, so she taught them how to cook. One lady would come over, and then she'd teach her, and she'd tell one of her friends. They also wanted to know how Ms. Frankie cooked. These were white women.

These white people were my parents' friends. They called one couple Bill and Chucky. They seemed like they all got along. You never hear that kind of story about blacks and whites moving across those train tracks that way socially in La Grande, but they did.

Mom didn't do handwork, though she knew how to do it. She did sew and taught me how to sew. I didn't learn how to crochet and make quilts and things from her. I didn't do any of that stuff. But she took time with us girls because she wanted us to learn how to sew and stuff like that.

I was a tomboy. So I would beat the boys up all the time. It didn't matter what age or what color. If you bothered me, I would just start fighting. My brothers used to punch me and stuff. They were going to make me strong. So I just started fighting.

I respect the teachers I had in La Grande now. I didn't then. They were stern. If you went to school and misbehaved, they would take a ruler and swat you on your behind or on your hand, where now they can't touch you. Of course I got swatted, I did. And the truth is, if you did something wrong, people heard about it as soon as you got in the neighborhood.

First you got chastised by some of the elders. Then when you got home, your parents chastised you again. That's what I call discipline!

Holidays were fun. We would all get together, and Mama would cook up big meals. Everybody would get around the table and eat and talk and have fun. It was cold in the

---

The article, below, from the Wallowa Sun is a example of just how dangerous it was in logging. There were also train delrailments and other kinds of accidents. Several deaths and serious injuries occurred, such as that of Mr. Anderson.

Ernest G. Flory of Maxville was instantly killed early last Wednesday morning when a lodged tree fell upon him fracturing his skull. Mr. Flory was cutting a tree at about 7 soon after starting to work. A Dead tree had lodged in the tree, and when the two trees fell, the lodged tree unexpectedly swung back, catching him in the head and crushing his skull against the other tree.

Mr. Flory was 24 years of age. He has been working for the Bowman-Hicks Lumber Co. at Maxville since last September. Ten months ago he was married, his bride coming from Sheridan, Ark. She was confined to the hospital at Maxville, seriously ill at the time of the accident. Mr. Flory was well like, and has many friends both at Maxville and in this city.

The body was shipped to Sheridan, Arkansas, where the funeral will be held. The father, W.A. Flory, and the heart broken wife accompanied the deceased. - *Wallowa Sun*

wintertime around Christmas. We got gifts, but not a lot. We were a family of thirteen, so we didn't get a whole lot of gifts. My favorite toy was a doll. We always got white dolls until I came to Portland.

We left La Grande in 1957 and moved to Portland. I was born in '45. I was just about twelve years old when we moved. My father had been injured before that, so we didn't move for work. My father wanted us to have a better life because he thought up in Portland we would have more opportunities to get better education and, for my older sisters, to find a good husband. Some of them did.

We moved to Portland on the Greyhound bus. It was a double-decker. We didn't have a car, so we all just got on the bus and came up to Portland. The stuff from the house got brought up in a truck. We already had a house ready for us down by the Steel Bridge.

Courtesy Luella Anderson Mazique
Luella Anderson Masique

I don't know who found it, but we moved in. That street doesn't exist anymore. There had been a flood, so most people started living over there. I vaguely remember hearing about Vanport when I was a child, that it had flooded. I think that's when the black people started staying over in North Portland. But I don't know too much about it.

We went to church in Portland. It was Reverend Mitchell's church. I forgot the name of it. My mom was very religious after we moved to Portland up until she died.

The difference between Portland and La Grande was huge. You had to learn how to mix with other kids differently, because up in Portland it was racist. And that was a big adjustment. We were used to playing with different nationalities in La Grande. It was so horrifying in Portland until I just really blocked a lot of memories from my mind.

The racism was mostly in school, because when we moved to Portland most of the blacks lived together down by the Steel Bridge over at Northeast Portland. Portland had flooded, so they moved them over there.

My other brothers and sisters talked about racism or being mistreated, but just a little bit. Most of them decided to just ignore it because there was nothing you could do about it.

So when we got to Portland, we stayed mostly just in the black community. It was okay. Everybody went over to each other's houses, and the kids got along. We had old friends too, because the Minor family, the Mays family, and the Lowrys moved from La Grande to Portland. It wasn't as if we were around strangers completely. Once they started coming, it was like family, people that we knew. I think they sold their houses in La Grande and moved up to Portland to have a better life and thought moving to Portland was a step up.

I enjoyed being a child in Portland—ripping and running and getting into trouble.

My brother Harry taught me how to ride a bicycle. He was about eight or ten years older than I am. Because I had so many brothers and sisters, I never had a chance to get lonesome.

In Portland, we went to school with white kids. I only had one bad encounter with a white girl. She called me out of my name quite a bit and said four-letter words. Finally she put her hand on me, and we had a confrontation. But later we became best friends, and we're best of friends still. I was about twelve or thirteen. She didn't understand because she had never been around black people, and her father was a racist. She thought she could just pick on me and call me names. And that wasn't acceptable. After she grew up, she had kids, and she didn't want her children to be raised that way. So her kids are all nationalities. But when I was in school, she picked on me, yes, she did. It changed when I kicked her butt. Then she became my friend. I got tired of being bullied.

I don't know if my brothers had problems. They were older, except for Dickie. We didn't get to go out with them or be around what they were doing. So I don't know. They're all deceased now. They didn't talk about it with us, put it like that.

Only Gladys and I are living now. She moved to Walla Walla, Washington, when she got married in the late '50s. Now I'm retired, and I retired from cooking too. That's right. I'm seventy-two. I don't need to cook now.

APPENDIX

Courtesy Irene Barklow, Wallowa County Museum

Maxville area train trestle.

Note: These stories are from *The North Woods*, Vols. 1 & 2, by Orvalla Hafer. They are included because they help enrich the memories of the African Americans who worked and lived in Maxville.

BOB BAGGETT

Lillie Trunell-Cook

Robert Lee Baggett was one of the early loggers and an important figure in the Maxville community. He was born on June 1, 1874. In some records, his birthplace is listed as Centralia, Illinois and in others Mississippi. He worked as a section foreman and camp manager for Bowman-Hicks. Throughout the community he was known as "Ol' Man Bob".

He married Rosie Charles in La Grande in 1927. Her nickname was Bobbie and she died sometime after 1930. Shortly after, the community got together and decided he needed a wife. So, they sent back to Brookhaven, MS and recruited Lily Trunell-Cook as his "mail order bride", "Miss Lilly", as she was called.

Hi died on October 21, 1946, in La Grande, OR, and the age of 1972, and is buried in Wallowa, OR.

BOB BAGGETT,
By Kenneth Brooks, as told to Pearl Alice Marsh

Remember old Bob Baggett? You know, I knew him when I was just a kid. And they were building, I don't know whether they were building railroad or cutting logs out there on that point. Never seen him after we got through there for many years.

Now, I must have been about oh, fourteen or fifteen. I was coming down from Promise to Maxville. And, cold... you can't believe how cold it was. And, I said to myself, I wonder if old Bob is still over there. I said, well, I'll go see. I went up there.

Sure enough, someone was in there. And, I knocked on the door. There was old Bob. I said, I'm froze to death. He said, sit down by the fire. He had one of them big old stoves like that and he threw in a few knots. That thing got hot in a hurry. Oh boy. Long time ago.

Robert L. Baggett was born about 1875 in Mississippi. He died on October 21, 1946, in

Courtesy Pearl Alice Marsh
This is Lilly Cook, Bob Baggett's second wife. This is her second husband after Bob died in 1946. His name is Roosevelt "Pick Handle" Coney. Bob is buried in Wallowa.

Union County, Oregon, at the age of 71, and was buried in Wallowa Cemetery, Wallowa, Oregon. In 1880, Bob. Baggett was 5 years old and lived in Lawrence, Mississippi with his father, mother, 2 brothers, and 4 sisters. In 1930, he was 57 years old and lived in Maxville, Oregon with his first wife, Bobbie. On April 1, 1940, he was 65 years old and lived in Promise, Oregon with his second wife, Lilly. Old Man Bob died on October 31, 1946.

OLD BOB BAGGETT
By Pearl Alice Marsh

Bob Baggett was the "elder" among the African American loggers. He was a bachelor and sent to Mississippi to get a bride. Lillie Cook answered the proposal and came to Maxville. Then her whole family moved out! My uncle Louie (Sssnett) married one of her sisters, Theola Cook.

BOB AND LILLY BAGGETT
by Ottis Garrett

Ottis Garrett, who was born and reared in Promise, related this story to me. He was born in 1933 and hadn't started to school yet, so he speculates he was four or five years old, making the time 1937 or '38. His dad, Dave Garrett, and Dave's brother, Arthur, was working at Wood Camp, at the top of the Summit, cutting wood to be delivered and sold at Maxville. They had four head of horses and sleds. Both of their wives, Hazel (Kenworthy) and Laura (Trump) and young son, Ottis, were with them, undoubtedly helping to stack and load the blocks of cut firewood.

Courtesy Pearl Alice Marsh
Bob Baggett's headstone. He is buried in the Wallowa Cemetery.

Darkness came early along with the snow and wind and it was "cold as the Dickens." The team and sled was bucking snow as they made their way north. The men decided it would be best to get the women and youngster out of the cold. When they got to Maxville, Dave asked Bob if the family could spend the night at his place. Bob and Lilly accommodated them and the men continued on to Promise to do the chores and take care of the horses. Ottis remembers the sheets were "clean white and shiny crisp." Ottis slept with his mom and Aunt Laura in a double bed.

When morning came Aunt Laura said, "I've heard it said that black people don't eat with white people." By the time they got up, got dressed and scurried around, Lilly had homemade pancakes and everything that goes with them, and they all sat down to the table and ate breakfast together.

"MY SUMMER IN MAXVILLE"
By Ona Hug Harwood, 2006

It was the summer of 1937 and my Dad, Harold Hug, was logging for Joe Henderson. After school was out Mother, my Grandpa and I went up to Maxville to be with Dad. Maxville is 16 miles out of Wallowa and it is an old logging camp. In its day it must have been booming as there were quite a few houses, Post Office, Schoolhouse, large beautiful Lodge. We lived in a house and the Hendersons lived in a house. We were the only white families there ...although I do remember an older lady that lived there too. (At 10 years of age I probably thought she was old). I do not remember her name.

We had our cow and I sold the milk we didn't need for ten cents a quart. I thought I had made a fortune. When school was to start Mother and I went to La Grande to shop. I bought a dress at Woolworth's for 50 cents. That was my favorite dress and I wanted to wear it every day. There were two black families that lived there too. The Wilfong's and the Pattersons. The Wilfongs were a lovely family and I thought Mr. Wilfong was a handsome man. They had a son, JD, who was about my age and we had such a good time together. We played in the Post Office and there were still the boxes and a lot of mail (maybe junk mail), and we played school. The desks and the blackboards, books and a lot of things were left. One day it would be JD's turn to be the teacher and the next day it would be mine.

We would go down to the lodge and there was water there and we would catch frogs. The Lodge was beautiful and it had a huge fireplace. Dick Henderson and Verle

Maxville Logging Camp, 1937. L-R:. Helen Wisdom Johnson Prince Collins, daughter of Nellie Coats Wisdom Henderson (SW), Adolph Williams CRT), J.D. Wilfong (OH), Nova Jean Henderson Heyduck, child of Joseph Franklin Henderson and Clara Johnson (step-daughter of Nellie Henderson (SW), Dave Allen (OH), Nadine's older brother (RT), Ona May Hug Harwood, the daughter of Millie (McClune) and Harold Hug (SW), Nadine, the daughter of Esther (OH), Nadine Patterson (RT). (OH) is Ona Hug who is #5 in photo. (RT) is Robert Terry of Seattle, (SW) is Sue Rae Collins Wells. Capital letters show who identified the children. The old photo has the initials RJ written on the middle front child.

D

Wisdom slept in the Lodge. The Pattersons, Pa and Ma Patterson and I believe it was their Grandchildren Dave Allen, who was three, and Nadine, a baby. Dave Allen loved my Mother and would come over every morning. Mother always got up early and fixed my Dad's breakfast and later when Grandpa and I got up she would fix breakfast for us. She would ask Dave Allen if he had had breakfast. He would always say, "I done ate but I haven't had breakfast." So he would eat with us every morning.

Sometimes we would go to Elgin for the weekend and Dave Allen would go with us. We would go to the movies and all my friends thought he was adorable. I liked to sing and dance and the Pattersons would teach me songs and dances. I loved all of them. After we moved back to Elgin they would come to see us on their way to La Grande. I would love to know where they are now.

Joe and Nellie Henderson were our life long friends. Joe had a son, Dick and a daughter, Nova Jean, and Nellie had a son, Verle James. He was so handsome. I think he must have been seventeen or so.

I had my birthday while we were in Maxville and I got a new bike. I turned ten years old. Maxville had sidewalks made out of boards. One day JD and I were running and I fell and my arms and legs were full of splinters. I know I cried a lot as my mother had to pull them all out. We went back to visit once and I ate with the Wilfongs. Mrs. Wilfong was a very gracious lady.

I have never been back (to Promise). Always wanted to, but now I understand they have torn down the lodge, so maybe I am glad, because I have such good memories of that summer, and want to remember how it was.

MAXVILLE CHILDREN
By Orvalla Hafer

Robert Terry, along with his daughter, visited Promise for the 2002 Memorial potluck and program. He was a child in the town of Maxville and later became a professor in a Seattle college. He was honored as a speaker at the Eastern Oregon State University graduation ceremony. The following is taken from the La Grande Observer article about his presentation: "The town (Maxville), about 15 miles north of Wallowa was owned by Bowman-Hicks Lumber Company.

Almost forty African Americans worked there during the town's brief history, according to the book, The History of Wallowa County, which was published in 1983 by the Wallowa County Museum Board. The town had a roundhouse, hotel, living quarters for the men who worked there, post office, and a lodge that served as a social center. The town's railway shut down in 1933 but the community remained in existence through a portion of the 1940's.

Ted McKenzie spent a lot of the summers at Maxville with Joseph Henderson and wife, Nellie Coates Henderson, who was a sister of Anna Coates McKenzie, his mother. Ted always called them Uncle Joe and Auntie Nell. Ted was born in 1931, stayed and visited with them in 1935 & 1936. Ted's account: "Auntie Nell said we kids could go anywhere in Maxville except on Saturday nights when the black men got to playing cards - and get mad - and drag out their knives and start cutting. They took one black man to the doctor in Wallowa with a bad cut. He told the doctor, "Doc, keep your needle and

E

thread out cause when I get back to Maxville you' re going to have another customer." Ted said, "another time those two Negro boys and I were playing in the hay barn. The older boy took out his knife and we were cutting the twines on the bales. Uncle Joe (Henderson) spanked both of the black boys. The youngest boy said, "Spank Teddy, too, he cut bales," Uncle Joe said, "No, Teddy wouldn't do that." McKenzie said years later he "fessed up."

Anyway the children played together and enjoyed their childhood in Maxville.

Pa Pat
By Wes Conrad

I was just a kid when I started in the woods. And I never used a crosscut saw. I drove the logging truck. And I was working out there when the Blacks were cutting logs.

I used to like to get out there in the woods at lunchtime and not be able to load my truck on account of the lunchtime for the log cutters. Pa Pat and Granddad used to bring their lunch in a syrup bucket. They just have everything dumped in there. Then they set it on the fire and warm it up at lunchtime and go eat. Always had a stew.

Pa Pay's sweatshirt was always worn out in front. And I was watching him one day out there. They had larger timber at that time and he was pretty short. Well, when he had to get on the other side of a log, he had a way of doing it. Looked easier than heck. He'd just tip up on his stomach there on that log and whip his feet around and drop on the other side ready to go. Didn't take but a couple of seconds. (See Map on inside front cover.)

RUBY SASNETT
By Pearl Alice Marsh

Ruby, Odell and Lightning (Ivan) came to Maxville in 1924.

In 1924, in the dust and weeds of Maxville, Oregon, Ruby Lee Sasnett often dressed like she lived in Portland, Chicago, or Harlem. Fine jewelry, fancy perfume, and elegant clothes, purchased from catalogues, looked out of place in the rough Maxville logging camp where she and her husband, Odell Sasnett, lived. But, she was happy. Of all the women in Maxville, Ruby loved fine things and dressed accordingly. In her wardrobe could be found prized shoes and other treasures collected from earlier times. Her dark smooth skin and plump curves made her standout as the community's fashion queen.

Ruby was born Ruby Lee Flagler on August 7, 1915, in Valdosta, Georgia, the child of Benjamin and Carrie B. (Dempsey) Flagler. She married Odell Sasnett on July 4, 1943, in Walla Walla, Washington. They had one child, Bobby, during their marriage. She died on April 30, 1999, in La Grande, Oregon, at the age of 83, and is buried in Island City, Oregon.

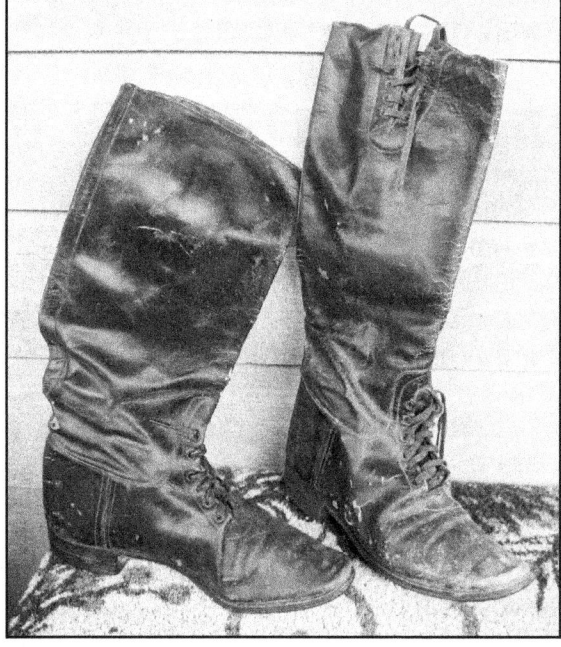

Photo of Ruby Courtesy Pearl Alice Marsh
Photo of Boots Courtesy Myrna Journot
Above, Ruby Sasnett.
Right, Ruby Sasnett's beautiful boots on display at the Promise Grange Hall at Promise.

G

REMEMBERING MY MAMA AND GRANDMA
AND LEARNING WOMEN'S WORK
By Pearl Alice Marsh

Mama and Grandma's work was from before sunup to after sundown, to amend the old saying. Early around four-thirty in the morning, they would rise in separate houses, make fires in the wood heaters to warm the house and begin the days work. During the night, Mama would wake several times to check on Penny who was handicapped from birth, and check on the rest of us. Well before sun-up, she had a full country breakfast prepared for Dad. She would call him, he would rise, put on the work clothes she had washed, patched, and laid out and come to breakfast – ham or bacon, eggs, grits, fresh homemade biscuits, jelly, and strong, freshly brewed coffee. While Dad ate breakfast, she made his lunch. By six-thirty, he was off to work and it was time to get the four healthy children up and ready for school. At Grandma's house, a similar scene took place – only the children were missing, unless one of us decided to sleep over that particular night.

Dad drove the men from Wallowa to the woods in a big red labor truck we called the "candy wagon." We were told that's what you called it because in labor camps, when the men got paid, the children got candy. The candy wagon was an old flat bed truck with a camper shell built on the bed. Inside the wagon were fixed bench seats on each side of the room and a small wood heater to keep the men warm. At day's end, Kay and I were always on the look out for the candy wagon. We would run out to the highway and gaze towards the Wallowa River Bridge. When the candy wagon came around the curve, we would run and announce its' arrival. One of our special treats when Dad came home was a lunch pail full of wild mushrooms. Mama would soak them over-night in heavy brine and the next day, season them with salt and pepper, dust a little flower, and lightly fry them for a treat.

Mama and Grandma cooked on wood stoves. With great skill, they manipulated various pots over different spots on the stove to regulate cooking temperatures for each dish. There was the area immediately over the firebox that was the hottest. You fried there. If something was cooking too fast, you moved it over to the center of the stove. And, if you wanted to slow cook a pot of beans, you put the pot on the left rear of the stove away from the firebox. Kay and I learned the art of managing cooking temperatures this way.

By the time, we were off to school, or in the summertime, out of the house to play, it was time for daily chores. With five children and a logger husband, Mama had to wash almost every day. Clothes' and bedding were washed in a wringer washing machine and hung to dry outside on the clothesline. By the time the wash was on the line, it was time to prepare our lunch. After a hot lunch – no peanut butter and jelly sandwiches – we were off to school or back at play and her afternoon chores were underway.

Grandma raised chickens so part of her morning was spent feeding the chickens and collecting eggs. She had a variety of chickens – Rhode Island Reds, Bantams, Plymouth Rocks, and Orpingtons. Sometimes the hens hatched baby chicks but usually, Grandma got her new brood of chicks from the feed store. There was always one rooster, usually a Rhode Island Red, strutting around the yard ruling over the hens. Sometimes, she

H

would have a couple of small Bantam roosters who always acted bigger than they were.

When it came time to fix a Sunday dinner, Grandma would go into the hen house and select a hen for the sacrifice. Grandma didn't hesitate to kill the chickens her self. She would catch the chicken by the neck and wring it around in the air several times and then – SNAP – I guess, break its neck! The chicken would flop around the yard for a minute or so until finally collapsing in death. The ritual was fascinating and amusing to us kids. Grandma would next scald the chicken in hot water and pluck all the feathers. The last step was to singe the "hair" or pinfeathers over an open flame. If the chicken was older, she made chicken and dumplings or baked it. If it were younger, it went into the frying pan.

The afternoon was spent house cleaning, ironing, running up to Shorty's to buy some groceries (f she had run out of something), and putting on supper. Usually, these were under control by three o'clock. That was when Mama, Grandma, and Beulah Crow, who lived across the highway, would gather in one of their houses to quilt, crochet, and embroider. Only Mama could read patterns. So, when Grandma and Beulah wanted to make something, Mama had to make it first. Sometimes she didn't mind their dependence; other times, she would get aggravated at their persistent inability to learn how to read patterns. She would really get mad when they would just sit around looking "mournful" until she relented. After she got them started or finished the piece, they would take off on their own. These activities preoccupied them for an hour or so until it was time to prepare the men to come home at five or six.

Courtesy Brenda Bell, Hancock, La Grande, OR
An old double oven wood cook stove similar to one used at Vincent to cook for logging crews. It is located in the Boise Cascade cabin in Grossman. Grossman was once Bowman-Hicks logging country.

When Papa and Dad arrived, the evening activities were underway. Dad and Papa would take care of their equipment – filing and repairing chains, mixing gasoline for the power saws, and organizing wedges. When they finished, supper had to be served, the kitchen cleaned, children set to task with their homework, or in the summer, a few more hours of outdoor play, children cleaned and put to bed. In the winter, these few hours after supper were spent with all of us – Mama, Grandma and us kids – gathered together to quilt, crochet, embroider, patch clothes, and sew. This was story time too. Mama would tell us a lot of stories about her early life. She also would recite poetry, her favorite being "The Village Blacksmith" by Henry Wadsworth Longfellow. After getting everyone settled down for the night, Mama would go to bed only to wake several times to see about Penny, to look in on the rest of us and get up the next morning long before sunrise.

Fall was a special time for women's work. It was the time of harvest, hunting, and preparing for the winter. From spring planting until the fall harvest, Papa had nurtured his gardens, usually one at the house and one uptown. He didn't just have a green thumb; he had a green hand and maybe even a green arm. He grew huge heads of cabbage and massively wide leafed collard greens; jumbo carrots and beets; turnips and mustard greens, strawberries, and corn.

Each fall, Mama and Grandma mulled over the merits of new methods for canning fruits and vegetables or making quilts and other preparations for the winter. I remember once when Mama got a quilting frame that she installed herself from the ceiling over their bed. The alleged advantage came from hoisting the quilt above the bed after you had finished working for the evening. Somehow, that didn't last, though she never announced a decision to abandon it. But, I could tell Mama missed sleeping under her quilt canopy while it was in progress.

Fall was not only harvest and canning season, it was also hunting season. Mama had proven she could kill a deer a long time before I was born, so she had give up hunting herself. Occasionally, we would drive out to a hunting area and wait for Dad and Papa. But Mama handled no guns anymore. I think she liked having the skill of shooting but didn't like killing the animals. It was also the time to slaughter the hogs raised since early spring. Anyway, the fall was when the men slaughtered hogs and killed deer for the freezer.

The day of the hunt started early with Dad and Papa leaving the house around five or six o'clock in the morning after a big breakfast. We all waited all day in anticipation for their return.   The later it got, the less likely there would be a kill. But, sooner or later, the kids, keeping the outside vigil, would see the truck with the deer strapped across the fender coming around the bend at the Wallowa River Bridge. Mama and grandma would get ready.

The first order was to cook the liver, smothered in onions and eaten with syrup and biscuits for everybody, including the neighbors, to celebrate the kill. The deer was gutted out in the woods but the liver was brought back as a special meal to celebrate a successful hunt.

Dad and Papa skinned the deer while recounting the kill. At this point, when the euphoria was high, there wasn't much disagreement about the facts. Later in the winter when recounting the same kill, friendly arguments would fly over who really did the best job of bringing down their deer and who had the best gun. Dad like an efficient 270 Winchester caliber rifle while Papa like a 30-30 Winchester or a 30-06 Springfield. Dad said Papa liked it because it didn't require any skill. That would make Papa real mad.

After skinning the deer, the men would be ready to eat the liver and Mama and Grandma would begin to cut up the deer for the freezer. Regardless of the size of the deer, it got shared to some degree among neighbors and friends. If there was plenty, everybody got steak. If there wasn't, somebody got stuck with heck bones and shanks. Never mind, it would be better the next time.

Mama and Grandma talked like hens while doing this work. Sometimes, they let us girls do some of it. We couldn't handle the butcher knives but we could move pans around and pick up stuff. After getting everything cut up, it either went in the freezer in the refrigerator or, if a big deer, to the rented freezer locker at the local store. Usually, Mama would put some aside to make homemade jerky. A Native American passing by during Chief Joseph Days had taught her how to make jerky and to smoke fish in a pit. These were real treats.

Mama was a great wife and mother. But, she wasn't a 1950s slave to domesticity. She had a lot of pride in her independence, her work, and her achievements. When other women in Arizona thought it feminine not to drive a car, in 1939, Mama drove herself, Amos Jr., her sister and nephew from Flagstaff, Arizona to Maxville. In Wallowa, Mama loved barreling her Oldsmobile Rocket 88 down the road between Wallowa and Enterprise. On a straight stretch, she would have the car sailing along at eighty miles and hour like a 50-foot sloop off the Catalina islands.

The car had power and she had power over the car. Between Wallowa and Elgin, Mama and that big old Oldsmobile would hug those curves – rocking us kids from side to side like a carnival ride. Then, hitting that straight stretch to La Grande, she would turn the grain fields into blurry oceans of wheat as the car flew by. One hot day, we would have all the windows open with the warm wind peppered against our round brown faces.

We spent a lot of time riding around with Mama and Grandma. Every Sunday, Mama drove Grandma and us to Minam for treats of candy bars and soda pop. Starting in the spring and lasting through early fall, Mama gathered all of us up and took us fishing in the sloughs of the Grande Ronde River. Being from the south, the fishing pole of choice was a long cane pole. Mama and Grandma would tie them on the passenger side of the care – they usually were as long as the car. We kids would harvest some worms from the garden and soon, with tackle boxes stocked with hooks, bobbers, and lead, we were off to the river.

Usually, the Grande Ronde River or Willow Creek were very good to us. We brought home a bounty of yellow perch, blue gill, bass, catfish, and crappie to both eat and put in the freezer. After cleaning the fish, Mama and Grandma would season them with salt and pepper, coat them with corn meal and fry them nice and crisp on the outside in hot oil.

Grandma loved fishing in the lethargic rivers but Mama like fishing for trout in the Wallowa River. She abandoned the cane pole for a takedown rod and reel and forsook the old red and white bobber. She learned how to fly fish and to tie her own flies. But, Grandma believed in her cane pole with 80-pound test line despite never catching a fish over a few pounds. Mama opted for six-pound test line. Grandma liked to drag her fish out over her head. Mama liked to play the fish in the water until it was tired and she could drag it out to the bank.

Wallowa was a safe place for our African American family. Mama was in charge of socializing her children for the big world that lay outside the Wallowa Valley. Because of Dad's work, she had to raise her five black children in this rural, white county in northeastern Oregon.

We had many friends and enjoyed school, sports and church along with everybody else. The only time we were exposed to race stuff was when we left the confined our little town. When we went to the Wallowa Lake for picnics and people moved away when we arrived, Mama would tell us kids in her strong voice that we had a right to be there. Though uncomfortable with the white children pointing and laughing at us, we would go ahead and have our picnic. On their way down to the water, children would leave when we arrived. Mama said, if the white kids were foolish enough to let our

K

family's presence spoil their day at the Lake that was their problem. They could either accept us and enjoy the Lake or go on back to their table and cars and long for the Lake. We would laugh when we saw little white kids sitting at their picnic tables looking miserable while watching us splash in the Lake and wishing they could. Sometimes, we would see them ask their parents if they could please come and play in the water. Their parents would always say "no". Too bad. There was enough Lake to go around.

Aside from being a full time wife and mother, Mama also had her moments. She made us proud of her a lot. One time, the Wallowa PTA decided to have a play at the school. Mama had starred in Romeo and Juliet in the eighth grades and the experience stuck with her. She confided that she even wanted to go to Hollywood at one time but never had the nerve to really try. She was too security oriented and thought Hollywood would try and compromised her morals.

Anyway, it came time for the auditions and Mama tried out for the lead part but didn't get it. They gave her the role of narrator – off stage. As her family, we were highly offended and, for one of the few times, wondered among ourselves if they organizers passed her up because she wasn't white. Anyway, it didn't matter to Mama. She rehearsed as if she was going off to Hollywood and w wee her grateful audience. Regardless the challenge, she always did her best.

And, I will never forget the night of the play. Mama French braided her hair and put on a new cobalt blue dress with a rhinestone choker around her neck. It didn't matter that she would be off-stage. She dressed to star in the play. She was so proud of herself, it made me too proud of her to care about the second choice part she had gotten.

Mama quit her church when I was nine and moved on to a more "enlightened" religion, so she thought. She ruffled a few feathers with some of her church friends, particularly since she was going to be celebrating the Sabbath on Saturday instead of Sunday and wouldn't be eating pork or shellfish. Mama announced it one by one to her fellow congregants to make sure they understood her decision. It wasn't that Mama felt superior with her new religion. It was just that God had revealed another level of understanding to her for which she was grateful.

Mama was my great teacher. After several stokes and heart failure in her old age, she didn't have many new lessons to share. But, when I looked at her frail face, I saw all of the lessons from Wallowa and I took them with me wherever I went.

SLAUGHTERING HOGS: A CHILDHOOD MEMORY
by Pearl Alice Marsh

One of the exciting events when I was a child in Wallowa, Oregon happened every Fall. That's when our grandfather Joseph Patterson, who everyone called "Pa Pat" but we called Papa, and my father Amos Marsh, slaughtered the hogs we had raised that year.

In very early spring, we went with Papa to buy three or four baby pigs. All spring and summer, Papa fed them "slop", made from table scraps and corn mixed with water. Then, around September or early October, he fed them just corn so their meat would taste good.

All summer, as the pigs grew bigger and fatter, my sister Kay and I would go "visit the pigs" on the way to pick wild flowers, even though they smelled really bad. As we approached the pig pen they would start squealing and grunting and come running over to see us. The pigs were always looking for something to eat.

By the end of Fall, the pigs were big and fat enough to slaughter. Early on a frosty morning, Papa and Daddy built a fire under a big metal barrel full of water and got the water scalding hot.

My brothers Amos Jr. and Frank, Kay and I got up early and went to Grandma's house to wait for Papa to get his 22-caliber rifle ready. Then, we followed him to the pigpen. Papa put some corn in the feeding trough and as the pigs ate, shot them in that soft spot right behind their ear. The pigs squealed for a second or two, then drop dead quickly.

Courtesy Orvalla Carper Hafer

Frank Shine, Charley Shine and Bird Sarrett butchering hogs at one of the Shine places. These men were contemporary to Bowman-Hicks logging in later years. This photo was taken in 1911.

M

After shooting the pigs, Papa and Daddy slit their throats to bleed them, cut them open, pulled out all of the organs into a big tub and gave them to Mama and Grandma to clean.   Next, Papa and Daddy brought the dead pigs in a wheelbarrow to the yard and lifted them over the barrel with a rope pulley set between two pine trees. Then they scalded the pigs in the boiling hot water, scrape off their hair, and readied the pigs for butchering.

They removed lots of fat that Mama and Grandma rendered to make cooking lard and lye soap. We loved the cracklin's that were left after they drained the grease from the kettle.

Papa and Daddy butchered the pigs into parts ready to cook later during the winter -- roasts, ribs, chops, hocks, shanks, neck bones, and feet. The meat was wrapped carefully in thick pink freezer paper to avoid freezer burn.

While Papa and Daddy were butchering, Mama and Grandma got the intestines (called chit'lins), liver, stomach, brains, lungs, and other internal parts. They shared them with neighbors like Ms. Lucy Lowry and Ms. Carrie Powell. Since we did not have indoor plumbing, they spent many hours and hours at the outdoor water pump cleaning the chit'lins and other organs in No. 3 tubs.

Mama and Grandma cooked the liver smothered in onion gravy and served with rice, hot biscuits, and syrup. They boiled the pigs' heads until the meat fell off the bone. They took the meat, mixed it with vinegar and spices and made hog headcheese. Neighbors scrambled the brains with eggs. I do not remember how anyone cooked the lungs (called lights) and other things. Mama stopped at the chitt'lin's and liver.

Papa took the raw hams, ham hocks, and slabs of belly (for bacon) up town and had them smoked. Mama and Grandma ground the scrap meat to make sausage. He then took the meat, after Mama and Grandma had wrapped it in the special freezer paper, and stored it in a rented freezer locker behind Shell's Mercantile store.

Our home-raised pigs' meat would last us through the whole winter along with the vegetables from Papa's garden that Mama and Grandma canned. We also had jars of home-canned jelly and fruits gathered from wild orchards, and frozen deer meat from a successful autumn hunt.

Footnote for Pearl Alice Marsh's "Slaughtering Hogs" story. Pa Pat had slaughtered a hog and wanted Ma Pat to go through the arduous task of making hog head cheese. She was tired from all of the cleaning and butchering. Papa kept fussing so she stuck the whole head in the oven, roasted it, and set it out on the table for him.

MAP OF WALLOWA COUNTY, OREGON

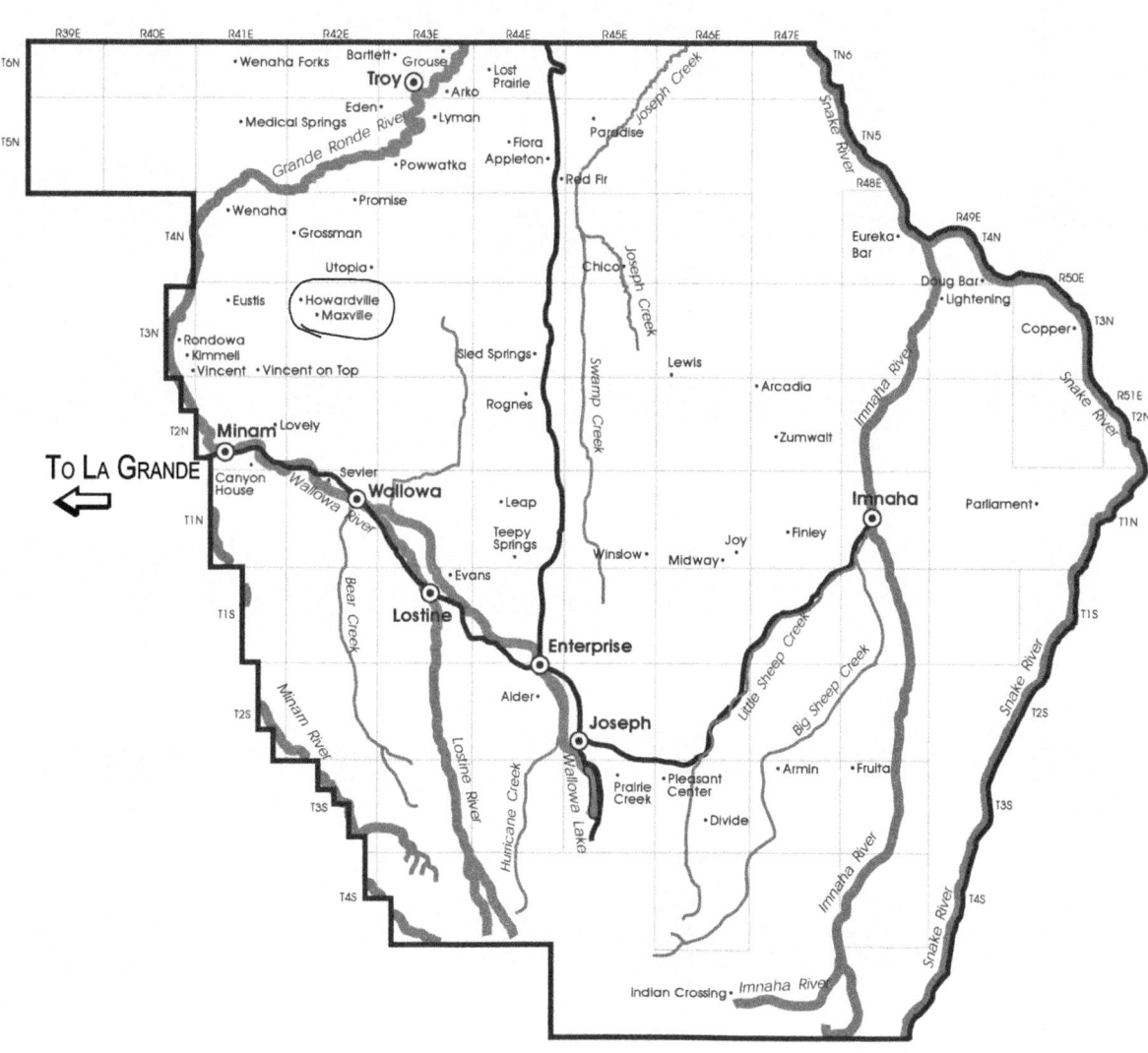

This map shows most of the places in Wallowa County mentioned in the memories. Maxville lies in the upper right quadrant of the map. Washington state borders Wallowa County on the north, Idaho on the east, Umatilla County, Oregon on the west, and Baker County on the south.

La Grande is 50 miles west from the town of Wallowa. Maxville was about 20 miles north of the town of Wallowa, the closest town with stores. After the post office at Maxville close, residents received their mail at Promise, about 10 miles north of Maxville. Many of the families left the rough living conditions in Maxville and moved to Wallowa or La Grande.

On the following page is a Google contour map of the Maxville area.

GOOGLE CONTOUR MAP
OF THE MAXVILLE AREA OF WALLOWA COUNTY OREGON

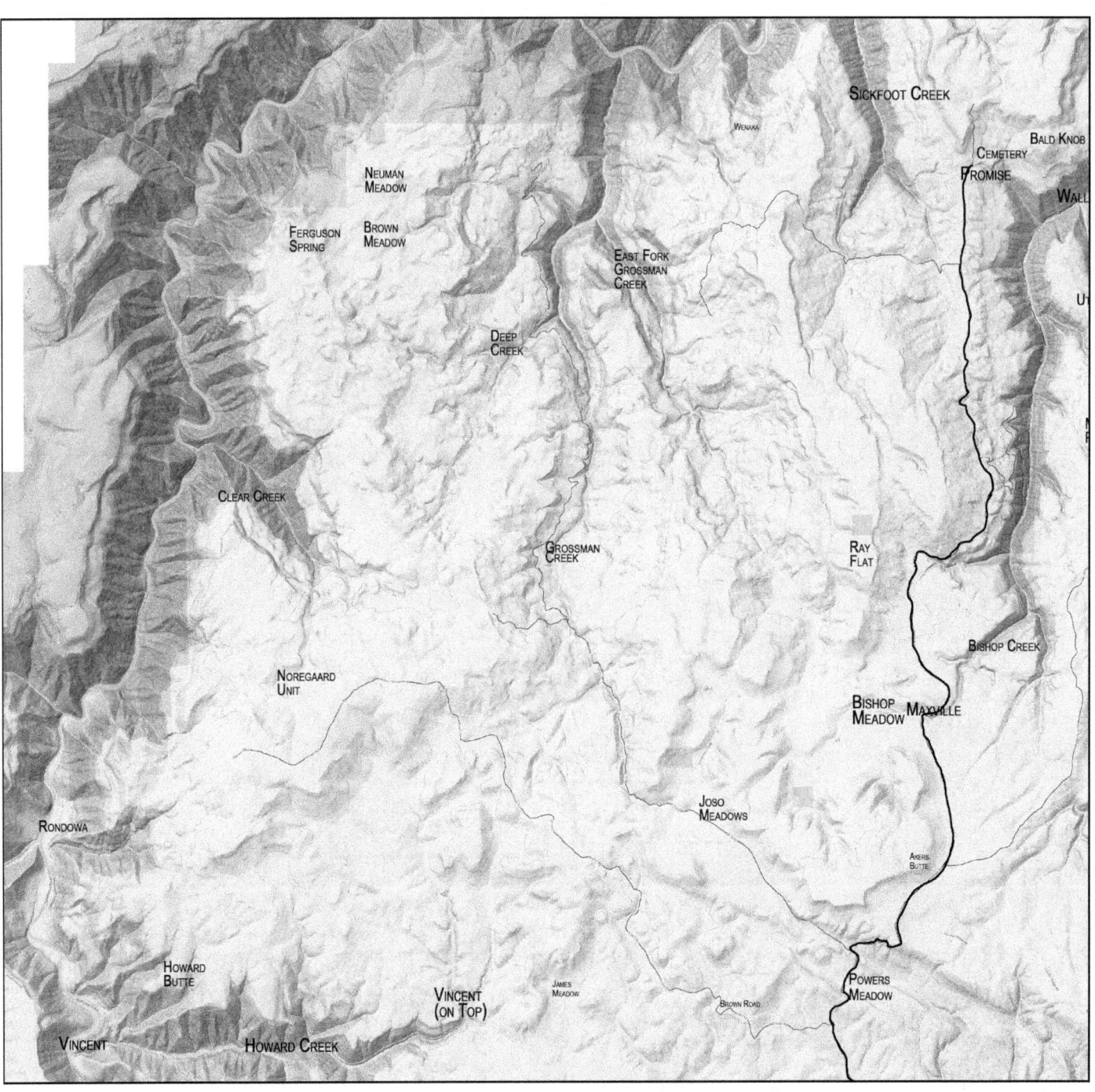

Bowman Hicks moved the living quarters from Vincent, down on the Grande Ronde river to Maxville using the railroad tracks that ran from Vincent on the river, along the tracks that followed Howard Creek (Lower edge of map ont the left), to Vincent on Top on the rail line that ran from Vincent on Top to Maxville. Until the tracks were built from Maxville to Wallowa (mostly using the Promise road of today) the logs were hauled to the mill using the tracks along Howard Creek to the Grande Ronde river around to Wallowa.

P

INDEX

Courtesy Vearl Lewis from album of Verna Silvers, wife of Jake Silvers
"Weedie" Williams sitting back by window. Ester Wilfong, 2nd from left, "Fourspot" Williams, 3rd from left, Verna Silvers, far right.

I

CPSIA information can be obtained
at www.ICGtesting.com
Printed in the USA
LVHW100313160919
631107LV00009B/193/P